DOVER · THRIFT · EDITIONS

Great Speeches by Native Americans

EDITED BY

BOB BLAISDELL

DOVER PUBLICATIONS, INC.
Mineola, New York

DOVER THRIFT EDITIONS

GENERAL EDITOR: PAUL NEGRI

To Sandy

Bibliographical Note

Great Speeches by Native Americans is a new anthology, first published by Dover Publications, Inc., in 2000.

Library of Congress Cataloging-in-Publication Data

Great speeches by Native Americans / edited by Bob Blaisdell.
  p. cm.
 ISBN-13: 978-0-486-41122-4 (pbk.)
 ISBN-10: 0-486-41122-2 (pbk.)
  1. Speeches, addresses, etc., Indian—North America—History. 2. Indians of North America—History. I. Blaisdell, Robert.

E98.O7 G74 2000
970'.00497—dc21

00-024041

Manufactured in the United States by Courier Corporation
41122211   2014
www.doverpublications.com

Note

"YOU DO not know who appears before you to speak," announced Chief Red Cloud of the Sioux to an overflowing audience at New York City's Cooper Union Institute on June 16, 1870. "He is a representative of the original American race, the first people of this continent." After his speech, Red Cloud's audience and the readers of the next day's *New York Times* had at least an appreciative inkling of who Red Cloud and his people were. The present collection of speeches, some famous, some little known, has a similar intent: to give readers of the twenty-first century an extensive appreciation of Native American oratory and some understanding of the history of America through the perspectives of its indigenous peoples.

The speeches included here tell of five hundred years of Native American encounters and conflicts with Spanish, French, Dutch, British, and "American" presumptions, aggression, and influence. They are individual expressions of outrage, wonder, exhortation, persuasion, sadness, pity, reflection, and meditation. Consider, for instance, this 1832 speech of Black Hawk:

> You have taken me prisoner with all my warriors. I am much grieved, for I expected, if I did not defeat you, to hold out much longer, and give you more trouble before I surrendered. I tried hard to bring you into ambush, but your last general understands Indian fighting. The first one was not so wise. When I saw that I could not beat you by Indian fighting, I determined to rush on you, and fight you face to face. I fought hard. But your guns were well aimed. The bullets flew like birds in the air, and whizzed by our ears like the wind through the trees in the winter. My warriors fell around me; it began to look dismal. I saw my evil day at hand. The sun rose dim on us in the morning, and at night it sunk in a dark cloud, and looked like a ball of fire. That was the last sun that shone on Black Hawk.

In general the language of Native American oratory is remarkable, as the Black Hawk example illustrates, for its directness, its metaphors and vivid images, its comprehension of clashing worlds. These are the literary qualities that give these speeches their freshness, power, and poignancy; read them within the context of America's history and they take on an even deeper pathos.

Some of the speeches that follow were delivered on the run, some on the attack, some on the defensive, some spontaneously, some after moments or years of reflection. The orators display a deep understanding (and usually voice a harsh criticism) of the imposing ways of European-American culture. Behind and within their words are shocking histories of tragedy and devastation. Though many of them call for war, there are more that simply call for a return "to the old ways," a fight to preserve native cultures in the flood of new cultures that brought amazing technology, fascinating know-how, and an often captivating religion.

While oratory is necessarily public, circumstances of time and place determine what is recorded and what is passed on to posterity. Many great speeches must have disappeared with the deaths of their speakers and listeners. In some tribes, a speech was made, and then a speaker could return to his speech several minutes later and recant or modify or elaborate upon what he had said. Even in the debates included here between, for example, Tecumseh and Pushmataha, there seems to have been a period of silence or reflection before Pushmataha rebutted Tecumseh's brilliant and seemingly irresistible call to war. Sometimes women were the tribespeople responsible for keeping a memorized "record" of the important speeches. Our culture is apt to regard written records as more trustworthy than oral ones, but there are colonial and American documents that show that Native Americans were remarkably capable of remembering the very words of treaties that the U.S. Government, for instance, would itself forget or conveniently overlook.

Although many of the speakers represented here have been the subjects of biographies and histories, others are hardly known. I have attempted to provide pertinent information about each speech and orator, noting as well each speech's published source. Most of the speeches were made by chiefs, and almost all by men, but it should be remembered that not all native chiefs were natural orators. One of the most admired Native Americans of the nineteenth century, Crazy Horse, was an unsurpassed warrior but said very little on record. Sitting Bull, on the other hand, was a celebrity in his own time. He received American journalists and fans by the score over the last dozen years of his life and made many wonderful quoted remarks. (Five of his speeches are included in this collection.)

The speakers' words were transcribed in a variety of ways: some were written and spoken in English (William Apes' "Eulogy on King Philip," for instance); some were spoken in native languages in the presence of mutually approved translators at French, British, Canadian, or U.S. Government hearings (White Eagle's "We were as grass that is trodden down"); some were remembered and retold by Native witnesses (Sitting Bull's "Behold, my friends, the spring is come"); and some were noted down, interpreted, or recreated by non-native auditors (Seattle's famous but suspect "Yonder sky"). Always, the orator spoke the words to (or dictated them for reception by) an audience.

In almost all cases, I have provided complete versions of the speeches, except when, given as testimony, the main thrust of the speech seems to have ended and further words have been drawn out. A notable exception is this collection's longest speech, the 1836 "Eulogy on King Philip," by the Pequot William Apes, a Methodist minister. His moving and controversial oration was performed before paid audiences in Boston; I have tried to follow his lead in abridging its presentation. Some speeches, on the other hand, have been warped, shaped, and chipped by time and use—Seattle's "Yonder sky" is the most notable example of that. In such cases, I have tried to provide the earliest and most "accurate" version available. In addition, whenever the language of a speech is obscure or seems to require explanation, clarification has been provided in brackets.

While the authenticity of a few of the following (more famous) speeches remains in question, most of them, fortunately, come to us through almost instantaneous translations. Ever since the first histories of the European explorers, there has been no dispute about Native American oratory's affecting directness and beauty. In a speech later recounted by native auditors, Sitting Bull addressed his people with these words: "Behold, my friends, the spring is come; the earth has gladly received the embraces of the sun, and we shall soon see the results of their love! Every seed is awakened, and all animal life. It is through this mysterious power that we too have our being, and we therefore yield to our neighbors, even to our animal neighbors, the same right as ourselves to inhabit this vast land."

There have been equally extraordinary public speeches by Native Americans ever since (and, of course, before) Europeans arrived in the West Indies, Florida, Virginia, New England, and Canada, and there have been numerous explanations for their quality and quantity: among them that the indigenous peoples belonged to oral cultures, which encourage and necessitate the art of public speaking. Furthermore, many of the tribes were democratically organized; in most cases chiefs ruled only by acknowledged consent—they had to speak well, and they had to fit their actions to their words or they might lose their followers. Oratory was a particular specialty of the Iroquois (the Five Nations), with their highly developed democratic confederacy and its rules and procedures; their leaders gained support from the tribespeople through agreement rather than by force or right, and the Iroquois women had strong input to tribal decisions.

But the oratorical sophistication displayed by such speakers as Red Jacket, a chief by dint of his eloquence rather than war prowess, is only part of what makes the oratory of Native Americans outstanding. The European discovery of the Americas was a disaster for the Native peoples, who, if not shoved out of the way beyond the boundaries of desirable lands, often succumbed to European diseases like smallpox, which could wipe out the majority of a tribe within months and leave the rest vulnerable to other tribes or, at best, in devastated disarray for years to come. Understandably, Native Americans have spoken out—and continue to speak out—about the difficulties they have encountered in the more than five hundred years of their shared habitation with settlers from Europe and elsewhere. It is the gravity of their statements, the enormity of their message, that makes Native American speeches so riveting—their stories command our attention and understanding.

Finally, these speeches are representative of, among other qualities, heroism, of particular individuals speaking in defense of the integrity of the lives their people have known.

Sources

Readers will find that there is a huge and exciting library of materials on almost all of the speakers, tribes, periods, and events touched upon in this collection, although the original sources I have cited in the footnotes to each speech are, in some cases, difficult to find. I wish to express my gratitude to the reference librarians of the New York Public Library, the City University of New York, and, most especially, Columbia University's Butler Library. I would also like to acknowledge the editors and compilers of earlier collections of Native American speeches, writings, and words, whose work inspired my investigations into further speeches and speakers: Virginia Irving Armstrong, *I Have Spoken: American History through the Voices of the Indians*; Charles Hamilton, *Cry of the Thunderbird: The American Indian's Own Story*; T.C. McLuhan, *Touch the Earth: A Self-Portrait of Indian Existence*; Lee Miller, *From the Heart: Voices of the American Indian*; Wayne Moquin and Charles Van Doren, *Great Documents in American Indian History*; Peter Nabokov, *Native American Testimony*; and W.C. Vanderwerth, *Indian Oratory*.

Other books (not cited as primary sources in this book) that have helped me discover speeches or historical background include: Robert A. Clark (editor), *The Killing of Chief Crazy Horse*; Vine DeLoria, Jr., *We Talk, You Listen: New Tribes, New Turf*; Ian Frazier, *Great Plains* and *On the Rez*; Albert Furtwangler, *Answering Chief Seattle*; Susan Hazen-Hammond, *Timelines of Native American History*; Bruce E. Johansen and Donald A. Grinde, Jr., *The Encyclopedia of Native American Biography*; Alvin M. Josephy, *The Patriot Chiefs* and *500 Nations*; Carl F. Klinck (editor), *Tecumseh: Fact and Fiction in Early Records*; Malcolm Margolin (editor), *The Way We Lived: California Indian Stories, Songs, and Reminiscences*; Peter Matthiessen, *In the Spirit of Crazy Horse*; Russell Means, *Where White Men Fear to Tread*; Frederick W. Turner III, *The Portable North American Indian Reader*; Stanley Vestal, *Sitting Bull* and *Warpath and Council Fire*; Carl Waldman and Molly Braun, *Atlas of the North American Indian*.

Contents

PART II. NINETEENTH CENTURY

PART III. TWENTIETH CENTURY

Part I.

SIXTEENTH, SEVENTEENTH, AND EIGHTEENTH CENTURIES

ACUERA (Timucua)

"With such a people I want no peace" (c. 1540)

In 1539, about twenty-five years after Juan Ponce de Leon had "discovered" Florida and enslaved south Floridan tribes, Spanish explorer Hernando de Soto and an army arrived in Florida. When de Soto sent a few Native Americans he had captured to ask Acuera to meet him, the Timucua chief had this to say.

Others of your accursed race have, in years past, poisoned our peaceful shores. They have taught me what you are. What is your employment? To wander about like vagabonds from land to land, to rob the poor, to betray the confiding, to murder in cold blood the defenceless. No! with such a people I want no peace—no friendship. War, never-ending war, exterminating war, is all the boon I ask.

You boast yourselves valiant, and so you may be; but my faithful warriors are not less brave, and this too you shall one day prove; for I have sworn to maintain an unsparing conflict while one white man remains in my borders—not only in battle, though even thus we fear not to meet you, but by stratagem, ambush, and midnight surprisal.

I am king in my own land, and will never become the vassal of a mortal like myself. Vile and pusillanimous is he who will submit to the yoke of another when he may be free. As for me and my people, we choose death—yes! a hundred deaths—before the loss of our liberty and the subjugation of our country.

Keep on, robbers and traitors: in Acuera and Apalachee we will treat you as you deserve. Every captive will we quarter and hang up to the highest tree along the road.

SOURCE: Francis S. Drake. *The Indian Tribes of the United States.* Volume 2. Philadelphia: J.B. Lippincott and Co., 1884. 34.

POWHATAN, WAHUNSONACOCK (Powhatan)

"Why should you destroy us, who have provided you with food?" (c. 1609)

Powhatan (c. 1547–1618) was the head of a confederacy that spanned hundreds of miles and thirty-two tribes. (He is well known today because of his favorite daughter, Pocahontas, who rescued the English captain John Smith from execution in 1608.) In 1607 Powhatan's confederacy allowed the English to establish their first colony at Jamestown. In 1609, when the same Captain Smith, dissatisfied with trade negotiations, resorted to bluster and threats, Powhatan made the following reply.

I am now grown old, and must soon die; and the succession must descend, in order, to my brothers, Opitchapan, Opekankanough, and Catataugh, and then to my two sisters, and their two daughters. I wish their experience was equal to mine; and that your love to us might not be less than ours to you. Why should you take by force that from us which you can have by love? Why should you destroy us, who have provided you with food? What can you get by war? We can hide our provisions, and fly into the woods; and then you must consequently famish by wronging your friends. What is the cause of your jealousy? You see us unarmed, and willing to supply your wants, if you will come in a friendly manner, and not with swords and guns, as to invade an enemy. I am not so simple, as not to know it is better to eat good meat, lie well, and sleep quietly with my women and children; to laugh and be merry with the English; and, being their friend, to have copper, hatchets, and whatever else I want, than to fly from all, to lie cold in the woods, feed upon acorns, roots, and such trash, and to be so hunted, that I cannot rest, eat, or sleep. In such circumstances, my men must watch, and if a twig should but break, all would cry out, "Here comes Capt. Smith;" and so, in this miserable manner, to end my miserable life; and, Capt. Smith, this *might* be soon your fate too, through your rashness and unadvisedness. I, therefore, exhort you to peaceable councils; and, above all, I insist that the guns and swords, the cause of all our jealousy and uneasiness, be removed and sent away.

SOURCE: Samuel G. Drake. *Biography and History of the Indians of North America, from Its First Discovery.* Boston: Benjamin B. Mussey & Co., 1851 (11th ed.). 353.

CHIKATAUBUT (Massachuset)

"Thy mother doth complain, implores thy aid against this thievish people new come hither" (c. 1620)

The first Plymouth settlers of 1620 thoughtlessly desecrated the grave of Chikataubut's mother, stealing the bear-skins that covered her body. When Chikataubut found out about this, he gathered his people and called for vengeance. Chikataubut died in 1633, one of many New England Native Americans who succumbed to a smallpox epidemic.

When last the glorious light of all the sky was underneath this globe, and birds grew silent, I began to settle, as my custom is, to take repose. Before mine eyes were fast closed, me tho't I saw a vision, at which my spirit was much troubled, and trembling at that doleful sight, a spirit cried aloud, "Behold! my son, whom I have cherished; see the paps that gave thee suck, the hands that clasped thee warm, and fed thee oft; canst thou forget to take revenge of those wild people, that hath my monument defaced in a despiteful manner; disdaining our ancient antiquities, and honorable customs. See now the sachem's grave lies like unto the common people, of ignoble race defaced. Thy mother doth complain, implores thy aid against this thievish people new come hither; if this be suffered, I shall not rest in quiet within my everlasting habitation."

SOURCE: Samuel G. Drake. *Biography and History of the Indians of North America, from Its First Discovery.* Boston: Benjamin B. Mussey & Co., 1851 (11th ed.). 107.

MIANTINOMO (Narraganset)

"Brothers, we must be one as the English are, or we shall soon all be destroyed" (c. 1642–1643)

Miantinomo (c. 1600–1643) tried to organize an intertribal resistance to the English colonists, and in the following speech he exhorted the Montauks of Long Island, New York, to join him. For his efforts, unsuccessful though they were, he was executed by the colonial government's Mohegan allies.

Brothers, we must be one as the English are, or we shall soon all be destroyed. You know our fathers had plenty of deer and skins, and our plains were full of deer and of turkeys, and our coves and rivers were full of fish. But, brothers, since these English have seized upon our country, they cut down the grass with scythes, and the trees with axes. Their cows and horses eat up the grass, and their hogs spoil our beds of clams; and finally we shall starve to death! Therefore, stand not in your own light, I beseech you, but resolve with us to act like men. All the sachems both to the east and west have joined with us, and we are all resolved to fall upon them, at a day appointed, and therefore I have come secretly to you, because you can persuade the Indians to do what you will. Brothers, I will send over fifty Indians to Manisses, and thirty to you from thence, and take a hundred of Southampton Indians, with a hundred of your own here. And, when you see the three fires that will be made at the end of forty days hence, in a clear night, then act as we act, and the next day fall on and kill men, women and children, but no cows; they must [not] be killed as we need them for provisions, till the deer come again.

SOURCE: Samuel G. Drake. *Biography and History of the Indians of North America, from Its First Discovery.* Boston: Benjamin B. Mussey & Co., 1851 (11th ed.). 127–128.

KING PHILIP, METACOM (Wampanoag)

"The English who came first to this country were but a handful of people" (1676)

The occasion for the following speech came when a Rhode Islander named John Borden tried to dissuade King Philip (c. 1637–1676) from launching his planned campaign against the inhabitants of New England, which became known as "King Philip's War." (For biographical details of King Philip's heroic life and tragic death, see William Apes's "Eulogy on King Philip," pages 93–115.)

The English who came first to this country were but a handful of people, forlorn, poor and distressed. My father did all in his power to serve them. Others came. Their numbers increased. My father's counselors were alarmed. They urged him to destroy the English before they became strong enough to give law to the Indians and take away their country. My father was also the father to the English. He remained their friend. Experience shows that his counselors were right. The English disarmed my people. They tried them by their own laws, and assessed damages my people could not pay. Sometimes the cattle of the English would come into the cornfields of my people, for they did not make fences like the English. I must then be seized and confined till I sold another tract of my country for damages and costs. Thus tract after tract is gone. But a small part of the dominion of my ancestors remains. I am determined not to live till I have no country.

SOURCE: Norman B. Wood. *Lives of Famous Indian Chiefs.* Aurora, Illinois: American Indian Historical Publishing Co., 1906. 94–95.

SWERISE (Oneida)

"But where are our prisoners?" (May 24, 1679)

After the Five Nations of Iroquois (the Mohawks, Onondagas, Cayugas, Oneidas, and Senecas) made a treaty, they would request their prisoners of war to be returned; if any of them were dead, they usually asked for members of the other tribe as substitutes. Here, Swerise, a chief about whom little is known, addressed the commandant and commissioner for Indian Affairs at Albany, New York. (He called these English colonial governors "Corlear" as something of an honorary title of respect, after the Dutch governor Arent van Corlear, who negotiated a treaty with the Mohawks in 1643.)

Brethren, we are come to this place with much trouble, as we did last winter, and renew the request we then made, that six Indians be delivered to us in the room of these six Christians, in case our people, who are prisoners, be dead. None of us have gone out against the Christians since we were last here; but we told you then that some were then out, who knew nothing of the Governor's orders, and we desired that if any thing happened it might not be taken ill. Now thirteen of our people, who went out against our Indian enemies, met eighteen men on horseback, as far from any of the English plantations as Cahnuaga is from Albany. They fired upon our people; our men, being soldiers, returned their fire, and killed two men and two horses, and brought away their scalps.

It would be convenient that the Governor tell the people of Virginia not to send their men so far from home; for if they should meet our parties in their way against our enemies, the Cahnowas, whom the English call Arogisti, we cannot answer for the consequences.

We have now observed the Governor's orders, in bringing the three other Christian prisoners; and we trust the affair of our prisoners wholly to the Governor.

We have now performed our promises: But where are our prisoners; or, if they be dead, the others in their room; now when it is so late in the spring? However, we will still trust this to the Governor.

[Then delivering the prisoners one by one, Swerise said:] We have, we say, now performed our promises, and are not ashamed. We hope

SOURCE: Cadwallader Colden. *The History of the Five Indian Nations Depending on the Province of New-York in America.* 1727. [Reprint edition: New York: Allerton Book Co., 1904. 28–30.]

Corlear, who governs the whole country, will likewise do that of which he need not be ashamed.

Corlear governs the whole land, from New-York to Albany, and from thence to the Senecas' Land; we, who are his inferiors, shall faithfully keep the chain: Let him perform his promise, as we have ours, that the chain be not broken on his side, who governs the whole country.

[Then the Commissioners gave them presents for their kind usage of the prisoners. After which Swerise stood up again and said:] Let Corlear take care, that the Indian woman, that is wanting, be restored, and, for those that are killed, others in their room. If Corlear will not give ear to us in this affair, we will not hereafter give ear to him in any thing.

[Hearing afterwards, that these last words were ill taken, Swerise, with two more of the chief Oneida sachems, excused it, saying:] What we said, of not hearkening any more to Corlear, did not proceed from the heart, but was spoken by way of argument, to make Corlear more careful to release our people that are prisoners; and you may be convinced it was so, when you consider that it was said after your answer, and without laying down either beaver or any belt or wampum, as we always do, when we make propositions; therefore we desire that, if it be noted, it may be blotted out, and not made known to Corlear, for we hold firmly to our covenant, as we said in our propositions.

UNNAMED (Onondaga and Cayuga)

"Our young men are soldiers, and when they are provoked, they are like wolves" (August 2, 1684)

The Iroquois chiefs, making a treaty with the British against the French, addressed the governors of Virginia and New York, to assert their independence and rights.

Brother Corlear, your sachem is a great sachem, and we are but a small people; but when the English came first to Manhattan, to Aragiske [Virginia] and to Yakokranagary [Maryland], they were then but a small people, and we were great. Then, because we found you a good people, we treated you kindly, and gave you land; we hope therefore, now that you are great, and we small, you will protect us from the French. If you do not, we shall lose all our hunting and beavers: The French will get all the beavers. The reason they are now angry with us is, because we carry our beaver to our brethren.

We have put our lands and ourselves under the protection of the great Duke of York, the brother of your great sachem, who is likewise a great sachem.

We have annexed the Susquehanna River, which we won with the sword, to this government; and we desire it may be a branch of the great tree that grows in this place, the top of which reaches the sun, and its branches shelter us from the French, and all other nations. Our fire burns in your houses, and your fire burns with us; we desire it may be so always. But we will not that any of the great Penn's people settle upon the Susquehanna River, for we have no other land to leave to our children.

Our young men are soldiers, and when they are provoked, they are like wolves in the woods, as you, Sachem of Virginia, very well know.

We have put ourselves under the great Sachem Charles, that lives on the other side the great lake. We give you these two white dressed deerskins, to send to the great sachem, that he may write on them, and put a great red seal to them, to confirm what we now do; and put the Susquehanna River above the falls, and all the rest of our land under the great Duke of York, and give that land to none else. Our brethren, his people, have been like fathers to our wives and children, and have

SOURCE: Cadwallader Colden. *The History of the Five Indian Nations Depending on the Province of New-York in America.* 1727. [Reprint edition: New York: Allerton Book Co., 1904. 46–49.]

given us bread when we were in need of it; we will not therefore join ourselves, or our land, to any other government but this. We desire Corlear, our governor, may send this our proposition to the great Sachem Charles, who dwells on the other side the great lake, with this belt of wampum, and this other smaller belt to the Duke of York his brother. And we give you, Corlear, this beaver, that you may send over this proposition.

You great man of Virginia, we let you know, that great Penn did speak to us here in Corlear's house by his Agents and desired to buy the Susquehanna River of us, but we would not hearken to him, for we had fastened it to this government.

We desire you therefore to bear witness of what we now do, and that we now confirm what we have done before. Let your friend, that lives on the other side of the great lake, know this, that we being a free people, though united to the English, may give our lands, and be joined to the sachem we like best. We give this beaver to remember what we say.

GARANGULA (Onondaga)

> **"Yonnondio, you must have believed when you left Quebec that the sun had burnt up all the forests which render our country unaccessible to the French"** (1684)

General de la Barre, governor of Canada, rebuked Garangula and the Iroquois for having harassed French traders and for aiding the English: "All the time that Monsieur de la Barre spoke, Garangula kept his eyes fixed on the end of his pipe; as soon as the governor had done speaking, he rose up, and having walked five or six times round the circle, he returned to his place, where he spoke standing, while Monsieur de la Barre kept his elbow chair." After Garangula's speech had been interpreted, de la Barre was furious, and "retreated to his tent." ("Yonnondio" was the name the Iroquois used for governors of Canada.)

Yonnondio, I honor you, and the warriors that are with me all likewise honor you. Your interpreter has finished your speech; I now begin mine. My words make haste to reach your ears, hearken to them.

Yonnondio, you must have believed when you left Quebec that the sun had burnt up all the forests which render our country inaccessible to the French, or that the lakes had so far overflown their banks that they had surrounded our castles, and that it was impossible for us to get out of them. Yes, Yonnondio, surely you must have dreamt so, and the curiosity of seeing so great a wonder has brought you so far. Now you are undeceived, since that I and the warriors here present are come to assure you that the Senecas, Cayugas, Onondagas, Oneidas, and Mohawks are yet alive. I thank you, in their name, for bringing back into their country the calumet, which your predecessor received from their hands. It was happy for you that you left underground that murdering hatchet that has been so often dyed in the blood of the French. Hear, Yonnondio, I do not sleep, I have my eyes open, and the sun, which enlightens me, discovers to me a great captain at the head of a company of soldiers, who speaks as if he were dreaming. He says, that he only came to the lake to smoke on the great calumet with the Onondagas. But Garangula says that he sees the contrary, that it was to knock them on the head, if sickness had not weakened the arms of the French.

SOURCE: Cadwallader Colden. *The History of the Five Indian Nations Depending on the Province of New-York in America.* 1727. [Reprint edition: New York: Allerton Book Co., 1904. 67–71.]

I see Yonnondio raving in a camp of sick men, whose lives the great spirit has saved, by inflicting this sickness on them. Hear, Yonnondio, our women had taken their clubs, our children and old men had carried their bows and arrows into the heart of your camp, if our warriors had not disarmed them, and kept them back, when your messenger, Ohguesse, came to our castles. It is done, and I have said it. Hear, Yonnondio, we plundered none of the French, but those that carried guns, powder, and ball to the Iwikties and Chictaghicks, because those arms might have cost us our lives. Herein we follow the example of the Jesuits, who stave all the caggs of rum brought to our castles, lest the drunken Indians should knock them on the head. Our warriors have not beavers enough to pay for all these arms that they have taken, and our old men are not afraid of the war. This belt preserves my words.

We carried the English into our lakes, to trade there with the Utawawas and Quatoghies, as the Adirondacks brought the French to our castles, to carry on a trade which the English say is theirs. We are born free, we neither depend on Yonnondio nor Corlear.

We may go where we please, and carry with us whom we please, and buy and sell what we please: If your allies be your slaves, use them as such, command them to receive no other but your people. This belt preserves my words.

We knocked the Twihtwies and Chictaghicks on the head, because they had cut down the trees of peace, which were the limits of our country. They have hunted beavers on our lands: They have acted contrary to the customs of all Indians; for they left none of the beavers alive, they killed both male and female. They brought the Satanas into their country, to take part with them, after they had concerted ill designs against us. We have done less than either the English or French, that have usurped the lands of so many Indian nations, and chased them from their own country. This belt preserves my words. Hear, Yonnondio, what I say is the voice of all the Five Nations; hear what they answer, open your ears to what they speak: The Senecas, Cayugas, Onondagas, Oneidas, and Mohawks say that when they buried the hatchet at Cadarackui (in the presence of your predecessor) in the middle of the fort, they planted the tree of peace in the same place, to be there carefully preserved, that, in place of a retreat for soldiers, that fort might be a rendezvous for merchants; that, in place of arms and ammunition of war, beavers and merchandise should only enter there.

Hear, Yonnondio, take care for the future that so great a number of soldiers, as appear there, do not choke the tree of peace planted in so small a fort. It will be a great loss, if after it had so easily taken root, you should stop its growth, and prevent its covering your country and ours with its branches. I assure you, in the name of the Five Nations, that our warriors shall dance to the calumet of peace under its leaves, and shall remain quiet on their mats, and shall never dig up the hatchet, till their brethren, Yonnondio or Corlear, shall either jointly or separately endeavour to attack the country, which the great spirit has given to our ancestors. This belt preserves my words, and this other, the authority which the Five Nations has given me.

[Then Garangula addressing himself to Monsieur le Maine, said:]

Take courage, Ohguesse, you have spirit, speak, explain my words, forget nothing, tell all that your brethren and friends say to Yonnondio, your governor, by the mouth of Garangula, who loves you, and desires you to accept of this present of beaver, and take part with me in my feast, to which I invite you. This present of beaver is sent to Yonnondio on the part of the Five Nations.

UNNAMED (Iroquois)

"If the gentlemen of Virginia will send us a dozen of their sons, we will take great care of their education"   (1744)

Benjamin Franklin tells the story of the speech that follows, how at a council between them and the government of Virginia, the Iroquois were offered a college education for some of their young men.

We know that you highly esteem the kind of learning taught in those colleges, and that the maintenance of our young men, while with you, would be very expensive to you. We are convinced, therefore, that you mean to do us good by your proposal, and we thank you heartily. But you who are wise must know that different nations have different conceptions of things; and you will therefore not take it amiss if our ideas of this kind of education happen not to be the same with yours. We have had some experience of it: several of our young people were formerly brought up at the colleges of the northern provinces; they were instructed in all your sciences; but when they came back to us, they were bad runners; ignorant of every means of living in the woods; unable to bear either cold or hunger; knew neither how to build a cabin, take a deer, or kill an enemy; spoke our language imperfectly; were therefore neither fit for hunters, warriors, or counsellors; they were totally good for nothing. We are, however, not the less obliged by your kind offer, though we decline accepting it: and to show our grateful sense of it, if the gentlemen of Virginia will send us a dozen of their sons, we will take great care of their education, instruct them in all we know, and make *men* of them.

SOURCE: Samuel G. Drake. *Biography and History of the Indians of North America, from Its First Discovery.* Boston: Benjamin B. Mussey & Co., 1851 (11th ed.). 41.

MINAVAVANA (Chippewa/Ojibway)

"Englishman!—You know that the French king is our father" (1761)

Though identifying himself as Chippewa, Minavavana may well have been the Ottawa chief Pontiac, the leader of the area's large confederacy. In any case, on Lake Huron a British trader named Alexander Henry received the brunt of the following speech.

Englishman!—It is to you that I speak, and I demand your attention!

Englishman!—You know that the French king is our father. He promised to be such; and we, in return, promised to be his children. This promise we have kept.

Englishman!—It is you that have made war with this our father. You are his enemy; and how then could you have the boldness to venture among us, his children? You know that his enemies are ours.

Englishman!—We are informed that our father, the king of France, is old and infirm; and that being fatigued with making war upon your nation, he is fallen asleep. During his sleep, you have taken advantage of him, and possessed yourselves of Canada. But his nap is almost at an end. I think I hear him already stirring, and inquiring for his children the Indians—and, when he does awake, what must become of you? He will destroy you utterly!

Englishman!—Although you have conquered the French, you have not yet conquered us! We are not your slaves. These lakes, these woods and mountains were left to us by our ancestors. They are our inheritance, and we will part with them to none. Your nation supposes that we, like the white people, cannot live without bread, and pork, and beef! But, you ought to know, that He—the Great Spirit and Master of Life—has provided food for us in these broad lakes and upon these mountains.

Englishman!—Our father, the King of France, employed our young men to make war upon your nation. In this warfare, many of them have been killed; and it is our custom to retaliate, until such time as the spirits of the slain are satisfied. Now the spirits of the slain are to be satisfied in either of two ways. The first is by the spilling of the blood of the nation by which they fell; the other, by *covering the bodies of the dead,*

SOURCE: B.B. Thatcher. *Indian Life and Battles.* Akron: New Werner Company, 1910. 78–80.

and thus allaying the resentment of their relations. This is done by making presents.

Englishman!—Your king has never sent us any presents, nor entered into any treaty with us. Wherefore he and we are still at war; and, until he does these things, we must consider that we have no other father, nor friend, among the white men, than the king of France. But, for you, we have taken into consideration that you have ventured your life among us in the expectation that we should not molest you. You do not come armed, with an intention to make war. You come in peace, to trade with us, and supply us with necessaries, of which we are much in want. We shall regard you, therefore, as a brother; and you may sleep tranquilly without fear of the Chippewas. As a token of friendship, we present you with this pipe, to smoke.

PONTIAC (Ottawa)

"The Master of Life" (April 27, 1763)

Pontiac (c. 1720–1769) was the leader of the largest league of
Native Americans the Europeans had yet encountered. Like
Tecumseh after him, he saw Indian unification and resistance as the
only way to stop the further western settlement by European
Americans. Rallying to war a council of Ottawas, Potawatomies, and
Hurons near Fort Detroit, Pontiac concluded the following speech
with the story of a dream by "The Wolf," a Delaware prophet.
Pontiac's leadership led to the surprising capture of most of the
British forts on the frontier; his ally France's unexpected peace with
England, however, undermined the chances of a successful war,
and Pontiac made peace with the British in 1764.

It is important, my brothers, that we should exterminate from our land
this nation, whose only object is our death. You must be all sensible, as
well as myself, that we can no longer supply our wants in the way we
were accustomed to do with our fathers, the French. They sell us their
goods at double the price that the French made us pay, and yet their
merchandise is good for nothing; for no sooner have we bought a blanket or other thing to cover us, than it is necessary to procure others
against the time of departure for our wintering ground. Neither will
they let us have them on credit, as our brothers, the French, used to do.
When I visit the English chief and inform him of the death of any of
our comrades, instead of lamenting, as our brothers, the French, used
to do, they make game of us. If I ask him for anything for our sick, he
refuses, and tells us he does not want us, from which it is apparent he
seeks our death. We must, therefore, in return, destroy them without
delay; there is nothing to prevent us; there are but few of them, and we
shall easily overcome them—why should we not attack them? Are we
not men? Have I not shown you the belts I received from our Great
Father, the King of France? He tells us to strike—why should we not
listen to his words? What do you fear? The time has arrived. Do you
fear that our brothers, the French, who are now among us, will hinder
us? They are not acquainted with our designs, and if they did know
them, could they prevent them? You know as well as myself that when
the English came upon our lands to drive from them our father,

SOURCE: Norman B. Wood. *Lives of Famous Indian Chiefs.* Aurora, Illinois:
American Indian Historical Publishing Co., 1906. 133–136.

Bellestre, they took from the French all the guns that they have, so that they have now no guns to defend themselves with. Therefore, now is the time; let us strike. Should there be any French to take their part, let us strike them as we do the English. I have sent belts and speeches to our friends, the Chippewas of Saginaw, and our brothers, the Ottawas of Michillimacinac, and to those of the Riviere á La Trauche [Thames River], inviting them to join us, and they will not delay. In the meantime, let us strike. There is no longer any time to lose, and when the English shall be defeated, we will stop the way, so that no more shall return upon our lands.

[He also assured them that the Indians and their French brothers would again fight side by side against the common foe, as they did in other years on the Monongahela, when the banners of the English had been trampled in the bloody mire of defeat. The orator, having lashed his audience into fury, quickly soothed them with the story of the Delaware prophet "The Wolf," who had a dream in which it was revealed to him that by traveling in a certain direction he would at length reach the abode of the "Great Spirit," or Master of Life. — *Wood*]

After many days of journeying, full of strange incidents, he [The Wolf] saw before him a vast mountain of dazzling whiteness, so precipitous that he was about to turn back in despair, when a beautiful woman arrayed in white appeared and thus accosted him: "How can you hope, encumbered as you are, to succeed in your design? Go down to the foot of the mountain, throw away your gun, your ammunition, your provisions and your clothing; wash yourself in the stream which flows there, and you will then be prepared to stand before the Master of Life." The Indian obeyed, and again began to ascend among the rocks, while the woman, seeing him still discouraged, laughed at his faintness of heart and told him that, if he wished for success, he must climb by the aid of one hand and one foot only. After great toil and suffering, he at length found himself at the summit. The woman had disappeared, and he was left alone. A rich and beautiful plain lay before him, and at a little distance he saw three great villages, far superior to any he had seen in any tribe. As he approached the largest and stood hesitating whether he should enter, a man, gorgeously attired, stepped forth, and, taking him by the hand, welcomed him to the celestial abode. He then conducted him into the presence of the Great Spirit, where the Indian stood confounded at the unspeakable splendor which surrounded him. The Great Spirit bade him be seated, and thus addressed him: "I am the Maker of heaven and earth, the trees, lakes, rivers and all things else. I am the Maker of mankind; and because I love you, you must do my will. The land on which you live I have made for *you*, and not for others. Why do you suffer the white man to dwell among you? My children, you have forgotten the customs and traditions of your forefathers. Why do you not clothe yourselves in skins, as they did, and use the bows and arrows, and the stone-pointed lances, which they used? You have bought guns, knives, kettles, and blankets from the white man, until you can no longer do without them; and what is worse, you have drunk the poison fire-water, which turns you into fools. Fling all these things away; live as your wise forefathers lived before you. And as for these English—these dogs dressed in red, who have come to rob you of your hunting-grounds and drive away the game—you must lift the hatchet against them. Wipe them from the face of the earth, and then you will win my favor back again, and once more be happy and prosperous. The children of your great father, the King of France, are not like the English. Never forget that they are your brethren. They are very dear to me, for they love the red men, and understand the true mode of worshipping me."

PONTIAC (Ottawa)

"I am a Frenchman, and I wish to die a Frenchman"
(May 23, 1763)

During the siege of Fort Detroit, Pontiac (c. 1720–1769) reminded the French traders and settlers near Detroit of his past services, when Detroit was under French dominion, and assured them that he would recompense them for and, in the future, protect them from his hungry soldiers' looting.

I do not doubt, my brothers, that this war is very troublesome to you, for our warriors are continually passing and repassing through your settlement. I am sorry for it. Do not think I approve of the damage that is done by them; and as a proof of this, remember the war with the Foxes and the part which I took in it. It is now seventeen years since the Ojibways of Michillimackinac, combined with the Sauks and Foxes, came down to destroy you. Who then defended you? Was it not I and my young men? Mickinac, great chief of all these nations, said in council that he would carry to his village the head of your commandant—that he would eat his heart and drink his blood. Did I not take your part? Did I not go to his camp, and say to him, that if he wished to kill the French he must first kill me and my warriors? Did I not assist you in routing them and driving them away? And now you think I would turn my arms against you! No, my brothers; I am the same French Pontiac who assisted you seventeen years ago. I am a Frenchman, and I wish to die a Frenchman; and now I repeat to you that you and I are one—that it is for both our interests that I should be avenged. Let me alone. I do not ask you for aid, for it is not in your power to give it. I only ask provisions for myself and men. Yet, if you are inclined to assist me, I shall not refuse you. It would please me, and you yourselves would be sooner rid of your troubles; for I promise you, that as soon as the English are driven out, we will go back to our villages, and there await the arrival of our French father. You have heard what I have to say; remain at peace, and I will watch that no harm shall be done to you, either by my men or by the other Indians.

SOURCE: Norman B. Wood. *Lives of Famous Indian Chiefs.* Aurora, Illinois: American Indian Historical Publishing Co., 1906. 151–152.

RED HAWK (Shawnee)

"We saw you coming with an uplifted tomahawk in your hand"   (November 12, 1764)

Red Hawk was an ally of Pontiac, who, while the great leader laid siege to Detroit, helped lay siege to Fort Pitt (later Pittsburgh), to the south. British Colonel Henry Bouquet, who mistrusted the "haughty" Shawnees, broke up the latter attack. In agreeing to a treaty and giving up captives the next spring, Red Hawk addressed the colonel in the following remarks.

Brother, listen to us, your younger brothers. As we see something in your eyes that looks dissatisfaction, we now clear them. You have credited bad stories against us. We clean your ears, that you may hear better hereafter. We wish to remove every thing bad from your heart, that you may be as good as your ancestors. [*Handing Bouquet a belt.*] We saw you coming with an uplifted tomahawk in your hand. We now take it from you, and *throw it up to God.* Let him do with it as he pleases. We hope never to see it more. Brother, as you are a warrior, take hold of this chain [*handing a belt*] of friendship, and let us think no more of war, in pity of our old men, women, and children. We, too, are warriors.

SOURCE: Samuel G. Drake. *Biography and History of the Indians of North America, from Its First Discovery.* Boston: Benjamin B. Mussey & Co., 1851 (11th ed.). 695.

UNNAMED (Naudowessie)

"Thy soul yet lives in the great Country of Spirits" (c. 1767)

The explorer Jonathan Carver was allowed to be present at a traditional funeral oration (though not at the internment in a cave that followed). This is how he set it down.

You still sit among us, Brother, your person retains its usual resemblance, and continues similar to ours, without any visible deficiency, except that it has lost the power of action. But whither is that breath flown, which a few hours ago sent up smoke to the Great Spirit? Why are those lips silent, that lately delivered to us expressive and pleasing language? why are those feet motionless, that a short time ago were fleeter than the deer on yonder mountains? why useless hang those arms that could climb the tallest tree, or draw the toughest bow? Alas! every part of that frame which we lately beheld with admiration and wonder, is now become as inanimate as it was three hundred winters ago. We will not, however, bemoan thee as if thou wast for ever lost to us, or that thy name would be buried in oblivion; thy soul yet lives in the great Country of Spirits, with those of thy nation that are gone before thee; and though we are left behind to perpetuate thy fame, we shall one day join thee. Actuated by the respect we bore thee whilst living, we now come to tender to thee the last act of kindness it is in our power to bestow: that thy body might not lie neglected on the plain, and become a prey to the beasts of the field, or the fowls of the air, we will take care to lay it with those of thy predecessors who are gone before thee; hoping at the same time, that thy spirit will feed with their spirits, and be ready to receive ours, when we also shall arrive at the great Country of Souls.

SOURCE: Jonathan Carver. *Travels through the Interior Parts of North America in the Years 1766, 1767, and 1768.* London: 1781 (3rd ed.). 399–400.

JAMES LOGAN, TAHGAHJUTE (Cayuga)

"I appeal to any white man to say, if he ever entered Logan's cabin hungry, and he gave him not meat" (c. 1774)

It is supposed that after launching many vengeful attacks on Virginians, Logan (c. 1728–1780) sent the following short speech to be delivered by an interpreter to his adversaries. It is one of the most famous of Native American speeches and was greatly lauded by Thomas Jefferson, though its authenticity has since been questioned.

I appeal to any white man to say, if he ever entered Logan's cabin hungry, and he gave him not meat; if he ever came cold and naked, and he clothed him not. During the course of the last long and bloody war, Logan remained idle in his cabin, an advocate for peace. Such was my love for the whites, that my countrymen pointed as they passed, and said, "Logan is the friend of white men." I had even thought to have lived with you, but for the injuries of one man. Colonel Cresap, the last spring, in cold blood, and unprovoked, murdered all the relations of Logan, not sparing even my women and children. There runs not a drop of my blood in the veins of any living creature. This called on me for revenge. I have sought it: I have killed many: I have fully glutted my vengeance. For my country, I rejoice at the beams of peace. But do not harbor a thought that mine is the joy of fear. Logan never felt fear. He will not turn on his heel to save his life. Who is there to mourn for Logan?—Not one.

SOURCE: B.B. Thatcher. *Indian Life and Battles*. Akron: New Werner Company, 1910. 187.

CAPTAIN PIPE, HOPOCAN (Delaware)

"Who of us can believe that you can love a people of a different color from your own?" (1781)

The Delawares were among the tribes courted, divided, and ultimately betrayed by the British in the Revolutionary War. Though an ally of the English against the upstart Americans, Captain Pipe (c. 1725–1794), at a Fort Detroit Indian council, aggressively addressed the British commandant as follows.

Father! I have said *father*, though indeed I do not know why I should call *him* so—I have never known any father but the French—I have considered the English only as brothers. But as this name is imposed upon us, I shall make use of it and say:

Father! Some time ago you put a war-hatchet into my hands, saying, "Take this weapon and try it on the heads of my enemies, the Long-Knives [Americans], and let me know afterwards if it was sharp and good."

Father!—At the time when you gave me this weapon, I had neither cause nor wish to go to war against a foe who had done me no injury. But you say you are my father—and call me your child—and in obedience to you I received the hatchet. I knew that if I did not obey you, you would withhold from me the necessaries of life; which I could procure nowhere but here.

Father! You may perhaps think me a fool, for risking my life at your bidding—and that in a cause in which I have no prospect of gaining any thing. For it is your cause, and not mine—you have raised a quarrel among yourselves—and you ought to fight it out.—It is *your* concern to fight the Long-Knives.—You should not compel your children, the Indians, to expose themselves to danger for your sake.

Father!—Many lives have already been lost on *your account.*—The tribes have suffered, and been weakened.—Children have lost parents and brothers—Wives have lost husbands.—It is not known how many more may perish before *your war* will be at an end.

Father!—I have said, you may perhaps think me a fool, for thus thoughtlessly rushing on your enemy! Do not believe this, Father: Think not that I want sense to convince me, that although you now

SOURCE: B.B. Thatcher. *Indian Life and Battles.* Akron: New Werner Company, 1910. 158–160.

pretend to keep up a perpetual enmity to the Long-Knives, you may, before long, conclude a peace with them.

Father! You say you love your children, the Indians.—This you have often told them; and indeed it is your interest to say so to them; that you may have them at your service.

But, Father! Who of us can believe that you can love a people of a different color from your own; better than those who have a white skin, like yourselves?

Father! Pay attention to what I am going to say. While you, Father, are setting me on your enemy, much in the same manner as a hunter sets his dog on the game; while I am in the act of rushing on that enemy of yours, with the bloody destructive weapon you gave me, I may, perchance, happen to look back at the place from whence you started me, and what shall I see? Perhaps, I may see my father shaking hands with the Long-Knives; yes, with those very people he now calls his enemies. I may *then* see him laugh at my folly for having obeyed his orders; and yet I am now risking my life at his command!—Father! keep what I have said in remembrance.

Now, Father! here is what has been done with the hatchet you gave me [handing over a stick with scalps on it]. I have done with the hatchet what you ordered me to do, and found it sharp. Nevertheless, I did not do all that I might have done. No, I did not. My heart failed within me. I felt compassion for your enemy. Innocence had no part in your quarrels; therefore I distinguished—I spared. I took some live flesh, [and], while I was bringing [it] to you, I spied one of your large canoes, on which I put it for you. In a few days you will receive this flesh, and find that the skin is of the same color with your own.

Father! I hope you will not destroy what I have saved. You, Father, have the means of preserving that which would perish with us from want. The warrior is poor, and his cabin is always empty; but your house, Father, is always full.

BUCKONGAHELAS (Delaware)

"You see a great and powerful nation divided!" (1781)

Buckongahelas (c. 1750s–1804), a warrior chief who sided with the British against the Americans in the Revolutionary War, addressed Christian Delawares in Ohio in the following words. He did not mean for them to join the fighting, but he did hope to save their lives by persuading them to leave American territory. He later scolded Captain Pipe for having threatened the missionaries—who had left—and thus encouraged the Christian Delawares to follow them rather than the other Delawares.

Friends!—Listen to what I say to you! You see a great and powerful nation divided! You see the father fighting against the son, and the son against the father!—The father has called on his Indian children to assist him in punishing his children, the Americans, who have become refractory!—I took time to consider what I should do—whether or not I should receive the hatchet of my father, to assist him!—At first I looked upon it as a family quarrel, in which I was not interested.—However, at length it appeared to me that the father was in the right; and his children deserved to be punished a little.—That this must be the case, I concluded from the many cruel acts his offspring had committed from time to time on his Indian children; in encroaching on their land, stealing their property, shooting at, and murdering without cause, men, women and children.—Yes! even murdering those, who at all times had been friendly to them, and were placed for protection under the roof of their father's house—the father himself standing sentry at the door, at the time.

Friends! Often has the father been obliged to settle, and make amends for the wrongs and mischiefs done to us, by his refractory children, yet these do not grow better! No! they remain the same, and will continue to be so, as long as we have any land left us! Look back at the murders committed by the Long-Knives on many of our relations, who lived peaceable neighbors to them on the Ohio! Did they not kill them without the least provocation?—Are they, do you think, better now than they were then?—No, indeed not; and many days are not elapsed since you had a number of these very men at your doors, who panted to kill you, but fortunately were prevented from so doing by the *Great*

SOURCE: B.B. Thatcher. *Indian Life and Battles.* Akron: New Werner Company, 1910. 190–191.

Sun [Col. Dan Broadhead], who, at that time, had been ordained by the Great Spirit to protect you!

Friends and relatives!—Now listen to me and hear what I have to say to you.—I am myself come to bid you rise and go with me to a secure place! Do not, my friends, covet the land you now hold under cultivation. I will conduct you to a country equally good, where your fields shall yield you abundant crops, and where your cattle shall find sufficient pasture; where there is plenty of game; where your women and children, together with yourselves, will live in peace and safety; where no Long-Knife shall ever molest you!—Nay! I will live between you and them, and not even suffer them to frighten you!—There, you can worship your God without fear!—Here, where you are, you cannot do this!—Think on what I have now said to you, and believe, that if you stay where you now are, one day or another the Long-Knives will, in their usual way, speak fine words to you, and at the same time murder you!

CORNPLANTER, HALF TOWN and BIG TREE (Seneca)

"The land we live on our fathers received from God"
(December 1790)

In this dictated speech, three Seneca chiefs address President George Washington about the Iroquois' role in the Revolutionary War and the Senecas' rights to their land.

Father, the voice of the Seneca Nations speaks to you, the great counsellor, in whose heart the wise men of all the Thirteen Fires have placed their wisdom; it may be very small in your ears, and we therefore entreat you to hearken with attention, for we are about to speak of things which are to us very great.

When your army entered the country of the Six Nations, we called you the town-destroyer; and to this day, when your name is heard, our women look behind them and turn pale, and our children cling close to the necks of their mothers. Our counsellors and warriors are men, and cannot be afraid; but their hearts are grieved with the fears of our women and children, and desire that it may be buried so deep as to be heard no more.

When you gave us peace we called you father, because you promised to secure us in the possession of our lands. Do this, and so long as the land shall remain, that beloved name shall be in the heart of every Seneca.

Father, we mean to open our hearts before you, and we earnestly desire that you will let us clearly understand what you resolve to do.

When our chiefs returned from the treaty at Fort Stanwix, and laid before our council what had been done there, our nation was surprised to hear how great a country you had compelled them to give up to you, without your paying to us anything for it. Everyone said that your hearts were yet swelled with resentment against us for what had happened during the war, but that one day you would consider it with more kindness. We asked each other, what have we done to deserve such severe chastisement?

Father, when you kindled your Thirteen Fires separately [before the union of the States. —*Buchanan's note*], the wise men assembled at them told us that you were all brothers, the children of one great father,

---

SOURCE: James Buchanan. *Sketches of the History, Manners, and Customs of the North American Indians with a Plan for Their Amelioration*. New York: William Borradaile, 1824. 108–116.

who regarded the red people as his children. They called us brothers, and invited us to his protection. They told us that he resided beyond the great water where the sun first rises; that he was a king whose power no people could resist, and that his goodness was as bright as the sun: what they said went to our hearts. We accepted the invitation, and promised to obey him. What the Seneca Nation promises they faithfully perform; and when you refused obedience to that king, he commanded us to assist his beloved men in making you sober. In obeying him, we did no more than yourselves had led us to promise. The men who claimed this promise told us that you were children and had no guns; that when they had shaken you, you would submit. We hearkened unto them, and were deceived until your army approached our towns. We were deceived, but your people teaching us to confide in that king had helped to deceive us, and we now appeal to your heart, is all the blame ours?

Father, when we saw that we had been deceived, and heard the invitation which you gave us to draw near to the fire you had kindled and talk with you concerning peace, we made haste toward it. You then told us you could crush us to nothing, and you demanded from us a great country as the price of that peace which you had offered to us; as if our want of strength had destroyed our rights. Our chiefs had felt your power and were unable to contend against you, and they therefore gave up that country. What they agreed to has bound our nation; but your anger against us must by this time be cooled, and although our strength is not increased, nor your power become less, we ask you to consider calmly: Were the terms dictated to us by your commissioners reasonable and just?

Father, your commissioners, when they drew the line which separated the land then given up to you from that which you agreed should remain to be ours, did most solemnly promise that we should be secured in the peaceable possession of the land which we inhabited, east and north of that line.—Does this promise bind you?

Hear now, we entreat you, what has since happened concerning that land. On the day we finished the treaty at Fort Stanwix, commissioners from Pennsylvania told our chiefs that they had come there to purchase from lines of their state; and they told us that all the lands belonging to us within the line would strike the river Susquehanna below Tioga branch. They then left us to consider of the bargain until next day. The next day we let them know that we were unwilling to sell all the land within their state, and proposed to let them have a part of it, which we pointed out to them in their map. They told us that they must have the whole, that it was already ceded to them by the great king at the time of making peace with you, and was then their own; but they said that they would not take advantage of that, and were willing to pay us for it, after the manner of their ancestors. Our chiefs were unable to contend at that time, and therefore they sold the lands up to the line, which was then shown them as the line of that state. What the commissioners had said about the land having been ceded to them at the peace, they considered as intended only to lessen the price, and they passed it by with very little notice; but since that time we have heard so much from others about the right to our lands which the king gave when you made peace with him, that it is our earnest desire that you will tell us what it means.

Our nation empowered J. L. to let out a part of our lands; he told us that he was sent by Congress to do this for us, and we fear he has deceived us in the writing he obtained from us; for since the time of our giving that power, a man named P—— has come and claimed our whole country northward of the line of Pennsylvania, under a purchase from that L. to whom he said he had paid twenty thousand dollars for it; he also said, that he had bought it from the council of the Thirteen Fires, and paid them twenty thousand more for the same; and he also said that it did not belong to us, for that the great king had ceded the whole of it, when you made peace with him. Thus he claimed the whole country north of Pennsylvania, and west of the lands belonging to the Cayugas. He demanded it; he insisted on his demand, and declared to us that he would have it all. It was impossible for us to grant him this, and we immediately refused it. After some days he proposed to run a line a small distance eastward of our western boundary, which we also refused to agree to. He then threatened us with immediate war if we did not comply.

Upon this threat our chiefs held a council, and they agreed that no event of war could be worse than to be driven, with our wives and children, from the only country which we had any right to; and therefore, weak as our nation was, they determined to take the chance of war rather than submit to such unjust demands, which seemed to have no bounds. Mr. Street, the great trader at Niagara, was then with us, having come at the request of P——; and as he had always professed to be our great friend, we consulted him on this subject. He also told us that our lands had been ceded by the king, and that we must give them up. Astonished at what we heard from every quarter, with hearts aching with compassion for our women and children, we were thus compelled to give up all our country north of the line of Pennsylvania, and east of the Chenesee river up to the great forks, and east of a south-line drawn up from that fork to the line of Pennsylvania. For this land P—— agreed to pay us ten thousand dollars in hand, and one thousand dollars a year for ever. He paid us two thousand five hundred dollars, and he sent for us to come last spring and receive our money; but instead of paying us the residue (or remainder) of the ten thousand dollars, and the one thousand dollars due for the first year, he offered only five hundred dollars, and insisted that he had agreed with us for that sum to be paid yearly.

We debated with him for six days, during all which time he persisted in refusing to pay us our just demand; and he insisted that we should receive the five hundred dollars; and Street from Niagara also insisted on our receiving the money as it was offered us. The last reason which he assigned for continuing to refuse paying us was—that the king had ceded the land to the Thirteen Fires, and that he had bought them from you and paid you for them.

Father, we could bear this confusion no longer and determined to press through every difficulty, and lift up our voice so that you might hear us, and to claim that security in the possession of our lands, which your commissioners so solemnly promised us; and we now entreat you to inquire into our complaints, and to redress our wrongs.

Father, our writings were lodged in the hands of Street of Niagara, as we supposed him to be our friend; but when we saw P—— consulting Street on every occasion, we doubted of his honesty towards us; and we have since heard that he was to receive for his endeavours to deceive us a piece of land ten miles in width west of the Chenesee river; and near forty miles in length extending to Lake Ontario; and the lines of this tract have been run accordingly, although no part of it is within the bounds which limit this purchase.

Father, you have said that we were in your hand, and that by closing it you could crush us to nothing. Are you then determined to crush us? If you are, tell us so, that those of our nation who have become your children, and have determined to die so, may know what to do. In this case one chief has said he would ask you to put him out of his pain. Another, who will not think of dying by the hand of his father, or of his brother, has said he will retire to the Chataughque, eat of the fatal root, and sleep with his fathers in peace.

Before you determine a measure so unjust, look up to God, who made us as well as you; we hope he will not permit you to destroy the whole of our nation.

Father, hear our case: Many nations inhabited this country, but they had no wisdom, therefore they warred together; the Six Nations were powerful and compelled them to peace. The land for a great extent was given up to them, but the nations which were not destroyed all continued on those lands: and claimed the protection of the Six Nations, as brothers of their fathers. They were men, and when at peace had a right to live upon the earth.

The French came among us, and built Niagara; they became our fathers, and took care of us. Sir William Johnson came, and took that fort from the French; he became our father, and promised to take care of us, and he did so until you were too strong for his king. To him we gave four miles round Niagara, as a place of trade. We have already said how we came to join against you; we saw that we were wrong, we wished for peace, you demanded a great country to be given up to you, it was surrendered to you as the price of peace, and we ought to have peace and possession of the little land which you then left us.

Father, when that great country was given up to you there were but few chiefs present, and they were compelled to give it up. And it is not the Six Nations only that reproach those chiefs with having given up that country. The Chippewas, and all the nations who lived on these lands westward, call to us, and ask us, "Brothers of our fathers, where is the place which you have reserved for us to lie down upon?"

Father, you have compelled us to do that which makes us ashamed. We have nothing to answer to the children of the brothers of our fathers. When last spring they called upon us to go to war to secure them a bed to lie down upon, the Senecas entreated them to be quiet until we had spoken to you; but on our way down, we heard that your army had gone towards the country which those nations inhabited; and if they meet together, the best blood on both sides will stain the ground.

Father, we will not conceal from you that the great God, and not men, has preserved Cornplanter from the hands of his own nation. For they ask continually, "Where is the land on which our children, and their children after them, are to lie down upon? You told us," say they, "that the line drawn from Pennsylvania to Lake Ontario would mark it forever on the east, and the line running from Beaver Creek to Pennsylvania would mark it on the west, and we see that it is not so; for first one, and then another, come and take it away by order of that people which you tell us promised to secure it to us." He is silent, for he has nothing to answer. When the sun goes down he opens his heart before God; and earlier than the sun appears again upon the hills he gives thanks for his protection during the night; for he feels that among men, become desperate by the injuries they sustain, it is God only that can preserve him. He loves peace, and all he had in store he has given to those who have been robbed by your people, lest they should plunder the innocent to repay themselves. The whole season, which others have employed in providing for their families, he has spent in endeavours to preserve peace; and this moment his wife and children are lying on the ground, and in want of food: his heart is in pain for them, but he perceives that the Great Spirit will try his firmness in doing what is right.

Father, the game which the Great Spirit sent into our country for us to eat is going from among us. We thought he intended we should till the ground with the plough as the white people do, and we talked to one another about it. But before we speak to you concerning this, we must know from you whether you mean to leave us and our children any land to till. Speak plainly to us concerning this great business.

All the land we have been speaking of belonged to the Six Nations: no part of it ever belonged to the King of England, and he could not give it up to you. The land we live on our fathers received from God, and they transmitted it to us for our children, and we cannot part with it.

Father, we told you that we would open our hearts to you: hear us once more. At Fort Stanwix we agreed to deliver up those of our people who should do you any wrong, and that you might try them and punish them according to your law. We delivered up two men accordingly; but instead of trying them according to your law, the lowest of your people took them from your magistrate, and put them immediately to death. It is just to punish the murderer with death, but the Senecas will not deliver up their people to men who disregard the treaties of their own nation.

Father, innocent men of our nation are killed, one after another, and of our best families; but none of your people who have committed those murders have been punished. We recollect that you did promise to punish those who killed our people; and we ask, was it intended that your people should kill the Senecas, and not only remain unpunished, but be protected from the next of kin?

Father, these are to us very great things; we know that you are very strong, and we have heard that you are wise, and we shall wait to hear your answer that we may know that you are just.

UNNAMED WOMEN and RED JACKET (Seneca)

"We are the owners of this land, and it is ours!" (1791)

In 1791 President George Washington sent emissaries to pressure the Iroquois into declaring their neutrality. Seneca women often voiced their opinions on important issues—and sometimes decided them—and in this instance they lobbied for agreement with Washington and peace; Red Jacket (see further speeches, pages 41–48) took up and expanded their argument.

Brother, the Great Ruler has spared us until another day to talk together; for since you came here from General Washington, you and our uncles, the sachems, have been counseling together. Moreover, your sisters, the women, have taken the same into great consideration, because you and our sachems have said so much about it. Now, that is the reason we have come to say something to you, and to tell you that the Great Ruler hath preserved you, and that you ought to hear and listen to what we women shall speak, as well as the sachems; *for we are the owners of this land,* AND IT IS OURS! It is we that plant it for our and their use. Hear us, therefore, for we speak things that concern us and our children; and you must not think hard of us while our men shall say more to you, for we have told them.

[The women then designated Red Jacket as their speaker, and he took up the speech of his clients as follows:]

Brothers from Pennsylvania: You that are sent from General Washington and by the thirteen fires; you have been sitting side by side with us every day, and the Great Ruler has appointed us another pleasant day to meet again.

Now, listen, brothers; you know it has been the request of our head warriors that we are left to answer for our women, who are to conclude what ought to be done by both sachems and warriors. So hear what is their conclusion. The business you come on is very troublesome, and we have been a long time considering it; and now the elder of our women have said that our sachems and warriors must *help you,* for the good of them and their children, and you tell us the Americans are strong for peace.

SOURCE: Norman B. Wood. *Lives of Famous Indian Chiefs.* Aurora, Illinois: American Indian Historical Publishing Co., 1906. 247–248.

Now, all that has been done for you has been done by our women; the rest will be a hard task for us; for the people at the setting sun are bad people, and you have come in too much haste for such great matters of importance. And now, brothers, you must look when it is light in the morning, until the setting sun, and you must reach your neck over the land to take in all the light you can to show the danger. And these are the words of our women to you, and the sachems and warriors who shall go with you.

Now, brothers from Pennsylvania and from General Washington, I have told you all I was directed. Make your minds easy, and let us throw all care on the mercy of the Great Keeper, in hopes that he will assist us.

UNNAMED (Delaware and twelve other tribes)

"Our only demand is the peaceable possession of a small part of our once great country" (1793)

The Council of 1793 tried to persuade the U.S. government to honor its own treaties and use the Ohio River as a boundary across which settlement by whites would be forbidden. The government, meanwhile, wanted to push all the tribes across the Mississippi. The Native Americans proposed another plan, which follows.

Money to us is of no value, and to most of us unknown; and as no consideration whatever can induce us to sell the lands on which we get sustenance for our women and children, we hope we may be allowed to point out a mode by which your settlers may be easily removed, and peace thereby obtained.

We know that these settlers are poor, or they would never have ventured to live in a country which has been in continual trouble ever since they crossed the Ohio. Divide, therefore, this large sum of money which you have offered us among these people; give to each, also, a proportion of what you say you would give to us annually, over and above this very large sum of money, and we are persuaded they would most readily accept of it in lieu of the lands you sold them. If you add, also, the great sums you must expend in raising and paying armies with a view to force us to yield you our country, you will certainly have more than sufficient for the purpose of repaying these settlers for all their labor and their improvements.

You have talked to us about concessions. It appears strange that you should expect any from us, who have only been defending our just rights against your invasions. We want peace. Restore to us our country, and we shall be enemies no longer.

We desire you to consider, brothers, that our only demand is the peaceable possession of a small part of our once great country. Look back and review the lands from whence we have been driven to this spot. We can retreat no farther, because the country behind hardly affords food for its present inhabitants, and we have therefore resolved to leave our bones in this small space to which we are now confined.

SOURCE: Helen Hunt Jackson. A *Century of Dishonor: A Sketch of the United States Government's Dealings with Some of the Indian Tribes.* New York, Harper and Brothers, 1881. 42–43.

Part II.

NINETEENTH CENTURY

RED JACKET, SAGOYEWATHA (Seneca)

"You have got our country, but are not satisfied; you want to force your religion upon us" (1805)

The foremost embodiment of the tradition of Iroquois oratory and probably the greatest of orators in Native American history, Red Jacket (c. 1751–1830)—unlike, for instance, Pontiac, Tecumseh, Black Hawk, or Sitting Bull—was no warrior. His fiery, incisive eloquence, however, inspired cultural pride and resistance, and sometimes even affected the behavior of his non-Indian auditors. He understood English, but determinedly refused to speak it in public. His name—Sagoyewatha—means "He is prepared." In the following speech, he answered a young missionary named Cram who had come to convert the Senecas to Christianity.

Friend and Brother: It was the will of the Great Spirit that we should meet together this day. He orders all things, and has given us a fine day for our council. He has taken his garment from before the sun and caused it to shine with brightness upon us. For all these things we thank the Great Ruler, and Him *only!*

Brother, this council-fire was kindled by you. It was at your request that we came together at this time. We have listened with joy to what you have said. You requested us to speak our minds freely. This gives us great joy, for we now consider that we stand upright before you and can speak what we think. All have heard your voice and can speak to you as one man. Our minds are agreed.

Brother, listen to what we say. There was a time when our forefathers owned this great island. Their seats extended from the rising to the setting sun. The Great Spirit had made it for the use of Indians. He had created the buffalo, the deer and other animals for food. He had made the bear and the beaver. Their skins served us for clothing. He had scattered them over the country and taught us how to take them. He had caused the earth to produce corn for bread. All this he had done for his red children because he loved them. If we had some disputes about our hunting-ground, they were generally settled without the shedding of much blood. But an evil day came upon us. Your forefathers crossed the great water and landed upon this island. Their numbers were small. They found us friends and not enemies. They told us they had fled

SOURCE: Norman B. Wood. *Lives of Famous Indian Chiefs*. Aurora, Illinois: American Indian Historical Publishing Co., 1906. 254–256.

from their own country on account of wicked men, and had come here to enjoy their religion. They asked for a small seat. We took pity on them and granted their request, and they sat down amongst us. We gave them corn and meat; they gave us poison [rum] in return.

The white people, brother, had now found our country. Tidings were carried back, and more came amongst us. Yet we did not fear them. We took them to be friends. They called us brothers; we believed them, and gave them a larger seat. At length their numbers had greatly increased. They wanted more land; they wanted our country. Our eyes were opened, and our minds became uneasy. Wars took place. Indians were hired to fight against Indians, and many of our people were destroyed. They also brought strong liquor amongst us. It was strong and powerful and has slain thousands.

Brother, our seats were once large, and yours were small. You have now become a great people, and we have scarcely a place left to spread our blankets. You have got our country, but are not satisfied; you want to force your religion upon us.

Brother, continue to listen. You say that you are sent to instruct us how to worship the Great Spirit agreeable to his mind; and if we do not take hold of the religion which you white people teach, we shall be unhappy hereafter. You say that you are right, and we are lost. How do we know this to be true? We understand that your religion is written in a book. If it was intended for us as well as you, why has not the Great Spirit given to us—and not only to us, but to our forefathers—the knowledge of that book, with the means of understanding it rightly? We only know what you tell us about it. How shall we know when to believe, being so often deceived by the white people?

Brother, you say there is but one way to worship and serve the Great Spirit. If there is but one religion, why do you white people differ so much about it? Why not all agree, as you can all read the book?

Brother, we do not understand these things. We are told that your religion was given to your forefathers, and has been handed down from father to son. We, also, have a religion which was given to our forefathers, and has been handed down to us, their children. We worship in that way. It teaches us to be thankful for all the favors we receive; to love each other, and be united. We never quarrel about religion, because it is a matter which concerns each man and the Great Spirit.

Brother, we do not wish to destroy your religion or take it from you; we only want to enjoy our own.

Brother, we have been told that you have been preaching to the white people in this place. These people are our neighbors. We are acquainted with them. We will wait a little while and see what effect your preaching has upon them. If we find it does them good, makes them honest and less disposed to cheat Indians, we will consider again of what you have said.

Brother, you have now heard our talk, and this is all we have to say at present. As we are going to part, we will come and take you by the hand, and hope the Great Spirit will protect you on your journey, and return you safely to your friends.

RED JACKET, SAGOYEWATHA (Seneca)

"We like our religion, and do not want another" (May 1811)

Red Jacket (c. 1751–1830) addressed Reverend Alexander, from
New York City, during a Seneca council at Buffalo Creek.

Brother!—We listened to the talk you delivered us from the Council of
Black-Coats, in New York. We have fully considered your talk, and the
offers you have made us. We now return our answer, which we wish
you also to understand. In making up our minds, we have looked back
to remember what has been done in our days, and what our fathers
have told us was done in old times.

Brother!—Great numbers of Black-Coats have been among the
Indians. With sweet voices and smiling faces, they offered to teach
them the religion of the white people. Our brethren in the East listened to them. They turned from the religion of their fathers, and took
up the religion of the white people. What good has it done? Are they
more friendly one to another than we are? No, Brother! They are a divided people—we are united. They quarrel about religion—we live in
love and friendship. Besides, they drink strong waters. And they have
learned how to cheat, and how to practice all the other vices of the
white people, without imitating their virtues. Brother!—If you wish us
well, keep away; do not disturb us.

Brother!—We do not worship the Great Spirit as the white people
do, but we believe that the forms of worship are indifferent to the Great
Spirit. It is the homage of sincere hearts that pleases him, and we worship him in that manner.

According to your religion, we must believe in a Father and Son, or
we shall not be happy hereafter. We have always believed in a Father,
and we worship him as our old men taught us. Your book says that the
Son was sent on Earth by the Father. Did all the people who saw the
Son believe him? No! they did not. And if you have read the book, the
consequence must be known to you.

Brother!—You wish us to change our religion for yours. We like our
religion, and do not want another. Our friends here [pointing to Mr.
Granger, the Indian Agent, and two other whites] do us great good;
they counsel us in trouble; they teach us how to be comfortable at all

SOURCE: B.B. Thatcher. *Indian Life and Battles*. Akron: New Werner
Company, 1910. 312–314.

times. Our friends the Quakers do more. They give us ploughs, and teach us how to use them. They tell us we are accountable beings. But they do not tell us we must change our religion.—we are satisfied with what they do, and with what they say.

Brother!—for these reasons we cannot receive your offers. We have other things to do, and beg you to make your mind easy, without troubling us, lest our heads should be too much loaded, and by and by burst.

RED JACKET, SAGOYEWATHA (Seneca)

"We are determined not to sell our lands"   (May 1811)

At the same Buffalo Creek council where he answered Reverend
Alexander, Red Jacket (c. 1751–1830) responded to the request of a
land speculator named Mr. Richardson.

Brother!—We opened our ears to the talk you lately delivered to us, at
our council-fire. In doing important business it is best not to tell long
stories, but come to it in a few words. We therefore shall not repeat your
talk, which is fresh in our minds. We have well considered it, and the
advantage and disadvantages of your offers. We request your attention
to our answer, which is not from the speaker alone, but from all the
Sachems and Chiefs now around our council-fire.

Brother!—We know that great men, as well as great nations, have different interests and different minds, and do not see the same light—but
we hope our answer will be agreeable to you and your employers.

Brother!—Your application for the purchase of our lands is to our
minds very extraordinary. It has been made in a crooked manner. You
have not walked in the straight path pointed out by the great Council
of your nation. You have no writings from your great Father, the
President. In making up our minds we have looked back, and remembered how the Yorkers purchased our lands in former times. They
bought them, piece after piece—for a little money paid to a few men
in our nation, and not to all our brethren—until our planting and
hunting-grounds have become very small, and if we sell *them*, we know
not where to spread our blankets.

Brother!—You tell us your employers have purchased of the Council
of Yorkers a right to buy our lands. We do not understand how this can
be. The lands do not belong to the Yorkers; they are ours, and were
given to us by the Great Spirit.

Brother!—We think it strange that you should jump over the lands
of our brethren in the East to come to our council-fire so far off, to get
our lands. When we sold our lands in the East to the white people, we
determined never to sell those we kept, which are as small as we can
comfortably live on.

Brother!—You want us to travel with you and look for new lands. If
we should sell our lands and move off into a distant country towards the

SOURCE: B.B. Thatcher. *Indian Life and Battles*. Akron: New Werner
Company, 1910. 314–317.

setting sun, we should be looked upon in the country to which we go as foreigners and strangers. We should be despised by the red as well as the white men, and we should soon be surrounded by the white people, who will there also kill our game, and come upon our lands and try to get them from us.

Brother!—We are determined not to sell our lands, but to continue on them. We like them. They are fruitful, and produce us corn in abundance for the support of our women and children, and grass and herbs for our cattle.

Brother!—At the treaties held for the purchase of our lands, the white men, with sweet voices and smiling faces, told us they loved us, and that they would not cheat us, but that the king's children on the other side of the lake would cheat us. When we go on the other side of the lake, the king's children tell us *your* people will cheat us. These things puzzle our heads, and we believe that the Indians must take care of themselves, and not trust either in your people, or in the king's children.

Brother!—At a late council we requested our agents to tell you that we would not sell our lands, and we think you have not spoken to our agents, or they would have told you so, and we should not have met you at our council-fire at this time.

Brother!—The white people buy and sell false rights to our lands, and your employers have, you say, paid a great price for their rights. They must have a plenty of money to spend it in buying false rights to lands belonging to Indians. The loss of it will not hurt them, but our lands are of great value to us, and we wish you to go back with our talk to your employers, and tell them and the Yorkers that they have no right to buy and sell false rights to our lands.

Brother!—We hope you clearly understand the ideas we have offered. This is all we have to say.

RED JACKET, SAGOYEWATHA (Seneca)

"I am an aged tree and can stand no longer" (c. 1829)

In this farewell, his last public speech to the Senecas, Red Jacket (c. 1751–1830) foretold the loss of the tribe's homeland. Within ten years of Red Jacket's death, the Senecas were indeed cheated out of their lands, but, remarkably, won them back in a legal decision.

I am about to leave you, and when I am gone, and my warning shall no longer be heard or regarded, the craft and avarice of the white man will prevail. Many winters have I breasted the storm, but I am an aged tree and can stand no longer. My leaves are fallen, my branches are withered, and I am shaken by every breeze. Soon my aged trunk will be prostrate, and the foot of the exulting foe of the Indian may be placed upon it in safety; for I have none who will be able to avenge such an indignity. Think not I mourn for myself. I go to join the spirits of my fathers, where age can not come; but my heart fails me when I think of my people, who are so soon to be scattered and forgotten.

SOURCE: Norman B. Wood. *Lives of Famous Indian Chiefs*. Aurora, Illinois: American Indian Historical Publishing Co., 1906. 281.

BIG ELK, ONGPATONGA (Omaha)

"Death will come, and always comes out of season"
(July 1811)

Big Elk (c. 1765–1846) offered this funeral oration for Black Buffalo, a Teton Sioux, at Portage des Sioux. Big Elk would go on to live a long life and make several treaties with the U.S. government.

Do not grieve. Misfortunes will happen to the wisest and best men. Death will come, and always comes out of season. It is the command of the Great Spirit, and all nations and people must obey. What is passed, and cannot be prevented, should not be grieved for. Be not discouraged or displeased then, that in visiting your father here [the American commissioner], you have lost your chief. A misfortune of this kind may never again befall you, but this would have attended you perhaps at your own village. Five times have I visited this land, and never returned with sorrow or pain. Misfortunes do not flourish particularly in our path. They grow everywhere. What a misfortune for me, that I could not have died this day, instead of the chief that lies before us. The trifling loss my nation would have sustained in my death would have been doubly paid for by the honours of my burial. They would have wiped off everything like regret. Instead of being covered with a cloud of sorrow, my warriors would have felt the sunshine of joy in their hearts. To me it would have been a most glorious occurrence. Hereafter, when I die at home, instead of a noble grave and a grand procession, the rolling music and the thundering cannon, with a flag waving at my head, I shall be wrapped in a robe (an old robe perhaps) and hoisted on a slender scaffold to the whistling winds [It is a custom to expose the dead upon a scaffold among some of the tribes of the west.—*Drake's note*.], soon to be blown down to the earth; my flesh to be devoured by the wolves, and my bones rattled on the plain by the wild beasts. Chief of the soldiers [addressing Col. Miller], your labors have not been in vain. Your attention shall not be forgotten. My nation shall know the respect that is paid over the dead. When I return, I will echo the sound of your guns.

SOURCE: Samuel G. Drake. *Biography and History of the Indians of North America, from Its First Discovery.* Boston: Benjamin B. Mussey & Co., 1851 (11th ed.). 633.

TECUMSEH (Shawnee)

"Sleep not longer, O Choctaws and Chickasaws"
(September 1811)

Tecumseh (c. 1768–1813), a far-seeing and brave leader, a dynamo of war and oratory, respected and feared by whites and Native Americans alike, was indefatigable in trying to organize a confederacy of resistance to American encroachment on Native American lands. He traveled from his lands in Indiana to Florida, to Missouri, to the Plains, and into Canada in his efforts to galvanize a union of tribes. In spite of his charisma and persuasiveness, he was not always successful. Following Tecumseh's powerful speech is the Choctaw leader Pushmataha's impressive reply (page 54).

In view of questions of vast importance, have we met together in solemn council to-night. Nor should we here debate whether we have been wronged and injured, but by what measures we should avenge ourselves; for our merciless oppressors, having long since planned out their proceedings, are not about to make, but have and are still making attacks upon those of our race who have as yet come to no resolution. Nor are we ignorant by what steps, and by what gradual advances, the whites break in upon our neighbors. Imagining themselves to be still undiscovered, they show themselves the less audacious because you are insensible. The whites are already nearly a match for us all united, and too strong for any one tribe alone to resist; so that unless we support one another with our collective and united forces; unless every tribe unanimously combines to give a check to the ambition and avarice of the whites, they will soon conquer us apart and disunited, and we will be driven away from our native country and scattered as autumnal leaves before the wind.

But have we not courage enough remaining to defend our country and maintain our ancient independence? Will we calmly suffer the white intruders and tyrants to enslave us? Shall it be said of our race that we knew not how to extricate ourselves from the three most to be dreaded calamities—folly, inactivity and cowardice? But what need is there to speak of the past? It speaks for itself and asks, "Where today is the Pequot? Where the Narragansetts, the Mohawks, Pocanokets, and

SOURCE: H.B. Cushman. *History of the Choctaw, Chickasaw and Natchez Indians.* Greenville, TX: Headlight Printing House, 1899. [Reprint edition. Edited by Angie Debo. University of Oklahoma Press, 1999. 248–252.]

many other once powerful tribes of our race?" They have vanished before the avarice and oppression of the white men, as snow before a summer sun. In the vain hope of alone defending their ancient possessions, they have fallen in the wars with the white men. Look abroad over their once beautiful country, and what see you now? Naught but the ravages of the pale-face destroyers meet your eyes. So it will be with you Choctaws and Chickasaws! Soon your mighty forest trees, under the shade of whose wide spreading branches you have played in infancy, sported in boyhood, and now rest your wearied limbs after the fatigue of the chase, will be cut down to fence in the land which the white intruders dare to call their own. Soon their broad roads will pass over the graves of your fathers, and the place of their rest will be blotted out forever. The annihilation of our race is at hand unless we unite in one common cause against the common foe. Think not, brave Choctaws and Chickasaws, that you can remain passive and indifferent to the common danger, and thus escape the common fate. Your people too will soon be as falling leaves and scattering clouds before their blighting breath. You too will be driven away from your native land and ancient domains as leaves are driven before the wintry storms.

Sleep not longer, O Choctaws and Chickasaws, in false security and delusive hopes. Our broad domains are fast escaping from our grasp. Every year our white intruders become more greedy, exacting, oppressive and overbearing. Every year contentions spring up between them and our people and when blood is shed we have to make atonement whether right or wrong, at the cost of the lives of our greatest chiefs, and the yielding up of large tracts of our lands. Before the pale-faces came among us, we enjoyed the happiness of unbounded freedom, and were acquainted with neither riches, wants, nor oppression. How is it now? Wants and oppressions are our lot; for are we not controlled in everything, and dare we move without asking, by your leave? Are we not being stripped day by day of the little that remains of our ancient liberty? Do they not even now kick and strike us as they do their black-faces? How long will it be before they will tie us to a post and whip us, and make us work for them in their corn fields as they do them? Shall we wait for that moment or shall we die fighting before submitting to such ignominy?

Have we not for years had before our eyes a sample of their designs, and are they not sufficient harbingers of their future determinations? Will we not soon be driven from our respective countries and the graves of our ancestors? Will not the bones of our dead be plowed up, and their graves be turned into fields? Shall we calmly wait until they become so numerous that we will no longer be able to resist oppression? Will we wait to be destroyed in our turn, without making an

effort worthy our race? Shall we give up our homes, our country, be-
queathed to us by the Great Spirit, the graves of our dead, and everything that is dear and sacred to us, without a struggle? I know you will
cry with me. Never! Never! Then let us by unity of action destroy them
all, which we now can do, or drive them back whence they came. War
or extermination is now our only choice. Which do you choose? I know
your answer. Therefore, I now call on you, brave Choctaws and
Chickasaws, to assist in the just cause of liberating our race from the
grasp of our faithless invaders and heartless oppressors. The white
usurpation in our common country must be stopped, or we, its rightful
owners, be forever destroyed and wiped out as a race of people. I am
now at the head of many warriors backed by the strong arm of English
soldiers. Choctaws and Chickasaws, you have too long borne with
grievous usurpation inflicted by the arrogant Americans. Be no longer
their dupes. If there be one here tonight who believes that his rights
will not sooner or later be taken from him by the avaricious American
pale-faces, his ignorance ought to excite pity, for he knows little of the
character of our common foe. And if there be one among you mad
enough to undervalue the growing power of the white race among us,
let him tremble in considering the fearful woes he will bring down
upon our entire race, if by his criminal indifference he assists the designs of our common enemy against our common country. Then listen
to the voice of duty, of honor, of nature and of your endangered country. Let us form one body, one heart, and defend to the last warrior our
country, our homes, our liberty, and the graves of our fathers.

Choctaws and Chickasaws, you are among the few of our race who
sit indolently at ease. You have indeed enjoyed the reputation of being
brave, but will you be indebted for it more from report than fact? Will
you let the whites encroach upon your domains even to your very door
before you will assert your rights in resistance? Let no one in this council imagine that I speak more from malice against the pale-face
Americans than just grounds of complaint. Complaint is just toward
friends who have failed in their duty; accusation is against enemies
guilty of injustice. And surely, if any people ever had, we have good and
just reasons to believe we have ample grounds to accuse the Americans
of injustice; especially when such great acts of injustice have been
committed by them upon our race, of which they seem to have no
manner of regard, or even to reflect. They are a people fond of inno-
vations, quick to contrive and quick to put their schemes into effectual
execution, no matter how great the wrong and injury to us; while we
are content to preserve what we already have. Their design [is] to en-
large their possessions by taking yours in turn; and will you, can you
longer dally, O Choctaws and Chickasaws? Do you imagine that that

people will not continue longest in the enjoyment of peace who timely prepare to vindicate themselves, and manifest a determined resolution to do themselves right whenever they are wronged? Far otherwise. Then haste to the relief of our common cause, as by consanguinity of blood you are bound; lest the day be not far distant when you will be left single-handed and alone to the cruel mercy of our most inveterate foe.

PUSHMATAHA (Choctaw)

"Listen to the voice of prudence, oh, my countrymen"
(September 1811)

Pushmataha (c. 1764–1824), the Choctaw leader, convinced his tribespeople to resist Tecumseh's alluring call to arms against the American settlers. (See Tecumseh's "Sleep not Longer, O Choctaws and Chickasaws," page 50.)

It was not my design in coming here to enter into a disputation with any one. But I appear before you, my warriors and my people, not to throw in my plea against the accusations of Tecumseh; but to prevent your forming rash and dangerous resolutions upon things of highest importance, through the instigations of others. I have myself learned by experience, and I also see many of you, O Choctaws and Chickasaws, who have the same experience of years that I have, the injudicious steps of engaging in an enterprise because it is new. Nor do I stand up before you tonight to contradict the many facts alleged against the American people, or to raise my voice against them in useless accusations. The question before us now is not what wrongs they have inflicted upon our race, but what measures are best for us to adopt in regard to them; and though our race may have been unjustly treated and shamefully wronged by them, yet I shall not for that reason alone advise you to destroy them, unless it was just and expedient for you so to do; nor, would I advise you to forgive them, though worthy of your commiseration, unless I believe it would be to the interest of our common good. We should consult more in regard to our future welfare than our present. What people, my friends and countrymen, were so unwise and inconsiderate as to engage in a war of their own accord, when their own strength, and even with the aid of others, was judged unequal to the task? I well know causes often arise which force men to confront extremities, but, my countrymen, those causes do not now exist. Reflect, therefore, I earnestly beseech you, before you act hastily in this great matter, and consider with yourselves how greatly you will err if you injudiciously approve of and inconsiderately act upon Tecumseh's advice. Remember the American people are now friendly disposed toward us. Surely you are convinced that the greatest good will result to

SOURCE: H.B. Cushman. *History of the Choctaw, Chickasaw and Natchez Indians.* Greenville, TX: Headlight Printing House, 1899. [Reprint edition. Edited by Angie Debo. University of Oklahoma Press, 1999. 253–257.]

us by the adoption of and adhering to those measures I have before rec-
ommended to you; and, without giving too great a scope to mercy or
forbearance, by which I could never permit myself to be seduced, I
earnestly pray you to follow my advice in this weighty matter, and in
following it resolve to adopt those expedients for our future welfare. My
friends and fellow countrymen! You now have no just cause to declare
war against the American people, or wreak your vengeance upon them
as enemies, since they have ever manifested feelings of friendship towards you. It is besides inconsistent with your national glory and with
your honor, as a people, to violate your solemn treaty; and a disgrace to
the memory of your forefathers, to wage war against the American people merely to gratify the malice of the English.

The war, which you are now contemplating against the Americans,
is a flagrant breach of justice; yea, a fearful blemish on your honor and
also that of your fathers, and which you will find if you will examine it
carefully and judiciously forbodes nothing but destruction to our entire
race. It is a war against a people whose territories are now far greater
than our own, and who are far better provided with all necessary implements of war, with men, guns, horses, wealth, far beyond that of all
our race combined, and where is the necessity or wisdom to make war
upon such a people? Where is our hope of success, if thus weak and
unprepared we should declare it against them? Let us not be deluded
with the foolish hope that this war, if begun, will soon be over, even if
we destroy all the whites within our territories, and lay waste their
homes and fields. Far from it. It will be but the beginning of the end
that terminates in the total destruction of our race. And though we will
not permit ourselves to be made slaves, or, like inexperienced warriors,
shudder at the thought of war, yet I am not so insensible and inconsistent as to advise you to cowardly yield to the outrages of the whites, or
wilfully to connive at their unjust encroachments; but only not yet to
have recourse to war, but to send ambassadors to our Great Father at
Washington, and lay before him our grievances, without betraying too
great eagerness for war, or manifesting any tokens of pusillanimity. Let
us, therefore, my fellow countrymen, form our resolutions with great
caution and prudence upon a subject of such vast importance, and in
which such fearful consequences may be involved.

Heed not, O my countrymen, the opinions of others to that extent as
to involve your country in a war that destroys its peace and endangers
its future safety, prosperity and happiness. Reflect, ere it be too late, on
the great uncertainty of war with the American people, and consider
well, ere you engage in it, what the consequences will be if you should
be disappointed in your calculations and expectations. Be not deceived
with illusive hopes. Hear me, O my countrymen, if you begin this war

it will end in calamities to us from which we are now free and at a distance; and upon whom of us they will fall, will only be determined by the uncertain and hazardous event. Be not, I pray you, guilty of rashness, which I never as yet have known you to be; therefore, I implore you, while healing measures are in the election of us all, not to break the treaty, nor violate your pledge of honor, but to submit our grievances, whatever they may be, to the Congress of the United States, according to the articles of the treaty existing between us and the American people. If not, I here invoke the Great Spirit, who takes cognizance of oaths, to bear me witness, that I shall endeavor to avenge myself upon the authors of this war, by whatever methods you shall set me an example. Remember we are a people who have never grown insolent with success, or become abject in adversity; but let those who invite us to hazardous attempts by uttering our praise, also know that the pleasure of hearing has never elevated our spirits above our judgment, nor an endeavor to exasperate us by a flow of invectives to be provoked the sooner to compliance. From tempers equally balanced let it be known that we are warm in the field of battle, and cool in the hours of debate; the former, because a sense of duty has the greater influence over a sedate disposition, and magnanimity the keenest sense of shame; and though good we are at debate, still our education is not polite enough to teach us a contempt of laws, yet by its severity gives us so much good sense as never to disregard them.

We are not a people so impertinently wise as to invalidate the preparations of our enemies by a plausible harangue, and then absolutely proceed to a contest; but we reckon the thoughts of the pale-faces to be of a similar cast with our own, and that hazardous contingencies are not to be determined by a speech. We always presume that the projects of our enemies are judiciously planned, and then we seriously prepare to defeat them. Nor do we found our success upon the hope that they will certainly blunder in their conduct, but upon the hope that we have omitted no proper steps for our own security. Such is the discipline which our fathers have handed down to us; and by adhering to it, we have reaped many advantages. Let us, my countrymen, not forget it now, nor in short space of time precipitately determine a question in which so much is involved. It is indeed the duty of the prudent, so long as they are not injured, to delight in peace. But it is the duty of the brave, when injured, to lay peace aside, and to have recourse to arms; and when successful in these, to then lay them down again in peaceful quiet; thus never to be elevated above measure by success in war, nor delighted with the sweets of peace to suffer insults. For he who, apprehensive of losing the delight, sits indolently at ease, will soon be deprived of the enjoyment of that delight which interesteth his fears; and he whose passions are inflamed by military success, elevated too high by a treacherous confidence, hears no longer the dictates of judgment.

Many are the schemes, though unadvisedly planned, through the more unreasonable conduct of an enemy, which turn out successfully; but more numerous are those which, though seemingly founded on mature counsel, draw after them a disgraceful and opposite result. This proceeds from that great inequality of spirit with which an exploit is projected, and with which it is put into actual execution. For in council we resolve, surrounded with security; in execution we faint, through the prevalence of fear. Listen to the voice of prudence, oh, my countrymen, ere you rashly act. But do as you may, know this truth, enough for you to know, I shall join our friends, the Americans, in this war.

TECUMSEH (Shawnee)

"Let the white race perish" (October 1811)

> Tecumseh (c. 1768–1813), on a six-month campaign to recruit tribes across the country, traveled to the Deep South, where he exhorted the Creeks to join him in fighting the Americans.

In defiance of the white men of Ohio and Kentucky, I have traveled through their settlements—once our favorite hunting-grounds. No war-whoop was sounded, but there is blood upon our knives. The pale-faces felt the blow, but knew not from whence it came. Accursed be the race that has seized on our country, and made women of our warriors. Our fathers, from their tombs, reproach us as slaves and cowards. I hear them now in the wailing winds. The Muscogee were once a mighty people. The Georgians trembled at our war-whoop; and the maidens of my tribe, in the distant lakes, sung the prowess of your warriors, and sighed for their embraces. Now, your very blood is white, your toma-hawks have no edges, your bows and arrows were buried with your fathers. O Muscogees, brethren of my mother! brush from your eyelids the sleep of slavery; once more strike for vengeance—once more for your country. The spirits of the mighty dead complain. The tears drop from the skies. Let the white race perish! They seize your land, they corrupt your women, they trample on your dead! Back! whence they came, upon a trail of blood, they must be driven! Back! back—ay, into the great water whose accursed waves brought them to our shores! Burn their dwellings! Destroy their stock! Slay their wives and children! The red man owns the country, and the pale-face must never enjoy it! War now! War forever! War upon the living! War upon the dead! Dig their very corpses from the graves! Our country must give no rest to a white man's bones. All the tribes of the North are dancing the war-dance. Two mighty warriors across the seas will send us arms.

Tecumseh will soon return to his country. My prophets shall tarry with you. They will stand between you and your enemies. When the white man approaches you the earth shall swallow him up. Soon shall you see my arm of fire stretched athwart the sky. I will stamp my foot at Tippecanoe, and the very earth shall shake.

SOURCE: Wallace A. Brice. *History of Fort Wayne*. Fort Wayne, Indiana: D.W. Jones and Son, 1868. 193–194.

TECUMSEH (Shawnee)

"When the white men first set foot on our grounds, they were hungry" (Winter 1811–1812)

Continuing his efforts to unite many tribes against the whites, Tecumseh (c. 1768–1813) addressed the Osages in Missouri as follows.

Brothers.—We all belong to one family; we are all children of the Great Spirit; we walk in the same path; slake our thirst at the same spring; and now affairs of the greatest concern lead us to smoke the pipe around the same council fire!

Brothers.—We are friends; we must assist each other to bear our burdens. The blood of many of our fathers and brothers has run like water on the ground to satisfy the avarice of the white men. We, ourselves, are threatened with a great evil; nothing will pacify them but the destruction of all the red men.

Brothers.—When the white men first set foot on our grounds, they were hungry; they had no place on which to spread their blankets, or to kindle their fires. They were feeble; they could do nothing for themselves. Our fathers commiserated their distress, and shared freely with them whatever the Great Spirit had given his red children. They gave them food when hungry, medicine when sick, spread skins for them to sleep on, and gave them grounds, that they might hunt and raise corn.—Brothers, the white people are like poisonous serpents: when chilled, they are feeble and harmless; but invigorate them with warmth, and they sting their benefactors to death.

The white people came among us feeble; and now we have made them strong, they wish to kill us, or drive us back, as they would wolves and panthers.

Brothers.—The white men are not friends to the Indians: at first, they only asked for land sufficient for a wigwam; now, nothing will satisfy them but the whole of our hunting grounds, from the rising to the setting sun.

Brothers.—The white men want more than our hunting grounds; they wish to kill our warriors; they would even kill our old men, women, and little ones.

Brothers.—Many winters ago, there was no land; the sun did not rise

SOURCE: John D. Hunter. *Memoirs of a Captivity among the Indians of North America, from Childhood to the Age of Nineteen.* London, 1823. 45–48.

and set: all was darkness. The Great Spirit made all things. He gave the white people a home beyond the great waters. He supplied these grounds with game, and gave them to his red children; and he gave them strength and courage to defend them.

Brothers.—My people wish for peace; the red men all wish for peace: but where the white people are, there is no peace for them, except it be on the bosom of our mother.

Brothers.—The white men despise and cheat the Indians; they abuse and insult them; they do not think the red men sufficiently good to live. The red men have borne many and great injuries; they ought to suffer them no longer. My people will not; they are determined on vengeance; they have taken up the tomahawk; they will make it fat with blood; they will drink the blood of the white people.

Brothers.—My people are brave and numerous; but the white people are too strong for them alone. I wish you to take up the tomahawk with them. If we all unite, we will cause the rivers to stain the great waters with their blood.

Brothers.—If you do not unite with us, they will first destroy us, and then you will fall an easy prey to them. They have destroyed many nations of red men because they were not united, because they were not friends to each other.

Brothers.—The white people send runners amongst us; they wish to make us enemies, that they may sweep over and desolate our hunting grounds, like devastating winds, or rushing waters.

Brothers.—Our Great Father, over the great waters, is angry with the white people, our enemies. He will send his brave warriors against them; he will send us rifles, and whatever else we want—he is our friend, and we are his children.

Brothers.—Who are the white people that we should fear them? They cannot run fast, and are good marks to shoot at: they are only men; our fathers have killed many of them: we are not squaws, and we will stain the earth red with their blood.

Brothers.—The Great Spirit is angry with our enemies; he speaks in thunder, and the earth swallows up villages, and drinks up the Mississippi. The great waters will cover their lowlands; their corn cannot grow; and the Great Spirit will sweep those who escape to the hills from the earth with his terrible breath.

Brothers.—We must be united; we must smoke the same pipe; we must fight each other's battles; and more than all, we must love the Great Spirit: he is for us; he will destroy our enemies, and make all his red children happy.

TECUMSEH (Shawnee)

"Father!—Listen to your children!"   (September 18, 1813)

When the U.S. declared war on England in 1812, Tecumseh (c. 1768–1813) saw that with the help of the British, who were less interested in settlement of the land than in trade, he would have his best chance of forcing the United States to accept the establishment of a wholly independent Native American nation. But then, after a series of triumphs, which included the Indian-British capture of Detroit, a British general named Henry Proctor, lacking Tecumseh's nerve and passion, made plans to withdraw into eastern Ontario. In the following speech, Tecumseh scolded Proctor for his deceit and cowardice. Proctor's hasty retreat left Tecumseh's warriors to fight an overwhelming American force. Two weeks after this speech, on October 5, Tecumseh was killed by William Henry Harrison's soldiers.

Father!—Listen to your children! You have them now all before you. The war before this, our British father gave the hatchet to his red children, when our old chiefs were alive. They are now dead. In that war our father was thrown flat on his back by the Americans, and our father took them by the hand without our knowledge. We are afraid that our father will do so again at this time. Summer before last, when I came forward with my red brethren, and was ready to take up the hatchet in favor of our British father, we were told not to be in a hurry—that he had not yet determined to fight the Americans.

Listen!—When war was declared, our father stood up and gave us the tomahawk, and told us that he was then ready to strike the Americans, that he wanted our assistance—and that he would certainly get us our lands back, which the Americans had taken from us.

Listen!—You told us, at that time, to bring forward our families to this place, and we did so. You also promised to take care of them—they should want for nothing, while the men would go and fight the enemy—that we need not trouble ourselves about the enemy's garrison—that we knew nothing about them—and that our father would attend to that part of the business. You also told your red children that you would take good care of your garrison here, which made our hearts glad.

SOURCE: B.B. Thatcher. *Indian Life and Battles.* Akron: New Werner Company, 1910. 263–265.

Listen!—When we were last at the Rapids it is true we gave you lit-tle assistance. It is hard to fight people who live like ground-hogs.

Father, listen!—Our fleet has gone out; we know they have fought; we have heard the great guns; but we know nothing of what has hap-pened to our father with one arm. Our ships have gone one way, and we are much astonished to see our father tying up everything and preparing to run away the other, without letting his red children know what his intentions are. You always told us to remain here, and take care of our lands; it made our hearts glad to hear that was your wish. Our great father, the king, is the head, and you represent him: You al-ways told us you would never draw your foot off British ground. But now, father, we see you are drawing back, and we are sorry to see our father doing so without seeing the enemy. We must compare our fa-ther's conduct to a fat dog that carries its tail upon its back, but when affrighted, it drops it between its legs and runs off.

Father, listen!—The Americans have not yet defeated us by land— neither are we sure that they have done so by water—we therefore wish to remain here, and fight our enemy, should they make their appear-ance. If they defeat us, we will then retreat with our father. At the bat-tle of the rapids, last war, the Americans certainly defeated us; and when we returned to our father's fort, at that place the gates were shut against us. We were afraid that it would now be the case; but instead of that, we now see our British father preparing to march out of his garrison.

Father!—You have got the arms and ammunition which our great fa-ther sent for his red children. If you have an idea of going away, give them to us, and you may go and welcome for us. Our lives are in the hands of the Great Spirit. We are determined to defend our lands, and if it be his will, we wish to leave our bones upon them.

TENKSWATAWA, "THE PROPHET" (Shawnee)

"It is three years since I first began that system of religion which I now practice" (July 1808)

In 1805, Tenkswatawa (c. 1770–1837), formerly of little account among the Shawnees, had a revelation, a vision of God, and became known as "The Prophet." For a time he helped his brother Tecumseh try to organize an allied Native American resistance to American encroachment. In the speech that follows, he professed his peaceable intentions to Indiana Territory Governor William Henry Harrison at Post Vincennes.

Father, it is three years since I first began with that system of religion which I now practice. The white people and some of the Indians were against me; but I had no other intention but to introduce among the Indians those good principles of religion which the white people profess. I was spoken badly of by the white people, who reproached me with misleading the Indians; but I defy them to say I did anything amiss.

Father, I was told that you intended to hang me. When I heard this, I intended to remember it, and tell my father, when I went to see him, and relate the truth.

I heard, when I settled on the Wabash, that my father, the Governor, had declared that all the land between Vincennes and Fort Wayne was the property of the Seventeen Fires. I also heard that you wanted to know, my father, whether I was God or man; and that you said if I was the former, I should not steal horses. I heard this from Mr. Wells, but I believed it originated with himself.

The Great Spirit told me to tell the Indians that he had made them, and made the world—that he had placed them on it to do good and not evil.

I told all the red-skins that the way they were in was not good, and that they ought to abandon it.

That we ought to consider ourselves as one man; but we ought to live agreeably to our several customs, the red people after their mode, and the white people after theirs; particularly, that they should not drink whiskey; that it was not made for them, but the white people, who alone knew how to use it; and that it is the cause of all the mischiefs which the Indians suffer; and that they must always follow the

SOURCE: Wallace A. Brice. *History of Fort Wayne*. Fort Wayne, Indiana: D.W. Jones and Son, 1868. 178–179.

directions of the Great Spirit, and we must listen to him, as it was He that made us; determine to listen to nothing that is bad; do not take up the tomahawk, should it be offered by the British, or by the Long-Knives; do not meddle with any thing that does not belong to you, but mind your own business, and cultivate the ground, that your women and your children may have enough to live on.

I now inform you that it is our intention to live in peace with our father and his people forever.

My father, I have informed you what we mean to do, and I call the Great Spirit to witness the truth of my declaration. The religion which I have established for the last three years has been attended to by the different tribes of Indians in this part of the world. These Indians were once different people; they are now but one; they are all determined to practice what I have communicated to them that has come immediately from the Great Spirit through me.

Brother, I speak to you as a warrior. You are one. But let us lay aside this character, and attend to the care of our children, that they may live in comfort and peace. We desire that you will join us for the preservation of both red and white people. Formerly, when we lived in ignorance, we were foolish; but now, since we listen to the voice of the Great Spirit, we are happy.

I have listened to what you have said to us. You have promised to assist us. I now request you, in behalf of all the red people, to use your exertions to prevent the sale of liquor to us. We are all well pleased to hear you say that you will endeavor to promote our happiness. We give you every assurance that we will follow the dictates of the Great Spirit.

We are all well pleased with the attention you have showed us; also with the good intentions of our father, the President. If you give us a few articles, such as needles, flints, hoes, powder, etc., we will take the animals that afford us meat, with powder and ball.

PUSHMATAHA (Choctaw)

"From its riven trunk leaped a mighty man" (c. 1812)

Soon after Pushmataha's rebuttal to Tecumseh's call for an Indian
alliance against the Americans, Pushmataha (c. 1764–1824), or
"Apushamatahahubih" as he referred to himself below, traveled to
Washington, D.C. There, he became annoyed at future President
Andrew Jackson's persistent queries about his origins and ascen-
dancy among the Choctaws, and answered with the following fan-
ciful account.

Well, if the white chief must know, tell him that Apushamatahahubih
has neither father nor mother, nor kinsman upon the earth. Tell him
that once upon a time, far away from here in the great forests of the
Choctaw Nation, a dark cloud arose from the western horizon, and
with astonishing velocity traveled up the arched expanse. In silence
profound, all animate nature stood apart; soon the fearful cloud
reached the zenith, then as quickly spread its dark mantle o'er the sky
entire, shutting out the light of the sun, and wrapping earth in midnight gloom. Then burst the cloud and rose the wind; and while falling
rains and howling winds, lightnings gleam and thunders roar, in wild
confusion blended, a blinding flash blazed athwart the sky, then hurled
its strength against a mighty oak and cleft it in equal twain from utmost
top to lowest bottom; when, lo! from its riven trunk leaped a mighty
man; in stature, perfect; in wisdom, profound; in bravery, un-
equalled—a full-fledged warrior. 'Twas Apushamatahahubih.

SOURCE: H.B. Cushman. *History of the Choctaw, Chickasaw and Natchez
Indians.* Greenville, TX: Headlight Printing House, 1899. 264.

BETWEEN THE LOGS (Wyandot)

"Why would you devote yourselves, your women, and your children to destruction?" (c. 1812)

In this exchange (at an Indian council at Brownstown, Michigan) Tarhe, a Wyandot chief and opponent of Tecumseh's proposed confederacy, sent Between the Logs to deliver a speech encouraging other tribes and Wyandot bands to become American allies. Chief Round Head (Stiaghta) was a Wyandot who sided with Tecumseh and would help the Shawnee leader and British defeat the Americans in the Battle of the River Raisin in January 1813; Captain Elliot was a British Indian agent. Tarhé's Wyandots helped William Henry Harrison defeat and kill Tecumseh in 1813.

Brothers!—the red men, who are engaged in fighting for the British king—listen! These words are from me, Tarhé, and they are also the words of the Wyandots, Delawares, Shawaneese, and Senecas.

Our American father has raised his war-pole, and collected a large army of his warriors. They will soon march to attack the British. He does not wish to destroy his red children, their wives, and families. He wishes you to separate yourselves from the British, and bury the hatchet you have raised. He will be merciful to you. You can then return to your own lands, and hunt the game, as you formerly did. I request you to consider your situation, and act wisely in this important matter; and not wantonly destroy your own people. Brothers! whoever feels disposed to accept this advice will come forward and take hold of this belt of wampum, which I have in my hand and offer to you. I hope you will not refuse to accept it in presence of your British father, for you are independent of him. Brothers! we have done, and we hope you will decide wisely.

[Not a hand moved to accept the offered pledge of peace. The spell was too potent to be broken by charms like these; but Round Head arose and addressed the embassy:]

Brothers!—the Wyandots from the Americans—we have heard your talk, and will not listen to it. We will not forsake the standard of our British father, nor lay down the hatchet we have raised. I speak the sentiments of all now present, and I charge you, that you faithfully deliver our talk to the American commander, and tell him it is our wish he would send more men against us; for all that has passed between us I

SOURCE: B.B. Thatcher. *Indian Life and Battles*. Akron: New Werner Company, 1910. 240–243.

do not call fighting. We are not satisfied with the number of men he sends to contend against us. We want to fight in good earnest.

[Elliot then spoke.] My children! — as you now see that my children here are determined not to forsake the cause of their British father, I wish you to carry a message back with you. Tell my wife, your American father, that I want her to cook the provisions for me and my red children more faithfully than she has done. She has not done her duty. And if she receives this as an insult, and feels disposed to fight, tell her to bring more men than she ever brought before, as our former skirmishes I do not call fighting. If she wishes to fight with me and my children, she must not burrow in the earth like a ground-hog, where she is inaccessible. She must come out and fight fairly.

[To this, Between the Logs replied:] Brothers! — I am directed by my American father to inform you that if you reject the advice given you, he will march here with a large army, and if he should find any of the red people opposing him in his passage through this country, he will trample them under his feet. You cannot stand before him.

And now for myself, I earnestly entreat you to consider the good talk I have brought, and listen to it. Why would you devote yourselves, your women, and your children to destruction? Let me tell you, if you should defeat the American army this time, you have not done. Another will come on, and if you defeat that, still another will appear that you cannot withstand; one that will come like the waves of the great water, and overwhelm you, and sweep you from the face of the earth. If you doubt the account I give of the force of the Americans, you can send some of your people in whom you have confidence to examine their army and navy. They shall be permitted to return in safety. The truth is, your British father tells you lies, and deceives you. He boasts of the few victories he gains, but he never tells you of his defeats, of his armies being slaughtered, and his vessels taken on the big water. He keeps all these things to himself.

And now, father, let me address a few words to you. Your request shall be granted. I will bear your message to my American father. It is true none of your children appear willing to forsake your standard, and it will be the worse for them. You compare the Americans to ground-hogs, and complain of their mode of fighting. I must confess that a ground-hog is a very difficult animal to contend with. He has such sharp teeth, such an inflexible temper, and such an unconquerable spirit, that he is truly a dangerous enemy, especially when he is in his own hole. But, father, let me tell you, you can have your wish. Before many days, you will see the ground-hog floating on yonder lake, paddling his canoe towards your hole; and then, father, you will have an opportunity of attacking your formidable enemy in any way you may think best.

WILLIAM WEATHERFORD, RED EAGLE (Creek)

"I am in your power—do with me as you please"
(April 1814)

Defeated by General Andrew Jackson, Weatherford (1780–1822) surrendered himself and delivered the following speech. Jackson pardoned him, and Weatherford forever after worked for peace.

I am in your power—do with me as you please—I am a soldier. I have done the whites all the harm I could. I have fought them, and fought them bravely. If I had an army, I would yet fight—I would contend to the last: but I have none. My people are all gone. I can only weep over the misfortunes of my nation. . . .

I could once animate my warriors to battle—but I cannot animate the dead. My warriors can no longer hear my voice. Their bones are at Talladega, Tallushatches, Emuckfaw and Tohopeka. I have not surrendered myself without thought. While there was a single chance of success, I never left my post, nor supplicated peace. But my people are gone, and I now ask it for my nation, not for myself. I look back with deep sorrow, and wish to avert still greater calamities. If I had been left to contend with the Georgia army, I would have raised my corn on one bank of the river, and fought them on the other. But your people have destroyed my nation. You are a brave man. I rely upon your generosity. You will exact no terms of a conquered people, but such as they should accede to. Whatever they may be, it would now be madness and folly to oppose them. If they are opposed, you shall find me amongst the sternest enforcers of obedience. Those who would still hold out can be influenced only by a mean spirit of revenge. To this they must not, and shall not, sacrifice the last remnant of their country. You have told our nation where we might go and be safe. This is good talk, and they ought to listen to it. They shall listen to it.

SOURCE: Samuel G. Drake. *Biography and History of the Indians of North America, from Its First Discovery.* Boston: Benjamin B. Mussey & Co., 1851 (11th ed.). 390–391.

WABASHAW (Sioux)

"A few knives and blankets?" (1815)

> After the War of 1812 and the Treaty of Ghent in 1815, in which
> the British failed to make provisions for their Native American al-
> lies, Wabashaw addressed the commanding officer of the British
> post on Drummond Island.

My father: What is this I see before me? a few knives and blankets? Is
this all you promised us at the beginning of the war?

Where is the fulfilment of those high speeches of promise you made
us at Michilimackinac and sent to our villages on the Mississippi? You
told us you would never let fall the hatchet till the Americans were
driven beyond the Alleghanies! You said we should again be put in possession of our ancient hunting-grounds! You said that our British fathers would never make peace without consulting his Red Children!
Has this come to pass?

We never knew of the peace! We are told it was made by our Great
Father beyond the big waters, without the knowledge of his officers and
generals here. We are told it is your duty to obey his orders. What is this
to us? Will these paltry presents pay for the men we have lost in battle
and on the road? Will they soothe the feelings of our friends? Will they
make good your promises?

For myself, I am an old man! I have lived long and always found the
means of support! And I can do so still! Perhaps my young men may
pick up the presents you have laid before us! I do not want them!

SOURCE: Francis S. Drake. *The Indian Tribes of the United States.* Volume 1.
Philadelphia: J.B. Lippincott and Co., 1884. 55.

METEA (Potawatomie)

"You are never satisfied!" (August 1821)

At the council of Chicago, where convened the Potawatomies,
Ojibways, and Ottawas, Chief Metea (c. 1780–1827), before his
peers, addressed U.S. government officials. Even though he casti-
gated the government for its greed, at this council he relented, sign-
ing a treaty that sold off five million acres of Michigan.

My father, we have listened to what you have said. We shall now retire
to our camps and consult upon it. You will hear nothing more from us
at present. [When the council was again convened, Metea continued,]
We meet you here today, because we had promised it, to tell you our
minds, and what we have agreed upon among ourselves. You will listen
to us with a good mind, and believe what we say. You know that we first
came to this country, a long time ago, and when we sat ourselves down
upon it, we met with a great many hardships and difficulties. Our country was then very large; but it has dwindled away to a small spot, and
you wish to purchase that! This has caused us to reflect much upon
what you have told us; and we have, therefore, brought all the chiefs
and warriors, and the young men and women and children of our tribe,
that one part may not do what the others object to, and that all may be
witness of what is going forward.

You know your children. Since you first came among them, they
have listened to your words with an attentive ear, and have always hearkened to your counsels. Whenever you have had a proposal to make to
us, whenever you have had a favor to ask of us, we have always lent a
favorable ear, and our invariable answer has been "yes." This you know!

A long time has passed since we first came upon our lands, and our
old people have all sunk into their graves. They had sense. We are all
young and foolish, and do not wish to do anything that they would not
approve, were they living. We are fearful we shall offend their spirits if
we sell our lands; and we are fearful we shall offend you, if we do *not*
sell them. This has caused us great perplexity of thought, because we
have counselled among ourselves, and do not know how we can part
with the land. Our country was given to us by the Great Spirit, who
gave it to us to hunt upon, to make our cornfields upon, to live upon,

SOURCE: Samuel G. Drake. *Biography and History of the Indians of North
America, from Its First Discovery.* Boston: Benjamin B. Mussey & Co., 1851
(11th ed.). 635–636.

and to make down our beds upon when we die. And he would never forgive us, should we bargain it away.

When you first spoke to us for lands at St. Mary's, we said we had a little, and agreed to sell you a piece of it; but we told you we could spare no more. Now you ask us again. You are never satisfied! We have sold you a great tract of land, already; but it is not enough! We sold it to you for the benefit of your children, to farm and to live upon. We have now but little left. We shall want it all for ourselves. We know not how long we may live, and we wish to have some lands for our children to hunt upon. You are gradually taking away our hunting-grounds. Your children are driving us before them. We are growing uneasy. What lands you have, you may retain forever; but we shall sell no more.

You think, perhaps, that I speak in passion; but my heart is good towards you. I speak like one of your own children. I am an Indian, a redskin, and live by hunting and fishing, but my country is already too small; and I do not know how to bring up my children if I give it all away. We sold you a fine tract of land at St. Mary's. We said to you then it was enough to satisfy your children, and the last we should sell: and we thought it would be the last you would ask for. We have now told you what we had to say. It is what was determined on, in a council among ourselves; and what I have spoken is the voice of my nation. On this account, all our people have come here to listen to me; but do not think we have a bad opinion of you. Where should we get a bad opinion of you? We speak to you with a good heart, and the feelings of a friend.

You are acquainted with this piece of land—the country we live in. Shall we give it up? Take notice, it is a small piece of land, and if we give it away, what will become of us? The Great Spirit, who has provided it for our use, allows us to keep it, to bring up our young men and support our families. We should incur his anger if we bartered it away. If we had more land, you should get more; but our land has been wasting away ever since the white people became our neighbors, and we have now hardly enough left to cover the bones of our tribe.

You are in the midst of your red children. What is due to us in money, we wish, and will receive at this place; and we want nothing more. We all shake hands with you. Behold our warriors, our women,. and children. Take pity on us and on our words.

CORNPLANTER (Seneca)

"When I was a child, I played with the butterfly, the grasshopper and the frogs" (February 2, 1822)

Cornplanter's father, John O'Bail, was a white liquor-trader who made a fortune selling alcohol to the Senecas. By the time Cornplanter (c. 1735–1836) addressed this dictated speech to Pennsylvania governor Joseph Heister, the long-lived Seneca leader was well experienced in dealing with American government officials. He equated the Americans' revolution against Britain's unfairly imposed taxes with his own protest over taxed lands.

I feel it my duty to send a speech to the Governor of Pennsylvania at this time, and inform him the place where I was from—which was at Conewaugus, on the Genesee River.

When I was a child, I played with the butterfly, the grasshopper and the frogs; and as I grew up, I began to pay some attention and play with the Indian boys in the neighborhood, and they took notice of my skin being a different color from theirs, and spoke about it. I inquired of my mother the cause, and she told me that my father was a residenter in Albany. I still ate my victuals out of a bark dish.—I grew up to be a young man, and married me a wife—and I had no kettle or gun. I then knew where my father lived, and went to see him, and found he was a white man, and spoke the English language. He gave me victuals whilst I was at his house, but when I started to return home, he gave me no provision to eat on the way. He gave me neither kettle nor gun; neither did he tell me that the United States were about to rebel against the government of England.

I will now tell you, brothers, who are in session of the legislature of Pennsylvania, that the Great Spirit has made known to me that I have been wicked; and the cause thereof was the Revolutionary War in America. The cause of Indians having been led into sin, at that time, was that many of them were in the practice of drinking and getting intoxicated. Great Britain requested us to join with them in the conflict against the Americans, and promised the Indians land and liquor. I, myself, was opposed to joining in the conflict, as I had nothing to do with the difficulty that existed between the two parties. I have now

---

SOURCE: James Buchanan. *Sketches of the History, Manners, and Customs of the North American Indians with a Plan for Their Amelioration.* New York: William Borradaile, 1824. 55–59.

informed you how it happened that the Indians took a part in the revolution, and will relate to you some circumstances that occurred after the close of the war. General Putnam, who was then at Philadelphia, told me there was to be a council at Fort Stanwix; and the Indians requested me to attend on behalf of the Six Nations—which I did, and there met with three commissioners, who had been appointed to hold the council. They told me they would inform me of the cause of the revolution, which I requested them to do minutely. They then said that it had originated on account of the heavy taxes that had been imposed upon them by the British government, which had been, for fifty years, increasing upon them; that the Americans had grown weary thereof, and refused to pay, which affronted the king. There had likewise a difficulty taken place about some tea (which they wished me not to use, as it had been one of the causes that many people had lost their lives). And the British government now being affronted, the war commenced, and the cannons began to roar in our country. General Putnam then told me at the council at Fort Stanwix that by the late war, the Americans had gained two objects: they had established themselves an independent nation, and had obtained some land to live upon—the division-line of which, from Great Britain, ran through the lakes. I then spoke, and said that I wanted some land for the Indians to live on, and General Putnam said that it should be granted, and I should have land in the state of New York, for the Indians. General Putnam then encouraged me to use my endeavours to pacify the Indians generally; and as he considered it an arduous task to perform, wished to know what I wanted for pay therefor? I replied to him, that I would use my endeavours to do as he had requested, with the Indians, and for pay therefor, I would take land. I told him not to pay me money or dry-goods, but land. And for having attended thereto I received the tract of land on which I now live, which was presented to me by Governor Mifflin. I told General Putnam that I wished the Indians to have the exclusive privilege of the deer and wild game—which he assented to. I also wished the Indians to have the privilege of hunting in the woods, and making fires—which he likewise assented to.

The treaty that was made at the aforementioned council has been broken by some of the white people, which I now intend acquainting the governor with. Some white people are not willing that Indians should hunt any more, whilst others are satisfied therewith; and those white people who reside near our reservation tell us that the woods are theirs, and they have obtained them from the governor. The treaty has been also broken by the white people using their endeavours to destroy all the wolves—which was not spoken about in the council at Fort Stanwix, by General Putnam, but has originated lately.

It has been broken again, which is of recent origin. White people wish to get credit from Indians, and do not pay them honestly, according to their agreement. In another respect it has also been broken by white people, who reside near my dwelling; for when I plant melons and vines in my field, they take them as their own. It has been broken again by white people using their endeavours to obtain our pine trees from us. We have very few pine trees on our land, in the state of New York; and white people and Indians often get into dispute respecting them. There is also a great quantity of whiskey brought near our reservation by white people, and the Indians obtain it and become drunken. Another circumstance has taken place which is very trying to me, and I wish the interference of the governor.

The white people, who live at Warren, called upon me, some time ago, to pay taxes for my land; which I objected to, as I had never been called upon for that purpose before; and having refused to pay, the white people became irritated, called upon me frequently, and at length brought four guns with them and seized our cattle. I still refused to pay, and was not willing to let the cattle go. After a time of dispute, they returned home, and I understood the militia was ordered out to enforce the collection of the tax. I went to Warren, and, to avert the impending difficulty, was obliged to give my note for the tax, the amount of which was forty-three dollars and seventy-nine cents. It is my desire that the governor will exempt me from paying taxes for my land to white people; and also cause that the money I am now obliged to pay may be refunded to me, as I am very poor. The governor is the person who attends to the situation of the people, and I wish him to send a person to Allegheny, that I may inform him of the particulars of our situation, and he be authorized to instruct the white people, in what manner to conduct themselves towards Indians.

The government has told us that when any difficulties arose between Indians and white people, they would attend to having them removed. We are now in a trying situation, and I wish the governor to send a person, authorized to attend thereto, the forepart of next summer, about the time that grass has grown high enough for pasture.

The governor formerly requested me to pay attention to the Indians, and take care of them: we are now arrived at a situation that I believe Indians cannot exist, unless the governor should comply with my request, and send a person authorized to treat between us and the white people the approaching summer. I have now no more to speak.

PETALESHARO (Pawnee)

"We have plenty of land, if you will keep your people off of it" **(February 4, 1822)**

The Pawnee brave Petalesharo (c. 1797–c. 1874), in the company of other midwestern Native Americans, addressed President James Monroe in Washington, D.C. He asked for nothing for the Indians but to be left alone.

My Great Father: I have travelled a great distance to see you—I have seen you and my heart rejoices. I have heard your words—they have entered one ear and shall not escape the other, and I will carry them to my people as pure as they came from your mouth.

My Great Father: I am going to speak the truth. The Great Spirit looks down upon us, and I call *Him* to witness all that may pass between us on this occasion. If I am here now and have seen your people, your houses, your vessels on the big lake, and a great many wonderful things far beyond my comprehension, which appear to have been made by the Great Spirit and placed in your hands, I am indebted to my Father here, who invited me from home, under whose wings I have been protected. Yes, my Great Father, I have travelled with your chief; I have followed him, and trod in his tracks; but there is still *another* Great Father *to whom I am much indebted—it is the Father of us all*. Him who made us and placed us on this earth. I feel grateful to the Great Spirit for strengthening my heart for such an undertaking, and for preserving the life which he gave me. The Great Spirit made us all—he made my skin red, and yours white; he placed us on this earth, and intended that we should live differently from each other.

He made the whites to cultivate the earth, and feed on domestic animals; but he made us, red skins, to rove through the uncultivated woods and plains; to feed on wild animals; and to dress with their skins. He also intended that we should go to war—to take scalps—steal horses from and triumph over our enemies—cultivate peace at home, and promote the happiness of each other. I believe there are no people of any color on this earth who do not believe in the Great Spirit—in rewards, and in punishments. We worship him, but we worship him not as you do. We differ from you in appearance and manners as well as in

SOURCE: James Buchanan. *Sketches of the History, Manners, and Customs of the North American Indians with a Plan for Their Amelioration.* New York: William Borradaile, 1824. 41–44.

our customs; and we differ from you in our religion; we have no large houses as you have to worship the Great Spirit in; if we had them today, we should want others tomorrow, for we have not, like you, a fixed habitation—we have no settled home except our villages, where we remain but two moons in twelve. We, like animals, rove through the country, whilst you whites reside between us and heaven; but still, my Great Father, we love the Great Spirit—we acknowledge his supreme power—our peace, our health, and our happiness depend upon him, and our lives belong to him—he made us and he can destroy us.

My Great Father: Some of your good chiefs, as they are called [missionaries], have proposed to send some of their good people among us to change our habits, to make us work and live like the white people. I will not tell a lie—I am going to tell the truth. You love your country— you love your people—you love the manner in which they live, and you think your people brave.—I am like you, my Great Father, I love my country—I love my people—I love the manner in which we live, and think myself and warriors brave. Spare me then, my Father; let me enjoy my country, and pursue the buffalo, and the beaver, and the other wild animals of our country, and I will trade their skins with your people. I have grown up, and lived thus long without work—I am in hopes you will suffer me to die without it. We have plenty of buffalo, beaver, deer and other wild animals—we have also an abundance of horses—we have every thing we want—we have plenty of land, if you will keep your people off of it. My father has a piece on which he lives [Council Bluffs], and we wish him to enjoy it—we have enough without it—but we wish him to live near us to give us good counsel—to keep our ears and eyes open that we may continue to pursue the right road—the road to happiness. He settles all differences between us and the whites, between the red skins themselves—he makes the whites do justice to the red skins, and he makes the red skins do justice to the whites. He saves the effusion of human blood, and restores peace and happiness on the land. You have already sent us a father; it is enough he knows us and we know him—we have confidence in him—we keep our eye constantly upon him, and since we have heard your words, we will listen more attentively to *his*.

It is too soon, my Great Father, to send those good men among us. *We are not starving yet*—we wish you to permit us to enjoy the chase until the game of our country is exhausted—until the wild animals become extinct. Let us exhaust our present resources before you make us toil and interrupt our happiness—let me continue to live as I have done, and after I have passed to the Good or Evil Spirit from off the wilderness of my present life, the subsistence of my children may become so precarious as to need and embrace the assistance of those good people.

There was a time when we did not know the whites—our wants were then fewer than they are now. They were always within our control—we had then seen nothing which we could not get. Before our intercourse with the *whites* (who have caused such a destruction in our game), we could lie down to sleep, and when we awoke we would find the buffalo feeding around our camp—but now we are killing them for their skins, and feeding the wolves with their flesh, to make our children cry over their bones.

Here, My Great Father, is a pipe which I present you, as I am accustomed to present pipes to all the red skins in peace with us. It is filled with such tobacco as we were accustomed to smoke before we knew the white people. It is pleasant, and the spontaneous growth of the most remote parts of our country. I know that the robes, leggings, mockasins, bear-claws, etc., are of little value to you, but we wish you to have them deposited and preserved in some conspicuous part of your lodge, so that when we are gone and the sod turned over our bones, if our children should visit this place, as we do now, they may see and recognize with pleasure the deposits of their fathers; and reflect on the times that are past.

SPECKLED SNAKE (Cherokee)

"Now he says, 'The land you live on is not yours'" (c. 1830)

In 1830, President Andrew Jackson signed the Removal Bill, which meant, more or less, that all Southern Native Americans had to move across the Mississippi or face the reprisals of the U.S. Army. After hearing a speech in which President Jackson proffered friendship to them, Chief Speckled Snake addressed his council. (The Cherokees, originally natives of Georgia, were forced to move to Oklahoma in 1838. Their agonizing cross-country removal, which became known as the "Trail of Tears," killed a quarter of the tribe.)

Brothers! We have heard the talk of our great father; it is very kind. He says he loves his red children. Brothers! When the white man first came to these shores, the Muskogees gave him land, and kindled him a fire to make him comfortable; and when the pale faces to the south made war on him [The Spaniards of Florida endeavored to break up the English settlement under Gen. Oglethorpe in Georgia. — *Drake's note.*], their young men drew the tomahawk, and protected his head from the scalping knife. But when the white man had warmed himself before the Indian's fire, and filled himself with the Indian's hominy, he became very large; he stopped not for the mountain tops, and his feet covered the plains and the valleys. His hands grasped the eastern and the western sea. Then he became our great father. He loved his red children; but said, "You must move a little farther, lest I should, by accident, tread on you." With one foot he pushed the red man over the Oconee, and with the other he trampled down the graves of his fathers.

But our great father still loved his red children, and he soon made them another talk. He said much; but it all meant nothing, but "move a little farther; you are too near me." I have heard a great many talks from our great father, and they all begun and ended the same. Brothers! When he made us a talk on a former occasion, he said, "Get a little farther; go beyond the Oconee and the Oakmulgee; there is a pleasant country." He also said, "It shall be yours forever." Now he says, "The land you live on is not yours; go beyond the Mississippi;

SOURCE: Samuel G. Drake. *Biography and History of the Indians of North America, from Its First Discovery.* Boston: Benjamin B. Mussey & Co., 1851 (11th ed.). 450.

there is game; there you may remain while the grass grows or the water runs."

Brothers! Will not our great father come there also? He loves his red children, and his tongue is not forked.

KEOKUK (Sauk)

"Their soldiers are springing up like grass on the prairies"
(1832)

Keokuk (c. 1783–1848) was the foil of his fellow Sauk Black Hawk
to the end of Black Hawk's days. Keokuk was accused by Black
Hawk and others of selling out tribal land and too readily agreeing
to peace treaties for his own benefit. He certainly was esteemed by
the whites to whom he made concessions, and was—in spite of his
low status among his own tribe—rewarded in 1833 by the U.S. government with official recognition as chief of the Sauks and Foxes.
The dramatic speech that follows—calling for a pre-battle act of eu-
thanasia of the Sauks' and Foxes' children, women, and aged—took
the wind out of the sails of Black Hawk's calls for attacking the
American settlers. Black Hawk had to rely on his own "British
band" of Sauks and other tribes for his war.

Head-men, chiefs, braves and warriors of the Sauks: I have heard and
considered your demand to be led forth upon the war-path against the
palefaces, to avenge the many wrongs, persecutions, outrages and murders committed by them upon our people. I deeply sympathize with
you in your sense and construction of these terrible wrongs. Few, indeed, are our people who do not mourn the death of some near and
loved one at the hands of the Long Guns [pioneers], who are becoming very numerous. Their cabins are as plenty as the trees in the forest,
and their soldiers are springing up like grass on the prairies. They have
the talking thunder [cannon], which carries death a long way off, with
long guns and short ones, long knives and short ones, ammunition and
provisions in abundance, with powerful war horses for their soldiers to
ride. In a contest where our numbers are so unequal to theirs we must
ultimately fail. All we can reasonably expect or hope is to wreak the utmost of our vengeance upon their hated heads, and fall, when fall we
must, with our faces to the enemy. Great is the undertaking, and desperate must be our exertions. Every brave and warrior able to throw a
tomahawk or wield a war-club must go with us. Once across the
Mississippi, let no one think of returning while there is a foe to strike
or a scalp to take, and when we fall—if our strength permit—let us drag
our feeble, bleeding bodies to the graves of our ancestors, and there die,

SOURCE: Perry A. Armstrong. *The Sauks and the Black Hawk War.* Springfield,
Illinois: H.W. Rokker, 1887. 265–268.

that our ashes may commingle with theirs, while our departing spirits shall follow the long trail made by them in their passage to the land of spirits.

It is my duty as your Chief to be your father while in the paths of peace, and your leader and champion while on the war-path. You have decided to follow the path of war, and I will lead you forth to victory if the Good Spirit prevails. If not, and the Bad Spirit rules, then will I perish at my post of duty. But what shall we do with our old and infirm, our women and children? We cannot take them with us upon the war-path, for they would hamper us in our movements and defeat us of our vengeance. We dare not leave them behind us, doomed to perish of hunger or fall captive to the palefaces, who would murder the old and the young, but reserve our wives and daughters for a fate worse than death itself.

I will lead you forth upon the war-path, but upon this condition: That we first put our wives and children, our aged and infirm, gently to sleep in that slumber which knows no waking this side the spirit land, and then carefully and tenderly lay their bodies away by the side of our sacred dead, from whence their freed spirits shall depart on the long journey to the happy home in the land of dreams beneath, beyond, the Evening Star. For we go upon the long trail which has no turn—from which, in a few short moons, we shall follow them, but they must not follow us. This sacrifice is demanded of us by the very love we bear those dear ones. Our every feeling of humanity tells us we cannot take them with us, and dare not leave them behind us. [Then turning to Black Hawk, he said:] To you, venerable Chief, do I appeal for an answer to what I have said. Your long experience upon the war-path tells you I have spoken the truth; yet, with all your wonderful eloquence, you have urged us to this terrible sacrifice. Brooding over the oft-repeated wrongs committed by the palefaces upon you and your people, your mind has grown weak, until you have lent a willing ear to the whisperings of evil counselors, who cannot speak the truth, because their tongues are forked, like the viper's.

They came to you under the guise and pretense of friendship, and by the use of base flattery and hypocrisy gained your confidence, only to lead you into the crooked path of ruin and destruction. They are enemies of yours and your band, instead of friends. They first told you the British Father has promised you aid and assistance, in warriors as well as guns, tomahawks, spears, knives, ammunition and provisions, as soon as you should recross the Mississippi at the head of a hostile army. Why has he not furnished you these things, to enable you to raise, arm and equip your army, ready for war? This fact proves the whole story a lie, prepared no doubt by Neapope or his cunning brother, Winnesheik, for the sole purpose of deceiving and misleading you and your band. The British Father is at peace with our Great Father at Washington, and neither knows of or cares for you or your grievances. The same evil counselors have told you that the moment you shall sound your war-whoop east of the Mississippi all the Indian tribes between that and the Illinois river will rise up as a single warrior and unite with you, and under your banner, to avenge their wrongs upon the white pioneers. What wrongs have they to avenge? They are on terms of peace and good-will with these white settlers, and have no cause of complaint or grievance whatever. Yet they have told you that these Indians across the river were not only ready but eager to join you in a general massacre of the frontier inhabitants of Northern Illinois, and are now only waiting your signal fires to be rekindled upon the watch-tower at Saukenuk to begin the slaughter. If this be true, why are not their great war-chiefs here tonight? Where are Wauponsee, The Red Devil, Big Thunder Shaata and Meachelle? Why are they not here in person, or by their representatives, if it be true they are anxious to go upon the war-path with you? Their absence is proof conclusive that they have no intention or desire to join you in this suicidal undertaking. You have been de-ceived—aye, cruelly deceived—by these counselors with a forked tongue, who are leading you into the crooked path of the Bad Spirit, and have no love for you or respect for your gray hairs or good name.

I beseech you, by the noble character you have always borne, by the honors and trophies you have won upon the war-path, by the love you bear your gallant little band, by everything you hold sacred and dear, abandon this wild, visionary and desperate undertaking, and return to your village. Seed time is here, but your grounds have not been pre-pared for the planting. Go back and plant the summer's crop. Arise to the dignity and grandeur of your honored position as the father of your gallant little band; shake off the base fetters of the Bad Spirit which bind you hand and foot, and turn your feet from the crooked war-path into the path that leads to peace. In this way only can you save your true and trusty band from certain defeat, if not utter annihilation. If you still persist in going upon the war-path against the white people, then in-deed may we bid farewell to Black Hawk, whose protecting spirit has forsaken him in his old age, and suffered his star of success—which has led him in triumph to a hundred victories on the war-path—to go down behind a cloud, never to rise again; and when the Pauguk comes, his lofty spirit will depart, groping its way doubtingly along the dark and crooked path to the land of dreams, unhonored, unlamented and unwept.

BLACK HAWK, MAKATAIMESHIEKIAKIAK (Sauk)

"I am going to send you back to your chief, though I ought to kill you" (c. 1832)

Black Hawk (c. 1770–1838) allied himself with Tecumseh in the War of 1812, and was the energetic, warrior spirit of the Sauks. He resented the broken treaties that continually pushed the Indians westward. He resisted white settlers who continually violated the U.S. Government's treaties, and finally he refused to abide by a treaty signed by Keokuk that gave up the Sauks' homeland. He mounted the "Black Hawk War" of 1832, but was quickly forced to capitulate, and agree to honor the treaty and acknowledge the government's choice of Keokuk as chief. Elijah Kilbourn, to whom Black Hawk made the following speech, was an American army scout captured in the War of 1812 by Black Hawk, and later, following an escape attempt, rescued from death by the leader.

I am going to send you back to your chief, though I ought to kill you for running away a long time ago after I had adopted you as a son, but Black Hawk can forgive as well as forget. When you return to your chief I want you to tell him all my words. Tell him that Black Hawk's eyes have looked upon many suns, but they shall not see many more, and that his back is no longer straight as in his youth, but is beginning to bend with age. The Great Spirit has whispered among the tree tops in the morning and in the evening, and says Black Hawk's days are few and he is wanted in the Spirit land. He is half dead, his arm shakes and is no longer strong, and his feet are slow on the war path. Tell him all this, and tell him too that Black Hawk would have been a friend to the whites, but they would not let him, and that the tomahawk was dug up by themselves and not by the Indians.

Tell your chief that Black Hawk meant no harm to the pale-faces when he came across the Mississippi, but came peaceably to raise corn for his starving women and children, and that even then he would have gone back, but when he sent his white flag the braves who carried it were treated like squaws, and one of them inhumanly shot. Tell him too that Black Hawk will have revenge and will never stop until the Great Spirit shall say to him *come away.*

SOURCE: Perry A. Armstrong. *The Sauks and the Black Hawk War.* Springfield, Illinois: H.W. Rokker, 1887. 533–534.

BLACK HAWK, MAKATAIMESHIEKIAKIAK (Sauk)

"Farewell to Black Hawk" (August 27, 1832)

> After his campaign of revenge on the settlers ("The Black Hawk War"), Black Hawk (c. 1770–1838), his braves, tribespeople, and allies were hunted down and killed or taken prisoner by U.S. soldiers and Sioux. Black Hawk surrendered at Prairie du Chien, and made the following speech.

You have taken me prisoner with all my warriors. I am much grieved, for I expected, if I did not defeat you, to hold out much longer, and give you more trouble before I surrendered. I tried hard to bring you into ambush, but your last general understands Indian fighting. The first one was not so wise. When I saw that I could not beat you by Indian fighting, I determined to rush on you, and fight you face to face. I fought hard. But your guns were well aimed. The bullets flew like birds in the air, and whizzed by our ears like the wind through the trees in the winter. My warriors fell around me; it began to look dismal. I saw my evil day at hand. The sun rose dim on us in the morning, and at night it sunk in a dark cloud, and looked like a ball of fire. That was the last sun that shone on Black Hawk. His heart is dead, and no longer beats quick in his bosom. —He is now a prisoner to the white men; they will do with him as they wish. But he can stand torture, and is not afraid of death. He is no coward. Black Hawk is an Indian.

He has done nothing for which an Indian ought to be ashamed. He has fought for his countrymen, the squaws and papooses, against white men, who came, year after year, to cheat them and take away their lands. You know the cause of our making war. It is known to all white men. They ought to be ashamed of it. The white men despise the Indians, and drive them from their homes. But the Indians are not deceitful. The white men speak bad of the Indian, and look at him spitefully. But the Indian does not tell lies; Indians do not steal.

An Indian who is as bad as the white men could not live in our nation; he would be put to death, and eat up by the wolves. The white men are bad schoolmasters; they carry false looks, and deal in false actions; they smile in the face of the poor Indian to cheat him; they shake them by the hand to gain their confidence, to make them drunk, to deceive them, and ruin our wives. We told them to let us alone, and keep

SOURCE: Perry A. Armstrong. *The Sauks and the Black Hawk War.* Springfield, Illinois: H.W. Rokker, 1887. 535–536.

away from us; but they followed on, and beset our paths, and they coiled themselves among us, like the snake. They poisoned us by their touch. We were not safe. We lived in danger. We were becoming like them, hypocrites and liars, adulterers, lazy drones, all talkers, and no workers.

We looked up to the Great Spirit. We went to our great father. We were encouraged. His great council gave us fair words and big promises; but we got no satisfaction. Things were growing worse. There were no deer in the forest. The opossum and beaver were fled; the springs were drying up, and our squaws and papooses without victuals to keep them from starving; we called a great council, and built a large fire. The spirit of our fathers arose and spoke to us to avenge our wrongs or die. We all spoke before the council fire. It was warm and pleasant. We set up the war-whoop, and dug up the tomahawk; our knives were ready, and the heart of Black Hawk swelled high in his bosom when he led his warriors to battle. He is satisfied. He will go to the world of spirits contented. He has done his duty. His father will meet him there, and commend him.

Black Hawk is a true Indian, and disdains to cry like a woman. He feels for his wife, his children and friends. But he does not care for himself. He cares for his nation and the Indians. They will suffer. He laments their fate. The white men do not scalp the head; but they do worse—they poison the heart; it is not pure with them.—His countrymen will not be scalped, but they will, in a few years, become like the white men, so that you can't trust them, and there must be, as in the white settlements, nearly as many officers as men to take care of them and keep them in order.

Farewell, my nation! Black Hawk tried to save you, and avenge your wrongs. He drank the blood of some of the whites. He has been taken prisoner, and his plans are stopped. He can do no more. He is near his end. His sun is setting, and he will rise no more. Farewell to Black Hawk.

BLACK HAWK, MAKATAIMESHIEKIAKIAK (Sauk)

"Your houses are as numerous as the leaves upon the trees"
(June 4, 1833)

After Black Hawk's surrender and imprisonment at Fort Armstrong, President Andrew Jackson brought him to Washington, D.C. Black Hawk (c. 1770–1838) was pardoned by the president on the condition of acknowledging Keokuk as the chief of his tribe. After his meeting with the president, he and his companions were detained for a short time at Fort Monroe, in Virginia. He made this speech to the post commander at Fort Monroe as he left on his tour of eastern cities before his final homeward journey.

Brother, I have come on my own part, and in behalf of my companions, to bid you farewell. Our great father has at length been pleased to permit us to return to our hunting-grounds. We have buried the tomahawk, and the sound of the rifle will hereafter only bring death to the deer and the buffalo. Brother, you have treated the red men very kindly. Your squaws have made them presents, and you have given them plenty to eat and drink. The memory of your friendship will remain till the Great Spirit says it is time for Black Hawk to sing his death-song.

Brother, your houses are as numerous as the leaves upon the trees, and your young warriors, like the sands upon the shore of the big lake which rolls before us. The red man has but few houses, and few warriors, but the red man has a heart which throbs as warmly as the heart of his white brother. The Great Spirit has given us our hunting-grounds, and the skin of the deer which we kill there is his favorite, for its color is white, and this is the emblem of peace. This hunting-dress and these feathers of the eagle are white. Accept them, my brother; I have given one like this to the *White-otter*. Accept of it as a memorial of Black Hawk. When he is far away, this will serve to remind you of him. May the Great Spirit bless you and your children—farewell.

SOURCE: Samuel G. Drake. *Biography and History of the Indians of North America, from Its First Discovery.* Boston: Benjamin B. Mussey & Co., 1851 (11th ed.). 662.

ARAPOOSH (Crow)

"There is no country like the Crow Country" (1833)

> The chief Arapoosh (c. 1790–1834) delivered the following testimonial on the glories of his homeland to a Rocky Mountain fur trader.

The Crow country is a good country. The Great Spirit has put it exactly in the right place; while you are in it you fare well; whenever you go out of it, which ever way you travel, you fare worse.

If you go to the south, you have to wander over great barren plains; the water is warm and bad, and you meet the fever and ague.

To the north it is cold; the winters are long and bitter, with no grass; you cannot keep horses there, but must travel with dogs. What is a country without horses?

On the Columbia they are poor and dirty, paddle about in canoes, and eat fish. Their teeth are worn out; they are always taking fish-bones out of their mouths. Fish is poor food.

To the east, they dwell in villages; they live well; but they drink the muddy water of the Missouri—that is bad. A Crow's dog would not drink such water.

About the forks of the Missouri is a fine country; good water; good grass; plenty of buffalo. In summer, it is almost as good as the Crow country; but in winter it is cold; the grass is gone; and there is no salt weed for the horses.

The Crow country is exactly in the right place. It has snowy mountains and sunny plains; all kinds of climates and good things for every season. When the summer heats scorch the prairies, you can draw up under the mountains, where the air is sweet and cool, the grass fresh, and the bright streams come tumbling out of the snow-banks. There you can hunt the elk, the deer, and the antelope, when their skins are fit for dressing; there you will find plenty of white bears and mountain sheep.

In the autumn, when your horses are fat and strong from the mountain pastures, you can go down into the plains and hunt the buffalo, or trap beaver on the streams. And when winter comes on, you can

SOURCE: Washington Irving. *The Adventures of Captain Bonneville, U.S.A., in the Rocky Mountains and the Far West.* New York: George P. Putnam, 1850. 189–191.

take shelter in the woody bottoms along the rivers; there you will find buffalo meat for yourselves, and cottonwood bark for your horses: or you may winter in the Wind River valley, where there is salt weed in abundance.

The Crow country is exactly in the right place. Every thing good is to be found there. There is no country like the Crow country.

OSCEOLA (Seminole)

"I love my home, and will not go from it"
(October 23, 1834)

Osceola (c. 1803–1838) claims in the following speech that agreement to the Treaty of Payne's Landing in 1832, which required the Seminoles to "remove" from Florida to Indian Territory, was obtained by dishonest means. Hiding in the swamps, Osceola led guerrilla forces for several years against the newcomers to Seminole land. At an official peace council with the U.S. Army in October 1837, he was arrested; soon after he died in prison.

My Brothers! The white people got some of our chiefs to sign a paper to give our lands to them, but our chiefs did not do as we told them to do; they done wrong; we must do right. The agent tells us we must go away from the lands which we live on—our homes, and the graves of our Fathers, and go over the big river among the bad Indians. When the agent tells me to go from my home, I hate him, because I love my home, and will not go from it.

My Brothers! When the great spirit tells me to go with the white man, I go: but he tells me not to go.—The white man says I shall go, and he will send people to make me go; but I have a rifle, and I have some powder and some lead. I say, we must not leave our homes and lands. If any of our people want to go west we won't let them; and I tell them they are our enemies, and we will treat them so, for the great spirit will protect us.

SOURCE: Woodburne Potter. *The War in Florida: Being an Exposition of Its Causes.* Baltimore: Lewis and Coleman, 1836. 53–54.

UNNAMED (Blackfoot)

"I was his dog; and not his wife"   (1835)

Washington Irving recounted Captain Bonneville's travels, drawing
on the explorer's journals and other sources. Captain Bonneville
met the Blackfoot wife of a white trapper near the Wind River
Mountains; she told him her story.

I was the wife of a Blackfoot warrior, and I served him faithfully. Who
was so well served as he? Whose lodge was so well provided, or kept so
clean? I brought wood in the morning, and placed water always at
hand. I watched for his coming; and he found his meat cooked and
ready. If he rose to go forth, there was nothing to delay him. I searched
the thought that was in his heart, to save him the trouble of speaking.
When I went abroad on errands for him, the chiefs and warriors smiled
upon me, and the young braves spoke soft things, in secret; but my feet
were in the straight path, and my eyes could see nothing but him.

When he went out to hunt, or to war, who aided to equip him, but
I? When he returned, I met him at the door; I took his gun; and he entered without further thought. While he sat and smoked, I unloaded
his horses; tied them to the stakes; brought in their loads, and was
quickly at his feet. If his moccasins were wet, I took them off and put
on others which were dry and warm. I dressed all the skins he had
taken in the chase. He could never say to me, why is it not done? He
hunted the deer, the antelope, and the buffalo, and he watched for the
enemy. Every thing else was done by me. When our people moved
their camp, he mounted his horse and rode away; free as though he had
fallen from the skies. He had nothing to do with the labor of the camp;
it was I that packed the horses, and led them on the journey. When we
halted in the evening, and he sat with the other braves and smoked, it
was I that pitched his lodge; and when he came to eat and sleep, his
supper and his bed were ready.

I served him faithfully; and what was my reward? A cloud was always
on his brow, and sharp lightning on his tongue. I was his dog; and not
his wife.

Who was it that scarred and bruised me? It was he. My brother saw
how I was treated. His heart was big for me. He begged me to leave my

SOURCE: Washington Irving. *The Adventures of Captain Bonneville, U.S.A., in
the Rocky Mountains and the Far West.* New York: George P. Putnam, 1850.
411–414.

tyrant and fly. Where could I go? If retaken, who would protect me? My brother was not a chief; he could not save me from blows and wounds, perhaps death. At length I was persuaded. I followed my brother from the village. He pointed the way to the Nez Percés, and bade me go and live in peace among them. We parted. On the third day I saw the lodges of the Nez Percés before me. I paused for a moment, and had no heart to go on; but my horse neighed, and I took it as a good sign, and suffered him to gallop forward. In a little while I was in the midst of the lodges. As I sat silent on my horse, the people gathered round me, and inquired whence I came. I told my story. A chief now wrapped his blanket close around him, and bade me dismount. I obeyed. He took my horse to lead him away. My heart grew small within me. I felt, on parting with my horse, as if my last friend was gone. I had no words, and my eyes were dry. As he led off my horse, a young brave stepped forward. "Are you a chief of the people?" cried he. "Do we listen to you in council, and follow you in battle? Behold! a stranger flies to our camp from the dogs of Blackfeet, and asks protection. Let shame cover your face! The stranger is a woman, and alone. If she were a warrior, or had a warrior by her side, your heart would not be big enough to take her horse. But he is yours. By the right of war you may claim him; but look!"—his bow was drawn, and the arrow ready!—"you never shall cross his back!" The arrow pierced the heart of the horse, and he fell dead.

An old woman said she would be my mother. She led me to her lodge: my heart was thawed by her kindness, and my eyes burst forth with tears; like the frozen fountains in spring time. She never changed; but as the days passed away, was still a mother to me. The people were loud in praise of the young brave, and the chief was ashamed. I lived in peace.

A party of trappers came to the village, and one of them took me for his wife. This is he. I am very happy; he treats me with kindness, and I have taught him the language of my people. As we were travelling this way, some of the Blackfeet warriors beset us, and carried off the horses of the party. We followed, and my husband held a parley with them. The guns were laid down, and the pipe was lighted; but some of the white men attempted to seize the horses by force, and then a battle began. The snow was deep; the white men sank into it at every step; but the red men, with their snow-shoes, passed over the surface like birds, and drove off many of the horses in sight of their owners. With those that remained we resumed our journey. At length words took place between the leader of the party and my husband. He took away our horses, which had escaped in the battle, and turned us from his camp. My husband had one good friend among the trappers. That is he [pointing to the man who had asked assistance for them]. He is a good man. His heart is big. When he came in from hunting, and found that we had been driven away, he gave up all his wages, and followed us, that he might speak good words for us to the white captain.

WILLIAM APES (Pequot)

"Eulogy on King Philip"   (January 6, 1836)

William Apes, or Apees, (1798–c. 1836) became a Christian at age fifteen. He was raised in Connecticut by his parents and then his grandparents, and finally by a white Presbyterian judge. After working odd jobs and putting in a stint in the U.S. Army, he became a Methodist preacher and an author. He fought for acknowledgment of his fellow Native Americans as human beings, and he argued that—as he pointedly makes clear in the following speech—even as "pagans," they practiced a purer and better Christianity than the Pilgrims who arrived on Plymouth Rock. Apes believed himself the great-great-grandson of King Philip. He delivered this controversial speech on the famous Wampanoag chief on three separate occasions (January 6–8, 1836) before a paid audience in Boston's Odeon Theater. Two weeks later he gave an abridged version at Boylston Hall. From the date of that last speech, there is no further record of Apes's life or death. The following excerpts comprise about two-thirds of his original speech.

I do not arise to spread before you the fame of a noted warrior, whose natural abilities shone like those of the great and mighty Phillip of Greece, or of Alexander the Great, or like those of Washington—whose virtues and patriotism are engraven on the hearts of my audience. Neither do I approve of war as being the best method of bowing the haughty tyrant, Man, and civilizing the world. No, far from me be such a thought. But it is to bring before you beings, made by the God of Nature, and in whose hearts and heads he has planted sympathies that shall live forever in the memory of the world, whose brilliant talents shone in the display of natural things, so that the most cultivated, whose powers shone with equal lustre, were not able to prepare mantles to cover the burning elements of an uncivilized world. What, then, shall we cease to mention the mighty of the earth, the noble work of God?

Yet those purer virtues remain untold. Those noble traits that marked the wild man's course lie buried in the shades of night; and who shall stand? I appeal to the lovers of liberty. But those few remaining descendants who now remain as the monument of the cruelty

SOURCE: William Apes. *Eulogy on King Philip*. Boston: Published by the Author, 1836. [Reprint edition, with notes and commentary by Lincoln A. Dexter. Brookfield, Massachusetts: {Pub. by} Lincoln A. Dexter, 1985.]

of those who came to improve our race, and correct our errors; and as the immortal Washington lives endeared and engraven on the hearts of every white in America, never to be forgotten in time — even such is the immortal Philip honored, as held in memory by the degraded, but yet grateful descendants, who appreciate his character; so will every patriot, especially in this enlightened age, respect the rude yet all-accomplished son of the forest, that died a martyr to his cause, though unsuccessful, yet as glorious as the *American* Revolution. Where, then, shall we place the hero of the wilderness? . . .

The first inquiry is, Who is Philip? He was the descendant of one of the most celebrated chiefs in the known world, for peace and universal benevolence towards all men; for injuries upon injuries, and the most daring robberies and barbarous deeds of death that were ever committed by the American Pilgrims, were with patience and resignation borne, in a manner that would do justice to any Christian nation or being in the world — especially when we realize that it was voluntary suffering on the part of the good old chief. His country extensive — his men numerous, so as the wilderness was enlivened by them, say a thousand to one of the white men, and they, also, sick and feeble — where, then, shall we find one nation submitting so tamely to another, with such a host at their command? For injuries of much less magnitude have the people called Christians slain their brethren, till they could sing, like Samson, "With a jaw bone of an ass have we slain our thousands, and laid them in heaps." It will be well for us to lay those deeds and depredations committed by whites upon Indians before the civilized world, and then they can judge for themselves.

It appears from history that in 1614, "There came one Henry Harley unto me, bringing with him a native of the Island of Capawick, a place at the south of Cape Cod, whose name was Epenuel. This man was taken upon the main by force, with some twenty-nine others," very probably good old Massasoit's men — see Harlow's Voyage, 1611, "by a ship, and carried to London, and from thence to be sold for slaves among the Spaniards; but the Indians being too shrewd, or, as they say, unapt for their use, they refused to traffic in Indians' blood and bones." This inhuman act of the whites caused the Indians to be jealous forever afterwards, which the white man acknowledges upon the first pages of the history of his country.

How inhuman it was in those wretches to come into a country where nature shone in beauty, spreading her wings over the vast continent, sheltering beneath her shades those natural sons of an Almighty Being, that shone in grandeur and lustre like stars of the first magnitude in the heavenly world; whose virtues far surpassed their more enlightened foes, notwithstanding their pretended zeal for religion and virtue. How they could go to work to enslave a free people, and call it religion, is beyond the power of my imagination, and out-strips the revelation of God's word. Oh, thou pretended hypocritical Christian, whoever thou art, to say it was the design of God, that we should murder and slay one another, because we have the power. Power was not given us to abuse each other, but a mere power delegated to us by the King of heaven, a weapon of defence against error and evil; and when abused, it will turn to our destruction. Mark, then, the history of nations throughout the world.

But notwithstanding the transgression of this power to destroy the Indians at their first discovery, yet it does appear that the Indians had a wish to be friendly. When the pilgrims came among them (Iyanough's men), there appeared an old woman, breaking out in solemn lamentations, declaring one Capt. Hunt had carried off three of her children, and they would never return here. The pilgrims replied, that they were bad and wicked men, but they were going to do better, and would never injure them at all. And to pay the poor mother, gave her a few brass trinkets, to atone for her three sons, and appease her present feelings, a woman nearly one hundred years of age. Oh, white woman! what would you think, if some foreign nation, unknown to you, should come and carry away from you three lovely children, whom you had dandled on the knee, and at some future time you should behold them, and break forth in sorrow, with your heart broken, and merely ask, sirs, where are my little ones, and some one should reply, it was passion, great passion; what would you think of them? Should you not think they were beings made more like rocks than men? Yet these same men came to these Indians for support, and acknowledge themselves, that no people could be used better than they were; that their treatment would do honor to any nation; that their provisions were in abundance; that they gave them venison, and sold them many hogsheads of corn to fill their stores, besides beans. This was in the year 1622. Had it not been for this humane act of the Indians, every white man would have been swept from the New England colonies. In their sickness too, the Indians were as tender to them as to their own children; and for all this, they were denounced as savages by those who had received all the acts of kindness they possibly could show them. After these social acts of the Indians towards those who were suffering, and those of their countrymen, who well knew the care their brethren had received by them: how were the Indians treated before that? Oh, hear! In the following manner, and their own words, we presume, they will not deny.

December (O. S.) 1620, the pilgrims landed at Plymouth, and without asking liberty from any one, they possessed themselves of a portion of the country, and built themselves houses, and then made a treaty, and commanded them to accede to it. This, if now done, would be called an insult, and every white man would be called to go out and act the part of a patriot, to defend their country's rights; and if every intruder were butchered, it would be sung upon every hill-top in the Union, that victory and patriotism was the order of the day. And yet the Indians (though many were dissatisfied), without the shedding of blood, or imprisoning any one, bore it. And yet for their kindness and resignation towards the whites, they were called savages, and made by God on purpose for them to destroy. We might say, God understood his work better than this. But to proceed, it appears that a treaty was made by the pilgrims and the Indians, which treaty was kept during forty years; the young chiefs during this time [were] showing the pilgrims how to live in their country, and find support for their wives and little ones; and for all this, they were receiving the applauses of being savages. The two gentlemen chiefs were Squanto and Samoset, that were so good to the pilgrims.

The next we present before you are things very appalling. We turn our attention to dates, 1623, January and March, when Mr. Weston Colony came very near starving to death; some of them were obliged to hire themselves to the Indians, to become their servants, in order that they might live. Their principal work was to bring wood and water; but not being contented with this, many of the whites sought to steal the Indian's corn; and because the Indians complained of it, and through their complaint, some one of their number being punished, as they say, to appease the savages. Now let us see who the greatest savages were; the person that stole the corn was a stout athletic man, and because of this, they wished to spare him, and take an old man who was lame and sickly, and that used to get his living by weaving, and because they thought he would not be of so much use to them, he was, although innocent of any crime, hung in his stead. Oh, savage, where art thou, to weep over the Christian's crimes. Another act of humanity for Christians, as they call themselves, that one Capt. Standish, gathering some fruit and provisions, goes forward with a black and hypocritical heart, and pretends to prepare a feast for the Indians; and when they sit down to eat, they seize the Indian's knives hanging about their necks, and stab them to the heart. The white people call this stabbing, feasting the savages. We suppose it might well mean themselves, their conduct being more like savages than Christians. They took one Wittumumet, the Chief's head, and put it upon a pole in their fort; and for aught we know, gave praise to their God for success in murdering a poor Indian; for we know it was their usual course to give praise to God for this kind of victory, believing it was God's will and command, for them to do so. We wonder if these same Christians do not think it the command of God, that they should lie, steal, and get drunk, commit fornication and adultery. The one is as consistent as the other. What say you, judges, is it not so, and was it not according as they did? Indians think it is. . . .

It does not appear that Massasoit or his sons were respected because they were human beings, but because they feared him; and we are led to believe that if it had been in the power of the Pilgrims, they would have butchered them out and out notwithstanding all the piety they professed. Only look for a few moments at the abuses the son of Massasoit received. Alexander being sent for with armed men, and while he and his men were breaking their fast in the morning, they were taken immediately away, by order of the governor, without the least provocation, but merely through suspicion. Alexander and his men saw them, and might have prevented it, but did not, saying the governor had no occasion to treat him in this manner; and the heartless wretch informed him that he would murder him upon the spot, if he did not go with him, presenting a sword at his breast; and had it not been for one of his men he would have yielded himself up upon the spot. Alexander was a man of strong passion, and of a firm mind; and this insulting treatment of him caused him to fall sick of a fever, so that he never recovered. Some of the Indians were suspicious that he was poisoned to death. He died in the year 1662. "After him," says that eminent divine, Dr. Mather, "there rose up one Philip, of cursed memory." Perhaps if the Dr. was present, he would find that the memory of Philip was as far before his, in the view of sound, judicious men, as the sun is before the stars, at noonday. But we might suppose that men like Dr. Mather, so well versed in Scripture, would have known his work better than to have spoken evil of any one, or have cursed any of God's works. He ought to have known that God did not make his red children for him to curse; but if he wanted them cursed, he could have done it himself. But, on the contrary, his suffering Master commanded him to love his enemies, and to pray for his persecutors, and to do unto others as he would that men should do unto him. Now, we wonder if the sons of the Pilgrims would like to have us, poor Indians, come out and curse the Doctor, and all their sons, as we have been, by many of them. And suppose that, in some future day, our children should repay all these wrongs, would it not be doing as we, poor Indians, have been done to? But we sincerely hope there is more humanity in us, than that.

In the history of Massasoit we find that his own head men were not satisfied with the Pilgrims; that they looked upon them to be intruders, and had a wish to expel those intruders out of their coast; and no wonder that from the least reports the Pilgrims were ready to take it up. A false report was made respecting one Tisquantum, that he was murdered by an Indian, one of Coubantant's men. Upon this news, one Standish, a vile and malicious fellow, took fourteen of his lewd Pilgrims with him, and at midnight, when a deathless silence reigned throughout the wilderness; not even a bird is heard to send forth her sweet songs to charm and comfort those children of the woods; but all had taken their rest, to commence anew on the rising of the glorious sun. But to their sad surprise there was no rest for them, but they were surrounded by ruffians and assassins; yes, assassins; what better name can be given them? At that late hour of the night, meeting a house in the wilderness, whose inmates were nothing but a few helpless females and children; soon a voice is heard—Move not, upon the peril of your life. I appeal to this audience if there was any righteousness in their proceedings? Justice would say no. At the same time some of the females were so frightened, that some of them undertook to make their escape, upon which they were fired upon. Now it is doubtless the case that these females never saw a white man before, or ever heard a gun fired. It must have sounded to them like the rumbling of thunder, and terror must certainly have filled all their hearts. And can it be supposed that these innocent Indians could have looked upon them as good and trusty men? Do you look upon the midnight robber and assassin as being a Christian, and trusty man? These Indians had not done one single wrong act to the whites, but were as innocent of any crime, as any beings in the world. And do you believe that Indians cannot feel and see, as well as white people? If you think so, you are mistaken. Their power of feeling and knowing is as quick as yours. Now this is to be borne, as the pilgrims did as their Master told them to; but what color he was I leave it. But if the real sufferers say one word, they are denounced, as being wild and savage beasts. . . .

The history of New England writers say, that our tribes were large and respectable. How then, could it be otherwise, but their safety rested in the hands of friendly Indians. In 1647, the pilgrims speak of large and respectable tribes. But let us trace them for a few moments. How have they been destroyed, is it by fair means? No. How then? By hypocritical proceedings, by being duped and flattered; flattered by informing the Indians that their God was a going to speak to them, and then place them before the cannon's mouth in a line, and then putting the match to it and kill thousands of them. We might suppose that meek Christians had better gods and weapons than cannon; weapons that were not carnal, but mighty through God, to the pulling down of strong holds. These are the weapons that modern Christians profess to have; and if the pilgrims did not have them, they ought not to be honored as such. But let us again review their weapons, to civilize the nations of this soil. What were they: rum and powder, and ball, together with all the diseases, such as the small pox, and every other disease imaginable; and in this way sweep off thousands and tens of thousands. And then it has been said, that these men who were free from these things, that they could not live among civilized people. We wonder how a virtuous people could live in a sink of diseases, a people who had never been used to them.

And who is to account for those destructions upon innocent families and helpless children. It was said by some of the New England writers, that living babes were found at the breast of their dead mothers. What an awful sight! and to think, too, that these diseases were carried among them on purpose to destroy them. Let the children of the pilgrims blush, while the son of the forest drops a tear, and groans over the fate of his murdered and departed fathers. He would say to the sons of the pilgrims, (as Job said about his birth day), let the day be dark, the 22d of December, 1622; let it be forgotten in your celebration, in your speeches, and by the burying of the Rock that your fathers first put their foot upon. For be it remembered, although the gospel is said to be glad tidings to all people, yet we poor Indians never have found those who brought it as messengers of mercy, but contrawise. We say, therefore, let every man of color wrap himself in mourning, for the 22d of December and the 4th of July are days of mourning and not of joy. (I would here say, there is an error in my book; it speaks of the 25th of December, but it should be the 22d. See *Indian Nullification*.) Let them rather fast and pray to the great Spirit, the Indian's God, who deals out mercy to his red children, and not destruction. . . .

But having laid a mass of history and exposition before you, the purpose of which is to show that Philip and all the Indians generally, felt indignantly towards whites, whereby they were more easily allied together by Philip, their King and Emperor, we come to notice more particularly his history. As to his Majesty, King Philip, it was certain that his honor was put to the test, and it was certainly to be tried, even at the loss of his life and country. It is a matter of uncertainty about his age; but his birth-place was at Mount Hope, Rhode Island, where Massasoit, his father, lived, till 1656, and died, as also his brother, Alexander, by the governor's ill-treating him (that is, Winthrop), which caused his death, as before mentioned, in 1662; after which, the kingdom fell into the hands of Philip, the greatest man that ever lived upon the American shores. Soon after his coming to the throne, it appears he began to be noticed, though, prior to this, it appears that he was not forward in the councils of war or peace. When he came into office it appears that he knew there was great responsibility resting upon himself and country; that it was likely to be ruined by those rude intruders around him; though he appears friendly, and is willing to sell them lands for almost nothing, as we shall learn from dates of the Plymouth Colony, which commence June 23, 1664. William Benton, of Rhode Island, a merchant, buys Matapoisett of Philip and wife, but no sum is set, which he gave for it. To this deed, his counsellors, and wife, and two of the Pilgrims, were witnesses. In 1665 he sold New Bedford and Compton for forty dollars. In 1667 he sells to Constant Southworth and others all the meadow lands from Dartmouth to Matapoisett, for which he received sixty dollars. The same year he sells to Thomas Willet a tract of land two miles in length, and perhaps the same in width, for which he received forty dollars. In 1668 he sold a tract of some square miles, now called Swanzey. The next year he sells five hundred acres in Swanzey, for which he received eighty dollars. His counsellors and interpreters, with the Pilgrims, were witnesses to these deeds.

Osamequan, for valuable considerations, in the year 1641 sold to John Brown and Edward Winslow a tract of land eight miles square, situated on both sides of Palmer's River. Philip, in 1668, was required to sign a quit-claim of the same, which we understand he did in the presence of his counsellors. In the same year Philip laid claim to a portion of land called New Meadows, alleging that it was not intended to be conveyed in a former deed for which Mr. Brown paid him forty-four dollars, in goods; so it was settled without difficulty. Also, in 1669, for forty dollars he sold to one John Cook a whole island, called Nokatay, near Dartmouth. The same year Philip sells a tract of land in Middleborough for fifty-two dollars. In 1671 he sold to Hugh Cole a large tract of land, lying near Swanzey, for sixteen dollars. In 1672 he sold sixteen square miles to William Breton and others, of Taunton, for which he and his chief received five hundred and seventy-two dollars. This contract, signed by himself and chiefs, ends the sales of lands with Philip, for all which he received nine hundred and seventy-four dollars, as far as we can learn by the records.

Here Philip meets with a most bitter insult, in 1673, from one Peter Talmon, of Rhode Island, who complained to the Plymouth Court against Philip, of Mount Hope, predecessor, heir, and administrator of his brother Alexander, deceased, in an action on the case, to the damage of three thousand and two hundred dollars, for which the Court gave verdict in favor of Talmon, the young Pilgrim; for which Philip had to make good to the said Talmon a large tract of land at Sapamet and other places adjacent; and for the want thereof, that is, more land that was not taken up, the complainant is greatly damnified. This is the language in the Pilgrims' Court. Now let us review this a little. The man who bought this land made the contract, as he says, with Alexander, ten or twelve years before; then why did he not bring forward his contract before the Court? It is easy to understand why he did not. Their object was to cheat, or get the whole back again in this way. Only look at the sum demanded, and it is enough to satisfy the critical observer. This course of proceedings caused the Chief and his people to entertain strong jealousies of the whites.

In the year 1668 Philip made a complaint against one Weston, who had wronged one of his men of a gun and some swine; and we have no account that he got any justice for his injured brethren. And, indeed, it would be a strange thing for poor unfortunate Indians to find justice in those Courts of the pretended pious, in those days, or even since; and for a proof of my assertion I will refer the reader or hearer to the records of Legislatures and Courts throughout New England; and also to my book, *Indian Nullification*.

We would remark still further; who stood up in those days, and since, to plead Indian rights? Was it the friend of the Indian? No; it was his enemies who rose; his enemies, to judge and pass sentence. And we know that such kind of characters as the Pilgrims were, in regard to the Indians' rights, who, as they say, had none, must certainly always give verdict against them, as, generally speaking, they always have. Prior to this insult it appears that Philip had met with great difficulty with the Pilgrims; that they appeared to be suspicious of him in 1671; and the Pilgrims sent for him, but he did not appear to move as though he cared much for their messenger, which caused them to be still more suspicious. What grounds the Pilgrims had is not ascertained, unless it is attributed to a guilty conscience for wrongs done to Indians. It appears that Philip, when he got ready, goes near to them, and sends messengers to Taunton, to invite the Pilgrims to come and treat with him; but the governor being either too proud, or afraid, sends messengers to him to come to their residence at Taunton, to which he complied. Among these messengers was the Honorable Roger Williams, a Christian and a patriot, and a friend to the Indians, for which we rejoice. Philip, not liking to trust the Pilgrims, left some of the whites in his stead, to warrant his safe return. When Philip and his men had come near the place, some of the Plymouth people were ready to attack him; this rashness was, however, prevented by the Commissioner of Massachusetts, who met there with the Governor, to treat with Philip; and it was agreed upon to meet in the meeting-house. Philip's complaint was, that the Pilgrims had injured the planting grounds of his people. The Pilgrims, acting as umpires, say the charges against them were not sustained; and because it was not, to their satisfaction, the whites wanted that Philip should order all his men to bring in his arms and ammunition; and the Court was to dispose of them as they pleased. The next thing was, that Philip must pay the cost of the treaty, which was four hundred dollars. The Pious Dr. Mather says, that Philip was appointed to pay a sum of money to defray the charges that his insolent clamors had put the Colony to. We wonder if the Pilgrims were as ready to pay the Indians for the trouble they put them to. If they were, it was with the instruments of death. It appears that Philip did not wish to make war with them, but compromised with them, and in order to appease the Pilgrims he actually did order his men, whom he could not trust, to deliver them up; but his own men withheld, with the exception of a very few.

Now what an unrighteous act this was in the people, who professed to be friendly and humane, and peaceable to all men. It could not be that they were so devoid of sense as to think these illiberal acts would produce peace: but contrawise, continual broils. And in fact it does appear that they courted war instead of peace, as it appears from a second council that was held by order of the Governor, at Plymouth, September 13, 1671. It appears that they sent again for Philip; but he did not attend, but went himself and made complaint to the governor, which made him write to the council, and ordered them to desist, to be more mild, and not to take such rash measures. But it appears that on the 24th, the scene changed; that they held another council, and the disturbers of the peace, the intruders upon a peaceable people, say they find Philip guilty of the following charges:

1. That he had neglected to bring in his arms, although competent time had been given him.

2. That he had carried insolently and proudly towards us on several occasions, in refusing to come down to our courts (when sent for), to procure a right understanding betwixt us.

What an insult this was to his Majesty, an independent Chief of a powerful nation, [that he] should come at the beck and call of his neighbors whenever they pleased to have him do it. Besides, did not Philip do as he agreed, at Taunton, that is in case there was more difficulty they were to leave it to Massachusetts, to be settled there in the high council, and both parties were to abide by their decision; but did the Pilgrims wait? No. But being infallible, of course they could not err.

The third charge was, harboring divers Indians not his own men; but vagabond Indians.

Now what a charge this was to bring against a King, calling his company vagabonds, because it did not happen to please them; and what right had they to find fault with his company. I do not believe that Philip ever troubled himself about the white people's company, and prefer charges against them for keeping company with whom they pleased. Neither do I believe he called their company vagabonds, for he was more noble than that.

The fourth charge is, that he went to Massachusetts with his council, and complained against them, and turned their brethren against them.

This was more a complaint against themselves than Philip, inasmuch it represents that Philip's story was so correct, that they were blameable.

5. That he had not been quite so civil as they wished him to be.

We presume that Philip felt himself much troubled by these intruders, and of course put them off from time to time, or did not take much notice of their proposals. Now such charges as those, we think are to no credit of the pilgrims. However, this council ended much as the other did, in regard to disarming the Indians, which they never were able to do. Thus ended the events of 1671.

But it appears that the pilgrims could not be contented with what they had done, but they must send an Indian, and a traitor, to preach to Philip and his men, in order to convert him and his people to Christianity. The preacher's name was Sassamon. I would appeal to this audience, is it not certain that the Plymouth people strove to pick a quarrel with Philip and his men. What could have been more insulting than to send a man to them who was false, and looked upon as such; for it is most certain that a traitor was above all others the more to be detested than any other. And not only so, it was the laws of the Indians, that such a man must die; that he had forfeited his life; and when he made his appearance among them, Philip would have killed him upon the spot, if his council had not persuaded him not to. But it appears that in March, 1674, one of Philip's men killed him, and placed him beneath the ice in a certain pond near Plymouth; doubtless by the order of Philip. After this, search was made for him, and he found there a certain Indian, by the name of Patuckson; Tobias, also, his son, were apprehended and tried. Tobias was one of Philip's counsellors, as it appears from the records that the trial did not end here, that it was put over, and that two of the Indians entered into bonds for $400, for the appearance of Tobias at the June term; for which a mortgage of land was taken to that amount, for his safe return. June having arrived, three instead of one are arraigned. There was no one but Tobias suspected at the previous Court. Now two others are arraigned, tried, condemned and executed (making three in all), in June the 8th, 1675, by hanging and shooting. It does not appear that any more than one was guilty, and it was said that he was known to acknowledge it; but the other two persisted in their innocency to the last.

This murder of the preacher brought on the war a year sooner than it was anticipated by Philip. But this so exasperated King Philip that from that day he studied to be revenged of the pilgrims; judging that his white intruders had nothing to do in punishing his people for any crime, and that it was in violation of treaties of ancient date. But when we look at this, how bold and how daring it was to Philip, as though they would bid defiance to him, and all his authority, we do not wonder at his exasperation. When the Governor finds that his Majesty was displeased, he then sends messengers to him, and wishes to know why he would make war upon him, (as if he had done all right), and wished to enter into a new treaty with him. The King answered them thus: Your Governor is but a subject of King Charles of England, I shall not treat with a subject; I shall treat of peace only with a King, my brother; when he comes, I am ready.

This answer of Philip's to the messengers is worthy of note throughout the world. And never could a prince answer with more dignity in regard to his official authority than he did; disdaining the idea of placing himself upon a par of the minor subjects of a King; letting them know at the same time that he felt his independence more than they thought he did. And indeed it was time for him to wake up, for now the subjects of King Charles had taken one of his counsellors and killed him, and he could no longer trust them. Until the execution of these three Indians, supposed to be the murderers of Sassamon, no hostility was committed by Philip or his warriors. About the time of their trial, he was said to be marching his men up and down the country in arms; but when it was known, he could no longer restrain his young men, who, upon the 24th of June, provoked the people of Swansey, by killing their cattle and other injuries, which was a signal to commence the war, and what they had desired, as a superstitious notion prevailed among the Indians that whoever fired the first gun of either party would be conquered. Doubtless a notion they had received from the pilgrims. It was upon a fast day, too, when the first gun was fired; and as the people were returning from church, they were fired upon by the Indians, when several of them were killed. It is not supposed that Philip directed this attack, but was opposed to it. Though it is not doubted that he meant to be revenged upon his enemies; for during some time he had been cementing his countrymen together, as it appears that he had sent to all the disaffected tribes, who also had watched the movements of the comers from the new world, and were as dissatisfied as Philip himself was with their proceedings. . . .

At this council it appears that Philip made the following speech to his chiefs, counsellors and warriors:

"Brothers, you see this vast country before us, which the great Spirit gave to our fathers and us; you see the buffalo and deer that now are our support.—Brothers, you see these little ones, our wives and children, who are looking to us for food and raiment; and you now see the foe before you, that they have grown insolent and bold; that all our ancient customs are disregarded; the treaties made by our fathers and us are broken, and all of us insulted; our council fires disregarded, and all the ancient customs of our fathers; our brothers murdered before our eyes, and their spirits cry to us for revenge. Brothers, these people from the unknown world will cut down our groves, spoil our hunting and planting grounds, and drive us and our children from the graves of our fathers and our council fires, and enslave our women and children."

This famous speech of Philip was calculated to arouse them to arms, to do the best they could in protecting and defending their rights. The blow had now been struck, the die was cast, and nothing but blood and carnage was before them. And we find Philip as active as the wind, as dextrous as a giant, firm as the pillows of heaven, and as fierce as a lion, a powerful foe to contend with indeed: and as swift as an eagle, gathering together his forces, to prepare them for the battle. And as it would swell our address too full to mention all the tribes in Philip's train of warriors, suffice it to say that from six to seven were with him at different times. When he begins the war, he goes forward and musters about 500 of his men, and arms them complete, and about 900 of the other, making in all about fourteen hundred warriors when he commenced. It must be recollected that this war was legally declared by Philip, so that the colonies had a fair warning. It was no savage war of surprise as some suppose, but one sorely provoked by the pilgrims themselves. But when Philip and his men fought, as they were accustomed to do, and according to their mode of war, it was no more than what could be expected. But we hear no particular acts of cruelty committed by Philip during the siege. But we find more manly nobility in him than we do in all the head pilgrims put together, as we shall see during this quarrel between them. Philip's young men were eager to do exploits, and to lead captive their haughty lords. It does appear that every Indian heart had been lighted up at the council fires, at Philip's speech, and that the forest was literally alive with this injured race. And now town after town fell before them. The pilgrims with their forces were ever marching in one direction, while Philip and his forces were marching in another, burning all before them, until Middleborough, Taunton and Dartmouth were laid in ruins, and forsaken by its inhabitants.

At the great fight at Pocasset, Philip commanded in person, where he also was discovered with his host in a dismal swamp. He had retired here with his army to secure a safe retreat from the pilgrims, who were in close pursuit of him, and their numbers were so powerful they thought the fate of Philip was sealed. They surrounded the swamp, in hopes to destroy him and his army. At the edge of the swamp Philip had secreted a few of his men to draw them into ambush, upon which the pilgrims showed fight; Philip's men retreating and the whites pursuing them till they were surrounded by Philip, and nearly all cut off. This was a sorry time to them; the pilgrims, however, reinforced, but ordered a retreat, supposing it impossible for Philip to escape, and knowing his forces to be great, it was conjectured by some to build a fort to starve him out, as he had lost but few men in the fight. The situation of Philip was rather peculiar, as there was but one outlet to the swamp, and a river before him nearly seven miles to descend. The pilgrims placed a guard around the swamp for thirteen days, which gave Philip and his men time to prepare canoes to make good his retreat; in which he did, to the Connecticut river, and in his retreat lost but fourteen men. We may look upon this move of Philip's to be equal, if not superior, to that of Washington crossing the Delaware. For while Washington was assisted by all the knowledge that art and science could give, together with all the instruments of defence, and edged tools to prepare rafts, and the like helps for safety across the river, Philip was naked as to any of these things, possessing only what nature, his mother, had bestowed upon him; and yet makes his escape with equal praise. But he would not even have lost a man, had it not been for Indians who were hired to fight against Indians, with promise of their enjoying equal rights with their white brethren; but not one of those promises have as yet been fulfilled by the pilgrims or their children, though they must acknowledge that without the aid of Indians and their guides, they must inevitably have been swept off. It was only then by deception that the pilgrims gained the country, as their word has never been fulfilled in regard to Indian rights.

Philip having now taken possession of the back settlements of Massachusetts, one town after another was swept off. A garrison being established at Northfield by the pilgrims, and while endeavoring to reinforce it with thirty-six armed, twenty out of their number was killed, and one taken prisoner. At the same time Philip so managed it as to cut off their retreat, and take their ammunition from them.

About the month of August, they took a young lad about fourteen years of age, whom they intended to make merry with the next day; but the pilgrims said God touched the Indians' heart, and they let him go. About the same time, the whites took an old man of Philip's, whom they found alone; and because he would not turn traitor, and inform them where Philip was, they pronounced him worthy of death; and by them was executed, cutting off first his arms and then his head. We wonder why God did not touch the pilgrims' heart and save them from cruelty, as well as the Indians.

We would now notice an act in King Philip that outweighs all the other princes and emperors in the world. That is, when his men began to be in want of money, having a coat neatly wrought with mampampeag (*i.e.*, Indian money), he cut it to pieces, and distributed it among all his chiefs and warriors; it being better than the old continental money of the revolution, in Washington's day, as not one Indian soldier found fault with it, as we could ever learn; so that it cheered their hearts still to persevere to maintain their rights and expel their enemies.

On the 18th of September, the pilgrims made a tour from Hadley to Deerfield, with about eighty men, to bring their valuable articles of clothing and provisions. Having loaded their teams and returning, Philip and his men attacked them, and nearly slew them all. The attack was made near Sugar-loaf Hill. It was said that in this fight, the pilgrims lost their best men of Essex, and all their goods; upon which there were many made widows and orphans in one day. Philip now having done what he could upon the Western frontiers of Massachusetts, and believing his presence was wanted among his allies, the Narragansets, to keep them from being duped by the pilgrims, he is next known to be in their country.

The pilgrims determined to break down Philip's power, if possible, with the Narragansets: thus they raised an army of 1500 strong, to go against them and destroy them if possible. In this, Massachusetts, Plymouth and Connecticut all join in severally, to crush Philip. Accordingly in December, in 1675, the pilgrims set forward to destroy them. Preceding their march, Philip had made all arrangements for the winter, and had fortified himself beyond what was common for his countrymen to do, upon a small island near South Kingston, R.I. Here he intended to pass the winter with his warriors and their wives and children. About five hundred Indian houses was erected of a superior kind, in which was deposited all their stores, tubs of corn, and other things, piled up to a great height, which rendered it bullet proof. It was supposed that about three thousand persons had taken up their residence in it. (I would remark, that Indians took better care of themselves in those days than they have been able to since.) Accordingly on the 19th day of December, after the pilgrims had been out in the extreme cold, for nearly one month, lodging in tents, and their provision being short, and the air full of snow, they had no other alternative than to attack Philip in the fort. Treachery however, hastened his ruin; one of his men by hope of reward from the deceptive pilgrims betrayed his country into their hands. The traitor's name was Peter. No white man was acquainted with the way, and it would have been almost impossible for them to have found it, much less to have captured it. There was but one point where it could have been entered or assailed with any success, and this was fortified much like a block house, directly in front of the entrance, and also flankers to cover a cross fire. Besides high palisides, an immense hedge of fallen trees of nearly a rod in thickness. Thus surrounded by trees and water, there was but one place that the pilgrims could pass. Nevertheless, they made the attempt. Philip now had directed his men to fire, and every platoon of the Indians swept every white man from the path one after another, until six captains with a great many of the men had fallen. In the mean time, one Captain Moseley with some of his men had some how or other gotten into the fort in another way, and surprised them; by which the pilgrims were enabled to capture the fort, at the same time setting fire to it, and hewing down men, women and children indiscriminately. Philip, however, was enabled to escape with many of his warriors. It is said at this battle eighty whites were killed, and one hundred and fifty wounded; many of whom died of their wounds afterwards, not being able to dress them till they had marched eighteen miles; also leaving many of their dead in the fort. It is said that seven hundred of the Narragansets perished. The greater part of them being women and children.

It appears that God did not prosper them much after all. It is believed that the sufferings of the pilgrims were without a parallel in history; and it is supposed that the horrors and burning elements of Moscow will bear but a faint resemblance of that scene. The thousands and tens of thousands assembled there with their well disciplined forces bear but little comparison to that of modern Europe, when the inhabitants, science, manners and customs are taken into consideration. We might well admit the above fact, and say, the like was never known among any heathen nation in the world; for none but those worse than heathens would have suffered so much, for the sake of being revenged upon those of their enemies. Philip had repaired to his quarters to take care of his people and not to have them exposed. We should not have wondered quite so much if Philip had gone forward and acted thus. But when a people, calling themselves Christians, conduct in this manner, we think they are censurable, and no pity at all ought to be had for them.

It appears that one of the whites had married one of Philip's countrymen; and they, the pilgrims, said he was a traitor, and therefore they said he must die. So they quartered him; and as history informs us, they said, he being a heathen, but a few tears were shed at his funeral. Here, then, because a man would not turn and fight against his own wife and family, or leave them, he was condemned as an heathen. We presume that no honest men will commend those ancient fathers for such absurd conduct. Soon after this, Philip and his men left that part of the country, and retired farther back, near the Mohawks; where, in July 1676, some of his men were slain by the Mohawks. Notwithstanding this, he strove to get them to join him; and here it is said that Philip did not do that which was right; that he killed some of the Mohawks and laid it to the whites, in order that he might get them to join him. If so, we cannot consistently believe he did right. But he was so exasperated that nothing but revenge would satisfy him. All this act was no worse than our political men do in our days, of their strife to wrong each other, who profess to be enlightened; and all for the sake of carrying their points. Heathen-like, either by the sword, calumny or deception of every kind; and the late duels among the called high men of honor is sufficient to warrant my statements. But while we pursue our history in regard to Philip, we find that he made many successful attempts against the pilgrims, in surprising and driving them from their posts, during the year 1676, in February, and through till August, in which time many of the Christian Indians joined him. It is thought by many that all would have joined him if they had been left to their choice, as it appears they did not like their white brethren very well. It appears that Philip treated his prisoners with a great deal more Christian-like spirit than the pilgrims did; even Mrs. Rolandson, although speaking with bitterness sometimes of the Indians, yet in her journal she speaks not a word against him. Philip even hires her to work for him, and pays her for her work, and then invites her to dine with him and to smoke with him. And we have many testimonies that he was kind to his prisoners; and when the English wanted to redeem Philip's prisoners, they had the privilege.

Now did Governor Winthrop or any of those ancient divines use any of his men so? No. Was it known that they received any of their female captives into their houses and fed them? No; it cannot be found upon history. Were not the females completely safe, and none of them were violated, as they acknowledge themselves? But was it so when the Indian women fell into the hands of the pilgrims? No. Did the Indians get a chance to redeem their prisoners? No. But when they were taken, they were either compelled to turn traitors and join their enemies, or be butchered upon the spot. And this is the dishonest method that the famous Capt. Church used in doing his great exploits; and in no other way could he ever have gained one battle. So after all, Church only owes his exploits to the honesty of the Indians, who told the truth, and to his own deceptive heart in duping them. Here it is to be understood that the whites have always imposed upon the credulity of the Indians. It is with shame, I acknowledge, that I have to notice so much corruption of a people calling themselves Christians. If they were like my people, professing no purity at all, then their crimes would not appear to have such magnitude. But while they appear to be by profession more virtuous, their crimes still blacken. It makes them truly to appear to be like mountains filled with smoke; and thick darkness covering them all around.

But we have another dark and corrupt deed for the sons of the pilgrims to look at, and that is the fight and capture of Philip's son and wife, and many of his warriors, in which Philip lost about one hundred and thirty men killed and wounded; this was in August 1676. But the most horrid act was in taking Philip's son, about ten years of age, and selling him to be a slave away from his father and mother. While I am writing, I can hardly restrain my feelings, to think a people calling themselves Christians should conduct so scandalous, so outrageous, making themselves appear so despicable in the eyes of the Indians; and even now in this audience, I doubt not but there is men honorable enough to despise the conduct of those pretended Christians. And surely none but such as believe they did right will ever go and undertake to celebrate that day of their landing, the 22d of December. Only look at it, then stop and pause. My fathers came here for liberty themselves, and then they must go and chain that mind, that image they professed to serve; not content to rob and cheat the poor ignorant Indians, but must take one of the King's sons, and make a slave of him. Gentlemen and ladies, I blush at these tales, if you do not, especially when they professed to be a free and humane people. Yes, they did; they took a part of my tribe, and sold them to the Spaniards in Bermuda, and many others; and then on the Sabbath day, these people would gather themselves together, and say that God is no respecter of persons; while the divines would pour forth, "he that says he loves God and hates his brother, is a liar, and the truth is not in him." And at the same time they hating and selling their fellow men in bondage. And there is no manner of doubt but that all my countrymen would have been enslaved if they had tamely submitted. But no sooner would they butcher every white man that come in their way, and even put an end to their own wives and children, and that was all that prevented them from being slaves; yes, *all.* It was not the good will of those holy pilgrims that prevented, no. But I would speak, and I could wish it might be like the voice of thunder, that it might be heard afar off, even to the ends of the earth. He that will advocate slavery is worse than a beast, is a being devoid of shame; and has gathered around him the most corrupt and debasing principles in the world; and I care not whether he be a minister or member of any church in the world; no, not excepting the head men of the nation. And he that will not set his face against its corrupt principles is a coward, and not worthy of being numbered among men and Christians. And conduct too that libels the laws of the country, and the word of God, that men profess to believe in.

After Philip had his wife and son taken, sorrow filled his heart; but notwithstanding, as determined as ever to be revenged, though was pursued by the duped Indians and Church, into a swamp; one of the men proposing to Philip that he had better make peace with the enemy,

upon which he slew him upon the spot. And the pilgrims being also repulsed by Philip, were forced to retreat with the loss of one man in particular, whose name was Thomas Lucas, of Plymouth. We rather suspect that he was some related to Lucas and Hedge, who made their famous speeches against the poor Marshpees, in 1834, in the Legislature,
in Boston, against freeing them from slavery, that their fathers, the pilgrims, had made of them for years.

Philip's forces had now become very small, so many having been
duped away by the whites, and killed, that it was now easy surrounding
him. Therefore, upon the 12th of August, Captain Church surrounded
the swamp where Philip and his men had encamped, early in the
morning, before they had risen, doubtless led on by an Indian who was
either compelled or hired to turn traitor. Church had now placed his
guard so that it was impossible for Philip to escape without being shot.
It is doubtful, however, whether they would have taken him if he had
not been surprised. Suffice it to say, however, this was the case. A sor-
rowful morning to the poor Indians, to lose such a valuable man. When
coming out of the swamp, he was fired upon by an Indian, and killed
dead upon the spot.

I rejoice that it was even so, that the Pilgrims did not have the pleasure of tormenting him. The white man's gun missing fire lost the
honor of killing the truly great man, Philip. The place where Philip fell
was very muddy. Upon this news, the Pilgrims gave three cheers; then
Church ordering his body to be pulled out of the mud, while one of
those tender-hearted Christians exclaims, what a dirty creature he looks
like. And we have also Church's speech upon that subject, as follows:
For as much as he has caused many a pilgrim to lie above ground un-
buried, to rot, not one of his bones shall be buried. With him fell five
of his best and most trusty men; one the son of a chief, who fired the
first gun in the war.

Captain Church now orders him to be cut up. Accordingly, he was
quartered and hung up upon four trees; his head and one hand given
to the Indian who shot him, to carry about to show. At which sight it so
overjoyed the pilgrims, that they would give him money for it; and in
this way obtained a considerable sum. After which, his head was sent
to Plymouth, and exposed upon a gibbet for twenty years; and his hand
to Boston, where it was exhibited in savage triumph; and his mangled
body denied a resting place in the tomb, as thus adds the poet,

"Cold with the beast he slew, he sleeps,
O'er him no filial spirit weeps."

I think that as a matter of honor, that I can rejoice that no such evil
conduct is recorded of the Indians; that they never hung up any of the

white warriors who were head men. And we add the famous speech of Dr. Increase Mather; he says, during the bloody contest, the pious fathers wrestled hard and long with their God, in prayer, that he would prosper their arms, and deliver their enemies into their hands. And when upon stated days of prayer, the Indians got the advantage, it was considered as a rebuke of divine providence (we suppose the Indian prayed best then), which stimulated them to more ardor. And on the contrary, when they prevailed, they considered it as an immediate interposition in their favor. The Doctor closes thus: Nor could they, the pilgrims, cease crying to the Lord against Philip, until they had prayed the bullet through his heart. And in speaking of the slaughter of Philip's people at Narraganset, he says, We have heard of two and twenty Indian captains slain, all of them, and brought down to hell in one day. Again, in speaking of a Chief who had sneered at the pilgrims' religion, and who had withal added a most hideous blasphemy, immediately upon which a bullet took him in the head, and dashed out his brains, sending his cursed soul in a moment among the devils and blasphemers in hell forever. It is true that this language is sickening, and is as true as the sun is in the heavens, that such language was made use of, and it was a common thing for all the pilgrims to curse the Indians, according to the order of their priests. It is also wonderful how they prayed, that they should pray the bullet through the Indian's heart, and their souls down into hell. If I had any faith in such prayers, I should begin to think that soon we should all be gone. However, if this is the way they pray, that is bullets through people's hearts, I hope they will not pray for me; I should rather be excused. But to say the least, there is no excuse for their ignorance how to treat their enemies, and pray for them. If the Dr. and his people had only turned to the 23d of Luke, and 34th verse, and heard the words of their Master, whom they pretended to follow, they would see that their course did utterly condemn them; or the 7th of Acts, and 60th verse, and heard the language of the pious Stephen, we think it vastly different from the pilgrims; he prayed, Lord, lay not this sin to their charge. No curses were heard from these pious martyrs.

I do not hesitate to say, that through the prayers, preaching, and examples of those pretended pious has been the foundation of all the slavery and degradation in the American Colonies towards colored people. Experience has taught me that this has been a most sorry and wretched doctrine to us poor ignorant Indians. . . .

But who was Philip, that made all this display in the world; that put an enlightened nation to flight, and won so many battles? It was a son of nature; with nature's talent alone. And who did he have to contend with? With all the combined arts of cultivated talents of the old and new world. It was like putting one talent against a thousand. And yet Philip with that accomplished more than all of them. Yea, he out-did the well-disciplined forces of Greece, under the command of Philip, the Grecian Emperor; for he never was enabled to lay such plans of allying the tribes of the earth together, as Philip of Mount Hope did. And even Napoleon patterned after him, in collecting his forces and surprising the enemy. Washington, too, pursued many of his plans in attacking the enemy, and thereby enabled him to defeat his antagonists and conquer them. What, then, shall we say; shall we not do right to say that Philip, with his one talent, out-strips them all with their ten thousand? No warrior of any age was ever known to pursue such plans as Philip did. And it is well known that Church and nobody else could have conquered, if his people had not used treachery, which was owing to their ignorance; and after all, it is a fact, that it was not the pilgrims that conquered him, it was Indians. And as to his benevolence, it was very great; no one in history can accuse Philip of being cruel to his conquered foes; that he used them with more hospitality than they, the pilgrims did, cannot be denied; and that he had knowledge and forethought cannot be denied. As Mr. Gooking, in speaking of Philip says, that he was a man of good understanding and knowledge in the best things. Mr. Gooking it appears was a benevolent man, and a friend to Indians.

How deep then was the thought of Philip, when he could look from Maine to Georgia, and from the ocean to the lakes, and view with one look all his brethren withering before the more enlightened to come; and how true his prophesy, that the white people would not only cut down their groves, but would enslave them. Had the inspiration of Isaiah been there, he could not have been more correct. Our groves and hunting grounds are gone, our dead are dug up, our council-fires are put out, and a foundation was laid in the first Legislature, to enslave our people, by taking from them all rights which has been strictly adhered to ever since. Look at the disgraceful laws, disfranchising us as citizens. Look at the treaties made by Congress, all broken. Look at the deep-rooted plans laid, when a territory becomes a State, that after so many years, the laws shall be extended over the Indians that live within their boundaries. Yea, every charter that has been given was given with the view of driving the Indians out of the States, or dooming them to become chained under desperate laws, that would make them drag out a miserable life as one chained to the galley; and this is the course that has been pursued for nearly two hundred years. A fire, a canker, created by the pilgrims from across the Atlantic, to burn and destroy my poor unfortunate brethren, and it cannot be denied. What then shall we do, shall we cease crying, and say it is all wrong, or shall we bury the hatchet and those unjust laws, and Plymouth Rock together, and become friends. And will the sons of the pilgrims aid in putting out the fire and destroying the canker that will ruin all that their fathers left behind them to destroy? (By this we see how true Philip spake.) If so, we hope we shall not hear it said from ministers and church members, that we are so good no other people can live with us, as you know it is a common thing for them to say, Indians cannot live among Christian people; no, even the President of the United States tells the Indians they cannot live among civilized people, and we want your lands, and must have them, and will have them. As if he had said to them, we want your lands for our use to speculate upon, it aids us in paying off our national debt and supporting us in Congress, to drive you off.

You see, my red children, that our fathers carried on this scheme of getting your lands for our use, and we have now become rich and powerful; and we have a right to do with you just as we please; we claim to be your fathers. And we think we shall do you a great favor, my dear sons and daughters, to drive you out, to get you away out of the reach of our civilized people, who are cheating you, for we have no law to reach them, we cannot protect you although you be our children. So it is no use, you need not cry, you must go, even if the lions devour you, for we promised the land you have to somebody else long ago, perhaps twenty or thirty years; and we did it without your consent, it is true. But this has been the way our fathers first brought us up, and it is hard to depart from it; therefore you shall have no protection from us. Now while we sum up this subject. Does it not appear that the cause of all wars from beginning to end was and is for the want of good usage? That the whites have always been the aggressors, and the wars, cruelties and blood shed is a job of their own seeking, and not the Indians? Did you ever know of Indians' hurting those who was kind to them? No. We have a thousand witnesses to the contrary. Yea, every male and female declare it to be the fact. We often hear of the wars breaking out upon the frontiers, and it is because the same spirit reigns there that reigned here in New England; and wherever there are any Indians, that spirit still reigns; and at present, there is no law to stop it. What, then, is to be done; let every friend of the Indians now seize the mantle of Liberty and throw it over those burning elements that has spread with such fearful rapidity, and at once extinguish them forever. It is true, that now and then a feeble voice has been raised in our favor. Yes, we might speak of distinguished men, but they fall so far short in the minority, that it is heard but at a small distance. We want trumpets that sound like thunder, and men to act as though they were going at war with those corrupt and degrading principles that robs one of all rights, merely because he is ignorant, and of a little different color. Let us have principles that will give every one his due; and then shall wars cease, and the weary find rest. Give the Indian his rights, and you may be assured war will cease.

But, by this time you have been enabled to see that Philip's prophesy has come to pass; therefore, as a man of natural abilities, I shall pronounce him the greatest man that was ever in America; and so it will stand, until he is proved to the contrary, to the everlasting disgrace of the pilgrims' fathers. . . .

THE FOUR BEARS, MATO TOPE (Mandan)

"To die with my face rotten" (July 30, 1837)

A fur trader named Francois A. Chardon, who kept a journal while living among the Mandans and Gros Ventres, described "the ravages of the smallpox epidemic of 1837." (Karl Bodmer, the Swiss artist, painted The Four Bears' famous portrait in 1830; George Catlin painted another striking portrait in 1832.) In the following speech, The Four Bears (c. 1795–1837) described the agony of the disease that was killing him; smallpox killed almost ninety percent of the sixteen hundred Mandans.

My friends one and all, listen to what I have to say. Ever since I can remember, I have loved the whites. I have lived with them ever since I was a boy, and to the best of my knowledge, I have never wronged a white man. On the contrary, I have always protected them from the insults of others, which they cannot deny. The Four Bears never saw a white man hungry, but what he gave him to eat, drink, and a buffalo skin to sleep on, in time of need. I was always ready to die for them, which they cannot deny. I have done everything that a red skin could do for them, and how have they repaid it! With ingratitude! I have never called a white man a dog, but today, I do pronounce them to be a set of black hearted dogs. They have deceived me. Them that I always considered as brothers have turned out to be my worst enemies. I have been in many battles, and often wounded, but the wounds of my enemies I exhalt in. But today I am wounded, and by whom? By those same white dogs that I have always considered, and treated as brothers. I do not fear *death*, my friends. You know it, but to *die* with my face rotten, that even the wolves will shrink with horror at seeing me, and say to themselves, that is The Four Bears, the friend of the whites.

Listen well what I have to say, as it will be the last time you will hear me. Think of your wives, children, brothers, sisters, friends, and in fact all that you hold dear—are all dead, or dying, with their faces all rotten, caused by those dogs the whites? Think of all that, my friends, and rise all together and not leave one of them alive. The Four Bears will act his part.

SOURCE: Annie Heloise Abel. *Chardon's Journal at Fort Clark, 1834–1839.* Pierre, South Dakota: Department of History, State of South Dakota, 1932. 124–125.

SEATH'TL, "SEATTLE" (Duwamish)

"Yonder sky has wept tears of compassion on our fathers" (c. 1854)

The following speech, attributed to Chief Seath'tl (c. 1788–1866), has endured overuse and misquotation, gaining fame through the late nineteenth and entire twentieth centuries in spite of its probably spurious origins. A Seattle journalist named Henry A. Smith recalled and recorded this speech in 1887 from, he claimed, notes he had taken more than thirty years before. No other record of such a speech has surfaced.

Yonder sky has wept tears of compassion on our fathers for centuries untold, and which, to us, looks eternal, may change. Today it is fair, tomorrow it may be overcast with clouds. My words are like the stars that never set. What Seattle says the great chief, Washington, can rely upon, with as much certainty as our pale-face brothers can rely upon the return of the seasons. The son of the white chief says his father sends us greetings of friendship and good-will. This is kind, for we know he has little need of our friendship in return, because his people are many. They are like the grass that covers the vast prairies, while my people are few, and resemble the scattering trees of a storm-swept plain.

The great, and I presume also good, white chief sends us word that he wants to buy our lands but is willing to allow us to reserve enough to live on comfortably. This indeed appears generous, for the red man no longer has rights that he need respect, and the offer may be wise, also, for we are no longer in need of a great country. There was a time when our people covered the whole land as the waves of a wind-ruffled sea cover its shell-paved floor. But that time has long since passed away with the greatness of tribes almost forgotten. I will not mourn over our untimely decay, nor reproach my pale-face brothers with hastening it, for we, too, may have been somewhat to blame.

When our young men grow angry at some real or imaginary wrong and disfigure their faces with black paint, their hearts also are disfigured and turn black, and then their cruelty is relentless and knows no bounds, and our old men are not able to restrain them.

But let us hope that hostilities between the red man and his pale-face

---

SOURCE: Frederic James Grant. *History of Seattle, Washington*. New York: American Publishing, 1891. 434–436.

brothers may never return. We would have everything to lose and nothing to gain.

True it is that revenge, with our young braves, is considered gain, even at the cost of their own lives, but old men who stay at home in times of war, and old women who have sons to lose, know better.

Our great father Washington, for I presume he is now our father as well as yours, since George has moved his boundaries to the north; our great and good father, I say, sends us word by his son, who, no doubt, is a great chief among his people, that if we do as he desires, he will protect us. His brave armies will be to us a bristling wall of strength, and his great ships of war will fill our harbors so that our ancient enemies far to the northward, the Simsiams and Hydas, will no longer frighten our women and old men. Then he will be our father and we will be his children. But can this ever be? Your God loves your people and hates mine; he folds his strong arms lovingly around the white man and leads him as a father leads his infant son, but he has forsaken his red children; he makes your people wax strong every day, and soon they will fill the land; while our people are ebbing away like a fast-receding tide, that will never flow again. The white man's God cannot love his red children or he would protect them. They seem to be orphans and can look nowhere for help. How then can we become brothers? How can your father become our father and bring us prosperity and awaken in us dreams of returning greatness?

Your God seems to us to be partial. He came to the white man. We never saw Him; never even heard His voice; He gave the white man laws but He had no word for His red children whose teeming millions filled this vast continent as the stars fill the firmament. No, we are two distinct races and must ever remain so. There is little in common between us. The ashes of our ancestors are sacred and their final resting place is hallowed ground, while you wander away from the tombs of your fathers seemingly without regret.

Your religion was written on tables of stone by the iron finger of an angry God, lest you might forget it. The red man could never remember nor comprehend it.

Our religion is the traditions of our ancestors, the dreams of our old men, given them by the great Spirit, and the visions of our sachems, and is written in the hearts of our people.

Your dead cease to love you and the homes of their nativity as soon as they pass the portals of the tomb. They wander far off beyond the stars, are soon forgotten and never return. Our dead never forget the beautiful world that gave them being. They still love its winding rivers, its great mountains and its sequestered vales, and they ever yearn in tenderest affection over the lonely hearted living and often return to visit and comfort them.

Day and night cannot dwell together. The red man has ever fled the approach of the white man, as the changing mists on the mountain side flee before the blazing morning sun.

However, your proposition seems a just one, and I think my folks will accept it and will retire to the reservation you offer them, and we will dwell apart and in peace, for the words of the great white chief seem to be the voice of nature speaking to my people out of the thick darkness that is fast gathering around them like a dense fog floating inward from a midnight sea.

It matters but little where we pass the remainder of our days. They are not many. The Indian's night promises to be dark. No bright star hovers about the horizon. Sad-voiced winds moan in the distance. Some grim Nemesis of our race is on the red man's trail, and wherever he goes he will still hear the sure approaching footsteps of the fell destroyer and prepare to meet his doom, as does the wounded doe that hears the approaching footsteps of the hunter. A few more moons, a few more winters and not one of all the mighty hosts that once filled this broad land or that now roam in fragmentary bands through these vast solitudes will remain to weep over the tombs of a people once as powerful and as hopeful as your own.

But why should we repine? Why should I murmur at the fate of my people? Tribes are made up of individuals and are no better than they. Men come and go like the waves of the sea. A tear, a *tamanamus*, a dirge, and they are gone from our longing eyes forever. Even the white man, whose God walked and talked with him, as friend to friend, is not exempt from the common destiny. We *may* be brothers after all. We shall see.

We will ponder your proposition, and when we have decided we will tell you. But should we accept it, I here and now make this the first condition: That we will not be denied the privilege, without molestation, of visiting at will the graves of our ancestors and friends. Every part of this country is sacred to my people. Every hillside, every valley, every plain and grove has been hallowed by some fond memory or some sad experience of my tribe. Even the rocks that seem to lie dumb as they swelter in the sun along the silent seashore in solemn grandeur thrill with memories of past events connected with the fate of my people, and the very dust under your feet responds more lovingly to our footsteps than to yours, because it is the ashes of our ancestors, and our bare feet are conscious of the sympathetic touch, for the soil is rich with the life of our kindred.

The sable braves, and fond mothers, and glad-hearted maidens, and the little children who lived and rejoiced here, and whose very names are now forgotten, still love these solitudes, and their deep fastnesses at eventide grow shadowy with the presence of dusky spirits. And when the last red man shall have perished from the earth and his memory among white men shall have become a myth, these shores shall swarm with the invisible dead of my tribe, and when your children's children shall think themselves alone in the field, the store, the shop, upon the highway or in the silence of the woods they will not be alone. In all the earth there is no place dedicated to solitude. At night, when the streets of your cities and villages shall be silent, and you think them deserted, they will throng with the returning hosts that once filled and still love this beautiful land. The white man will never be alone. Let him be just and deal kindly with my people, for the dead are not altogether powerless.

GERONIMO, GOYAHKLA (Chiricahua Apache)

"We will attack them in their homes" (c. 1859)

> At a war council, the warrior Geronimo (c. 1825–1909) addressed his band about taking revenge on the Mexican people. (Geronimo's mother, wife, and three children had been killed by Mexicans in 1858.)

Kinsman, you have heard what the Mexicans have recently done without cause. You are my relatives—uncles, cousins, brothers. We are men the same as the Mexicans are—we can do to them what they have done to us. Let us go forward and trail them—I will lead you to their city— we will attack them in their homes. I will fight in the front of the battle—I only ask you to follow me to avenge this wrong done by these Mexicans—will you come? It is well—you will all come.

Remember the rule in war—men may return or they may be killed. If any of these young men are killed I want no blame from their kinsmen, for they themselves have chosen to go. If I am killed no one need mourn for me. My people have all been killed in that country, and I, too, will die if need be.

SOURCE: S.M. Barrett. *Geronimo's Story of His Life*. New York: Duffield and Company, 1906. 47–48.

LITTLE CROW, TAÓYATEDÚTA (Santee Sioux)

"Taóyatedúta is not a coward, and he is not a fool!" (1862)

Little Crow (c. 1815–1863) found that his tribe was starving because the food the reservation had been promised had not come. Most of his people wanted to retaliate by going to war; in the speech that follows, Little Crow reminded them of how unlikely they were to triumph, at the same time pledging to stand with them if they chose to fight. The Great Sioux Uprising of 1862, which his people nevertheless led, resulted in the massacre of hundreds of Minnesota settlers and, later, in consequence, the mass hanging of thirty-eight of Little Crow's Santee braves. The next year, while picking berries, Little Crow was shot and killed by a settler.

Taóyatedúta is not a coward, and he is not a fool! When did he run away from his enemies? When did he leave his braves behind him on the war-path and turn back to his tepees? When he ran away from your enemies, he walked behind on your trail with his face to the Ojibways and covered your backs as a she-bear covers her cubs! Is Taóyatedúta without scalps? Look at his war-feathers! Behold the scalp-locks of your enemies hanging there on his lodge-poles! Do they call him a coward? Taóyatedúta is not a coward, and he is not a fool. Braves, you are like little children; you know not what you are doing.

You are full of the white man's *devil-water*. You are like dogs in the Hot Moon when they run mad and snap at their own shadows. We are only little herds of buffaloes left scattered; the great herds that once covered the prairies are no more. See!—the white men are like the locusts when they fly so thick that the whole sky is a snow-storm. You may kill one—two—ten; yes, as many as the leaves in the forest yonder, and their brothers will not miss them. Kill one—two—ten, and ten times ten will come to kill you. Count your fingers all day long and white men with guns in their hands will come faster than you can count.

Yes; they fight among themselves—away off. Do you hear the thunder of their big guns? No; it would take you two moons to run down to where they are fighting, and all the way your path would be among white soldiers as thick as tamaracks in the swamps of Ojibways. Yes; they fight among themselves, but if you strike at them they will all turn on you and devour you and your women and little children just as the

SOURCE: H. L. Gordon. Appendix to *The Feast of the Virgins and Other Poems*. Chicago: Laird and Lee, 1891. 343–344.

locusts in their time fall on the trees and devour all the leaves in one day. You are fools. You cannot see the face of your chief; your eyes are full of smoke. You cannot hear his voice; your ears are full of roaring waters. Braves, you are little children—you are fools. You will die like the rabbits when the hungry wolves hunt them in the Hard Moon [January]. Taóyedúta is not a coward: he will die with you.

STRUCK BY THE REE (Yankton Sioux)

"If we had been learned all these things we could support ourselves" (August 25–26, 1865)

In 1865 the Yankton chief Struck by the Ree (1804–1888) testified before a commission investigating graft by Indian reservation agents. These agents were not chosen by the tribes but were government-appointed employees. They administered food, funds, and housing, and they enforced laws and sanctions. On the first day of his testimony, Struck by the Ree talked about one agent; on the second day he discussed some of the problems the soldiers at surrounding forts caused the tribe.

[August 25]

My friend, you sent a letter to our agency requesting our presence here. My friend, I have a good leg; it is sound; there are no sores upon it, and I want to go to Washington to see my Great Father. The reason I want to see my Great Father is, I desire to make my report to him in person, but the agents say if I go he will not pay any attention to me; that he is full of business with the whites. My belly is full of what I want to say to him. My friend, you are sent by my grandfather. I think you will do just as all the rest—make money. I should think if my grandfather would want to see me to make my report in person.

I cannot say much. The Great Spirit knows that I speak the truth; knows what I say. When I went to see my grandfather, he told me I should have my reserve; that I should have fifty miles up and down the Missouri river for fifty years, and I might become rich and high up; but I am like one on a high snow bank; the sun shines and continually melts it away, and it keeps going down and down until there is nothing left. When I went to make my treaty, my grandfather agreed, if I would put three young men to work, he would put one white laborer with them to learn them; that I should put three young men to learn ploughing, and he would put one white man to learn them; also, three to sow, three to learn the carpenter's trade, three to learn the blacksmith's trade, and such other trades as we should want; and my great grandfather was to furnish one white man for each trade to learn the young men. My grandfather also said that a school should be established for

SOURCE: *Condition of the Indian Tribes*. Report of the Joint Special Committee, Appointed under Joint Resolution of March 3, 1865. Washington, D.C.: Government Printing Office, 1867. 366–368, 370–372.

the nation to learn them to read and write; that the young boys and girls should go to school, and that the young men who worked should have the same pay as the whites. My grandfather told me if my young men would go to work that the money going to those who would not work should be given to those who would work. None of these things have been fulfilled. If my grandfather had told me that I must split rails, I could have tried it, and then perhaps my young men would have tried; but they would say, how could I learn them when I did not know how myself. If I try to get my young men to plough, they would say, if you cannot plough how can we; there is no one to learn them, and the same thing would be true if I should try to get the young men to run the saw mill or work at any other trade; if I do not know myself, how can I learn the young men; and the same thing would be the case if I try to get the young men to build a house; if I don't know myself, how can I learn them. If I should get all the young men, half-breeds and Indians, and put them in a room, and pick out those who have big arms and hands, and take a big bar of iron and tell them to work it, they would not know how. If I were to take all the young men and girls, half-breeds and Indians, and tell them that we will go in that house and take pen and ink and write, how could I make letters as they ought to be made; I never learned myself.

My friend, I think if my young men knew how to sow, farm, carpenter, and do everything else, I could send the white men away; we ourselves should have the money paid the white men, and we should have plenty of money. If we had been learned all these things we could support ourselves, have plenty of money, have schools, and I could have written my great grandfather, and have got a letter from him; I could have written him myself what I wanted.

My grandfather sent me two agents, and I understood the governor was over them. I came down here [Yankton] and the governor was gone to Washington. I staid three days, and then went back home.

I think I gave my land to my grandfather. When I signed the treaty I told them I never would sign for the pipestone quarry. I wanted to keep it myself; but I understand white men are going there and getting and breaking up the stone.

I would have to tell my grandfather that I made a treaty with him, and I would have to ask him how many goods he is going to give me; and I would tell him that I want him to give me the invoices of my goods, that I may know what I am entitled to. I do not want corn thrown to me the same as to hogs. If I could get my invoices I should always know what belongs to me. Every time our goods come I have asked the agent for the invoices, but they never show me the invoices; they can write what they please, and they go and show it to my grandfather, and he thinks it all right. I think, my friend, my grandfather tells me lies. My friend, what I give a man I don't try to take back. I think, my friend, there is a great pile of money belonging to us which we never yet have received.

I think the Great Spirit hears what I say. When they bring the goods to the agency, my goods are all mixed up with the agent's goods; I can't tell my goods from the trader's goods. I think if you go to all the nations, you will not find any who has been used as I have been. My grandfather told me I should have a warehouse separate from the agents; he told me I should take one hundred and sixty acres of land for my own use, and that I should have plenty of land to raise hay for the stock. All the hay on my bottom land is cut by the white man to sell. I asked for hay, but I can get none—white man cut it; I can't tell who gets the money for the hay, but I think Redfield got some money for hay; my ponies can have no hay. I think, my friend, if you go up to my agency you will have a bad feeling; you will feel bad for me to see the situation I am in, and to see my buildings, after what my grandfather told me.

The first agent was Redfield; and when he came there he borrowed blankets from me to sleep upon, and agreed to return them, but never did, though I asked for them. Goods have been stored up stairs in the warehouse, and have all disappeared; perhaps the rats eat them; I don't know what became of them. If they bring any goods for the Indians to eat and put them in the warehouse, the agents live out of them, and the mess-house where travellers stop has been supplied from the Indians' goods, and pay has been taken by the agents, and they have put the money in their pockets and taken it away with them. I have seen them take the goods from the storehouse of the Indians and take them to the mess-house, and I have had to pay for a meal for myself at the mess-house, and so have others of our Indians had to pay for meals at the mess-house, prepared from their own goods.

I understand that the agents are allowed fifteen hundred dollars per year for salary. I think fifteen hundred dollars is not much—not more than enough to last a month, the way they live; they bring all their families there, and friends also. When the agents have been there one, two and three years, their property increases—the goods in their house and their household furniture increase. When Redfield left the agency, a steamboat came in the night and took away fifteen boxes of goods, so that the Indians would not know it; but the Indians were too sharp for him. When Redfield came up he brought his nephew to be trader for the Indians, and one night he took a load of flour out of the shed where the Indians' flour was, and carried it to his store to sell out to the Indians. My friend, what I say about his taking the flour I did not see with my own eyes, but my young men came and told me so. Because I wanted the blankets that I loaned Redfield, he got mad and never answered me, and never gave me the blankets.

My friend, a great many things have been going on, but they do them in the night, so as to blind me. What I say I see myself. After Redfield took away the fifteen boxes he sent back and took away more. I think all these young chiefs have eyes, the same as I, and that they have seen these things. I went down to Washington twice to see my grandfather, and the third time I went I came back by the Missouri. When I went down I saw many stores full of goods; the settlers come to our agency and make money and then go off. I think if we had two stores it would be better for us. If I had understood from what my grandfather told me, that I was to be treated as I have been, I would never have done as I have done; I never would have signed the treaty. Mr. Redfield said to me, "When I am gone you will meet with a great many agents; but you will never meet one like me." I think I never want to see one like him. . . .

[August 26]

My friend . . . we will now commence with the soldiers. The first year they came up in this country, I think my grandfather must have told them to commence on me, and that is the reason I commence thus with them. I would like to know if my grandfather told them to commence against me first; I should think so, the way they treated us. The first time they came up our young men had nothing to eat, and had gone over the Missouri river to hunt, and the soldiers killed seven of them. The Two-Kettle band and the Low Yanktonais were friendly, and were then on my reservation at the time, and some of them went out with my young men to hunt, and were among the seven that were killed; they were all friendly to the whites. When General Sully returned from his expedition, and was crossing my reserve, there were some of the Indian women married to half-breeds, and they had houses, and the soldiers went in and drove all the persons in them out, and robbed the houses of all there was in them. I would like to know if my grandfather told them to do so. I do not think he did. One of my chiefs, Little Swan, now here, had a house, and the soldiers broke in and destroyed all his goods, furniture, utensils and tools, and all the property of his band, the same being stored there. I would like to know if my grandfather told the soldiers when they returned from the expedition with their horses worn out, lost or stolen, to take horses from the Yanktons, in place of those they had lost or had worn out and broken down; I don't believe he did, but that is the way the soldiers did. I think the way the white men treated us is worse than the wolves do.

We have a way in the winter of putting our dead up on scaffolds up from the ground, but the soldiers cut down the scaffolds and cut off the hair of the dead, and if they had good teeth they pulled them out, and some of them cut off the heads of the dead and carried them away. One time one of my young men and two squaws went over the river to Fort Randall, and a soldier wanted one of the squaws to do something with; he wanted to sleep with her, and she refused to sleep with him; one of the Indians asked the other squaw if she would sleep with the soldier, and she said she would; but the soldier would not have her, but wanted the other squaw, and claimed that the Indian was trying to prevent him from sleeping with his (the Indian's) squaw, his wife, and the Indian, fearing trouble, started for the ferry, and the soldier shot the Indian, though the Indian got over it.

Another time when General Sully came up he passed through the middle of our field, turned all his cattle and stock into our corn and destroyed the whole of it. The ears of some were then a foot long; the corn was opposite Fort Randall, and they not only destroyed the corn but burnt up the fence. I think no other white man would do so; I do not think my grandfather told them to do so. The soldiers set fire to the prairie and burnt up four of our lodges and all there was in them, and three horses. When my corn is good to eat they cross the river from Fort Randall and eat it, and when it is not good they throw it in the river. I think my reserve is very small; the soldiers cut all my wood and grass, and I think this is bad treatment.

The above in regard to the soldiers applies to my three chiefs on the reserve opposite Fort Randall, and I will now speak of things at my agency when the soldiers came down from the expedition last fall. At that time myself and others were out on a hunt, and had put our goods under the floors; but when the expedition came down the soldiers broke open the houses, destroyed our pans and kettles, and fired into the stoves and kettles. The soldiers are very drunken and come to our place—they have arms and guns; they run after our women and fire into our houses and lodges; one soldier came along and wanted one of our young men to drink, but he would not, and turned to go away, and the soldier shot at him. Before the soldiers came along we had good health; but once the soldiers come along they go to my squaws and want to sleep with them, and the squaws being hungry will sleep with them in order to get something to eat, and will get a bad disease, and then the squaws turn to their husbands and give them the bad disease. . . .

Since I made the treaty I am an American. My new agent told me the other day that the old Commissioner of Indian Affairs had been stealing part of the annuities, and that a better man had been put in his place. At this I felt good, and I put on my hat, I felt so good, my heart so big. My new agent is an entirely different man; he shows me the invoices, and I think he is a good man for us. He hired a blacksmith right off. My friend, what I am going to tell you is the truth. We only get five dollars apiece; we have only had one trader; he often makes us feel bad; he sells us goods so high it makes us cry; I think there ought to be two traders; I want two traders. I think if you come up to our agency you will laugh in the first place, and then be mad to see our storehouse in the same building with the trader's store. I want the store moved away a mile, so that it won't be so handy to our goods; I want you to have this changed. I hope my grandfather will see that the store is moved away from my warehouse, because the trader's store is under the floor where my goods are stored. I sometimes have bad dreams; I feel that there may be cracks that my goods may fall through.

I am done. Again I say, my friend, I am glad you have come to see us, and I hope will report all I have said to the Great Father, and that you will do us good. The Great Spirit knows that I have spoken the truth.

RED CLOUD (Oglala Sioux)

"Shall we permit ourselves to be driven to and fro?"   (1866)

Charles A. Eastman, a Sioux biographer, says, "Red Cloud's position was uncompromisingly against submission," as is evident in the following speech. When most of the Sioux had accepted the reservations, to which Red Cloud (c. 1820–1909) and his band would go shortly as well, he remarked bitterly about a fellow chief: "We are told that Spotted Tail has consented to be the Beggars' Chief. Those Indians who go over to the white man can be nothing but beggars, for he respects only riches, and how can an Indian be a rich man? He cannot without ceasing to be an Indian. As for me, I have listened patiently to the promises of the Great Father, but his memory is short. I am now done with him. This is all I have to say." (Eastman, 14)

Friends, it has been our misfortune to welcome the white man. We have been deceived. He brought with him some shining things that pleased our eyes; he brought weapons more effective than our own: above all, he brought the spirit water that makes one forget for a time old age, weakness, and sorrow. But I wish to say to you that if you would possess these things for yourselves, you must begin anew and put away the wisdom of your fathers. You must lay up food, and forget the hungry. When your house is built, your storeroom filled, then look around for a neighbor whom you can take at a disadvantage, and seize all that he has! Give away only what you do not want; or rather, do not part with any of your possessions unless in exchange for another's.

My countrymen, shall the glittering trinkets of this rich man, his deceitful drink that overcomes the mind, shall these things tempt us to give up our homes, our hunting grounds, and the honorable teaching of our old men? Shall we permit ourselves to be driven to and fro—to be herded like the cattle of the white man?

SOURCE: Charles A. Eastman (Ohiyesa). *Indian Heroes and Great Chieftains*. Boston: Little, Brown, 1918. 14–15. [Reprint edition. Mineola, New York: Dover Publications, 1997. 6–7.]

RED CLOUD (Oglala Sioux)

"Dakotas, I am for war!" (1866)

> Shortly before the Sioux attack on Fort Phil Kearny in 1866, Red Cloud (c. 1820–1909) roused his warriors to the fight. (See Spotted Tail's speech against this war, page 134.)

Hear ye, Dakotas! When the Great Father at Washington sent us his chief soldier [General Harney] to ask for a path through our hunting grounds, a way for his iron road to the mountains and the western sea, we were told that they wished merely to pass through our country, not to tarry among us, but to seek for gold in the far west. Our old chiefs thought to show their friendship and good will, when they allowed this dangerous snake in our midst. They promised to protect the wayfarers.

Yet before the ashes of the council fire are cold, the Great Father is building his forts among us. You have heard the sound of the white soldier's ax upon the Little Piney. His presence here is an insult and a threat. It is an insult to the spirits of our ancestors. Are we then to give up their sacred graves to be plowed for corn? Dakotas, I am for war!

SOURCE: Charles A. Eastman (Ohiyesa). *Indian Heroes and Great Chieftains.* Boston: Little, Brown, 1918. 16. [Reprint edition. Mineola, New York: Dover Publications, 1997. 7.]

RED CLOUD (Oglala Sioux)

"The Great Spirit made us both"   (June 16, 1870)

Invited by Peter Cooper to tell "the Indian's story," the chief spoke
at Cooper Union Institute in New York City: "Red Cloud arose and
faced the audience, drawing his blankets around him majestically.
He was greeted with an outburst of applause and waving of hand-
kerchiefs. As soon as the tumult had subsided, he began on a somewhat high key and with a rapid utterance, his 'talk.' At the end of
each sentence he paused, and stood calmly surveying the audience,
while the interpreter explained his words to Dr. Crosby, and he
again in stentorian tones, gave them to the immense audience.
Almost every sentence was received with loud applause by the as-
sembly, while the other chieftains and warriors signified their assent
by a guttural 'Ugh.'"

My Brothers and my Friends who are before me today: God Almighty
has made us all, and He is here to hear what I have to say to you today.
The Great Spirit made us both. He gave us lands and He gave you
lands. You came here and we received you as brothers. When the
Almighty made you, He made you all white and clothed you. When He
made us He made us with red skins and poor. When you first came we
were very many and you were few. Now you are many and we are few.
You do not know who appears before you to speak. He is a representative of the original American race, the first people of this continent. We
are good, and not bad. The reports which you get about us are all on
one side. You hear of us only as murderers and thieves. We are not so.
If we had more lands to give to you we would give them, but we have
no more. We are driven into a very little island, and we want you, our
dear friends, to help us with the Government of the United States. The
Great Spirit made us poor and ignorant. He made you rich and wise
and skillful in things which we know nothing about. The good Father
made you to eat tame game and us to eat wild game. Ask any one who
has gone through to California. They will tell you we have treated them
well. You have children. We, too, have children, and we wish to bring
them up well. We ask you to help us do it. At the mouth of Horse
Creek, in 1852, the Great Father made a treaty with us. We agreed to
let him pass through our territory unharmed for fifty-five years. We kept
our word. We committed no murders, no depredations, until the troops

SOURCE: *New York Times*. June 17, 1870. 1.

132

came there. When the troops were sent there trouble and disturbance arose. Since that time there have been various goods sent from time to time to us, but only once did they reach us, and soon the Great Father took away the only good man he had sent us, Col. Fitzpatrick. The Great Father said we must go to farming, and some of our men went to farming near Fort Laramie, and were treated very badly indeed. We came to Washington to see our Great Father that peace might be continued. The Great Father that made us both wishes peace to be kept; we want to keep peace. Will you help us? In 1868 men came out and brought papers. We could not read them, and they did not tell us truly what was in them. We thought the treaty was to remove the forts, and that we should then cease from fighting. But they wanted to send us traders on the Missouri. We did not want to go on the Missouri, but wanted traders where we were. When I reached Washington the Great Father explained to me what the treaty was, and showed me that the interpreters had deceived me. All I want is right and justice. I have tried to get from the Great Father what is right and just. I have not altogether succeeded. I want you to help me to get what is right and just. I represent the whole Sioux nation, and they will be bound by what I say. I am no Spotted Tail, to say one thing one day and be bought for a pin the next. Look at me. I am poor and naked, but I am the Chief of the nation. We do not want riches, but we want to train our children right. Riches would do us no good. We could not take them with us to the other world. We do not want riches, we want peace and love.

The riches that we have in this world, Secretary Cox said truly, we cannot take with us to the next world. Then I wish to know why Commissioners are sent out to us who do nothing but rob us and get the riches of this world away from us! I was brought up among the traders, and those who came out there in the early times treated me well and I had a good time with them. They taught us to wear clothes and to use tobacco and ammunition. But, by and by, the Great Father sent out a different kind of men; men who cheated and drank whisky; men who were so bad that the Great Father could not keep them at home and so sent them out there. I have sent a great many words to the Great Father but they never reached him. They were drowned on the way, and I was afraid the words I spoke lately to the Great Father would not reach you, so I came to speak to you myself; and now I am going away to my home. I want to have men sent out to my people whom we know and can trust. I am glad I have come here. You belong in the East and I belong in the West, and I am glad I have come here and that we could understand one another. I am very much obliged to you for listening to me. I go home this afternoon. I hope you will think of what I have said to you. I bid you all an affectionate farewell.

SPOTTED TAIL (Brulé Sioux)

"This strange white man—consider him, his gifts are manifold!" (1866)

Shortly before the Sioux attack on Fort Phil Kearny in 1866, Spotted Tail (1823–1881) argued against fighting the American soldiers. (See Red Cloud's speech in favor of this war, page 131.) In the future, he and Red Cloud often disagreed, and their disputes may have led to Spotted Tail's assassination.

"Hay, hay, hay! Alas, alas!" Thus speaks the old man, when he knows that his former vigor and freedom is gone from him forever. So we may exclaim today, Alas! There is a time appointed to all things. Think for a moment how many multitudes of the animal tribes we ourselves have destroyed! Look upon the snow that appears today—tomorrow it is water! Listen to the dirge of the dry leaves, that were green and vigorous but a few moons before! We are a part of this life and it seems that our time is come.

Yet note how the decay of one nation invigorates another. This strange white man—consider him, his gifts are manifold! His tireless brain, his busy hand do wonders for his race. Those things which we despise he holds as treasures; yet he is so great and so flourishing that there must be some virtue and truth in his philosophy. I wish to say to you, my friends: Be not moved alone by heated arguments and thoughts of revenge! These are for the young. We are young no longer; let us think well, and give counsel as old men!

SOURCE: Charles A. Eastman (Ohiyesa). *Indian Heroes and Great Chieftains.* Boston: Little, Brown, 1918. 35–36. [Reprint edition. Mineola, New York: Dover Publications, 1997. 16.]

SPOTTED TAIL (Brulé Sioux)

"The people that you see before you are not men of a different country, but this is their country" (September 22, 1876)

When a commission came to Nebraska to negotiate with the various Sioux agencies for the Black Hills—a sacred center of Sioux land upon which gold had recently been found—Chief Spotted Tail (1823–1881) reminded the commissioners of the government's failure to uphold its previous treaties.

My friends that have come here to see me; you have brought to me words from the Great Father at Washington, and I have considered them now for seven days, and have made up my mind. I have considered the matter of these messages and words sent out by the Great Father to me.

This is the fifth time that you have come. At the time of the first treaty that was made on Horse Creek—the one we call the "great treaty"—there was provision made to borrow the overland road of the Indians, and promises made at the time of the treaty, though I was a boy at the time; they told me it was to last fifty years. These promises have not been kept. All the Dakotas that lived in this country were promised these things together at that time. All the words have proved to be false. The next conference was the one held with General Manydear, when there was no promises made in particular, nor for any amount to be given us, but we had a conference with him and made friends and shook hands.

Then after that there was a treaty made by General Sherman, General Sanborn, and General Harney. At that time the general told us we should have annuities and goods from that treaty for thirty-five years. He said this, but yet he didn't tell the truth. At that time General Sherman told me the country was mine; and that I should select any place I wished for my reservation and live in it. I told the general I would take the land from the headwaters of the White River to the Missouri, and he assented to it. My friends, I will show you well his words today. When he promised us we should have annuities for thirty-five years he told us there should be an issue of goods in the spring when the grass began to grow, and also another issue of goods every fall.

SOURCE: 44th Congress, 2nd Session, Senate Executive Document 9. #1718. Report of the Commission to Obtain Certain Concessions from the Sioux Indians. 37–39.

He said we should raise cattle; that they would give us cows to raise cattle with, and mares to raise horses with, and that they would give us yokes of oxen to haul logs with; that they would give us large wagons to haul goods with, in order that we might earn money in that way. He said also there should be issues of such things as we needed to learn the arts with, besides that there should be money given to every one. He told us that we should each have $15 for an annuity. I told him that was a bad amount—that we didn't understand money, and that it should be $20, and he assented to that. He told me that these things should be carried out; for me to go to the mouth of the Whetstone River and locate with my people and these things should be fulfilled, but it was not true. When these promises failed to be carried out, I went myself to see the Great Father, and went into his house and told him these things. The Great Father told me to go home, to select any place in my country I choose, and to go there and live with my people. I came home and selected this place to move here and settle. Then persons came to me, after I had settled, and said I must move from this place, and I came back here again and located the agency. You told me to come here and locate my agency and I should receive the fulfillment of these promises. You gave me some very small cows, some very bad cattle, and some old wagons that were worn out. Again: you came last summer to talk about the country, and we said we would consider the matter; we said we would leave the matter to the Great Father for settlement. In answer to that reply of ours, he has sent you out this summer. You have now come to visit our land, and we now ask you how many years there are for us to live?

My friends, you that sit before me are traders and merchants. You have come here to trade. You have not come here to turn anything out of the way without payment for it. When a man has a possession that he values, and another party comes to buy it, he brings with him such good things as the people that own it desire to have. My friends, your people have both intellect and hearts. You use these to consider in what way you had best live. My people, who are here before you today, are precisely the same. If you have much of anything you use it for your own benefit and in order that your children shall have food and clothing, and my people also are the same. I see that my friends before me are men of age and dignity. Men of that kind have good judgment to consider well what they do. I infer from this you are here to consider what shall be good for my people for a long time to come. I think that each of you have selected somewhere a good piece of land for himself, with the intention of living on it, that he may there raise up his children. My people, that you see here before you, are not different; they also live upon the earth and upon the things that come to them from above. We have the same thoughts and desires in that respect that white people have. The people that you see before you are not men of a different country, but this is their country, where they were born and where they have acquired all their property; their children, their horses, and other property were all raised here in this country. You have come here to buy this country of ours, and it would be well if you came with the things you propose to give us — the good price you propose to pay for it in your hands, so we could see the price you propose to pay for it, then our hearts would be glad. My people have grown up together with these white men, who have married into our tribe. A great many of them have grown up with their children; a great many of us have learned to speak their language; our children are with theirs in our school, and we want to be considered all one people with them.

My friends, when you get back to the Great Father, we wish you to tell him to send us goods; to send us oxen; to give us wagons, so we can earn money by hauling goods that may come to the railroad, and haul our own provisions. My friends, this seems to me to be a very hard day. You have come here to buy our country, and there is, at the time you come, half our country at war, and we have come upon very difficult times. This war did not spring up here in our land; this war was brought upon us by the children of the Great Father who came to take our land from us without price, and who, in our land, do a great many evil things. The Great Father and his children are to blame for this trouble. We have here a store-house to hold our provisions the Great Father sends us, but he sends very little provision to put in our store-house. When our people become displeased with their provision and have gone north to hunt in order that they might live, the Great Father's children are fighting them. It has been our wish to live here in our country peaceably, and do such things as may be for the welfare and good of our people, but the Great Father has filled it with soldiers who think only of our death. Some of our people who have gone from here in order they may have a change, and others who have gone north to hunt, have been attacked by the soldiers from this direction, and when they have got north have been attacked by soldiers from the other side, and now when they are willing to come back the soldiers stand between them to keep them from coming home. It seems to me there is a better way than this. When people come to trouble, it is better for both parties to come together without arms and talk it over and find some peaceful way to settle it.

My friends, you have come to me today, and mentioned two countries to me. One of them I know of old — the Missouri River. It is not possible for me to go there. When I was there before we had a great deal of trouble. I left, also, one hundred of my people buried there.

The other country you have mentioned is one I have never seen since I was born, but I agree to go and look at it. If it is possible to go with fifty of my young men, I will go down there and look at it. When men have a difficult business to settle it is not possible it should be well settled in one day; it takes at least twelve moons to consider it. In the meantime I want you to see to it that my people are well fed.

My friends, since I have lived in this country I have never had any evil thoughts. My only end has been to cultivate the ground and raise such things as may be for the good of my people. You are not different; you are good men; you are friends of the Great Father at Washington. My people also are good people, and we are friends of the Great Father in Washington. When this trouble first raised, the Great Father sent out word to stop the sale of ammunition at the stores. The ammunition my people needed to kill game, and the result has been great suffering to my people. It seems as if the wish of the Great Father was that my people should go into the ground, but notwithstanding we are all of sincere purpose to do what we can for the good of our people.

SATANTA (Kiowa)

"I love to roam over the prairies" (October 20, 1867)

At the Medicine Lodge Creek Council of 1867, Satanta (1830–1878), referred to at the time as "the orator of the plains," spoke to the U.S. Government treaty-making commission. Several years later, after being imprisoned for his alleged participation in raids on white settlers in Texas, Satanta committed suicide.

You, the Commissioners, have come from afar to listen to our grievances. My heart is glad, and I hide nothing from you. I understood that you were coming down to see us. I moved away from those disposed for war, and I also came along to see you. The Kiowas and Comanches have not been fighting. We were away down South when we heard you were coming to see us. The Cheyennes are those who have been fighting with you. They did it in broad daylight, so that all could see them. If I had been fighting I would have done it by day and not in the dark.

Two years ago I made peace with Gens. Harney, Sanborn and Col. Leavenworth, at the mouth of the Little Arkansas. That peace I have never broken. When the grass was growing in the spring a large body of soldiers came along on the Santa Fe road. I had not done anything and therefore I was not afraid. All the chiefs of the Kiowas, Comanches and Arrapahoes are here today; they have come to listen to good words. We have been waiting here a long time to see you, and are getting tired.

All the land south of the Arkansas belongs to the Kiowas and Comanches, and I don't want to give away any of it. I love the land and the buffalo, and will not part with it. I want you to understand well what I say. Write it on paper. Let the Great Father see it, and let me hear what he has to say. I want you to understand, also, that the Kiowas and Comanches don't want to fight, and have not been fighting since we made the treaty. I hear a good deal of good talk from the gentlemen whom the Great Father sends us, but they never do what they say. I don't want any of the Medicine lodges within the country. I want the children raised as I was.

When I make peace, it is a long and lasting one; there is no end to it. We thank you for your presents. All the head men and braves are happy. They will do what you want them, for they know you are doing the best you can. I and they will do our best also. When I look upon

---

SOURCE: *New York Times.* October 30, 1867. "The Indian Commission," 1.

you I know you are all big chiefs. While you are in this country we go to sleep happy and are not afraid.

I have heard that you intend to settle us on a reservation near the mountains. I don't want to settle. I love to roam over the prairies. I feel free and happy; but when we settle down we grow pale and die. I have laid aside my lance, bow and shield, and yet I feel safe in your presence. I have told you the truth. I have no little lies hid about me; but I don't know how it is with the Commissioners. Are they as clear as I am?

A long time ago this land belonged to our fathers; but when I go up to the river I see camps of soldiers on its banks. These soldiers cut down my timber, they kill my buffalo; and when I see that my heart feels like bursting; I feel sorry. I have spoken.

BLACKFOOT (Crow)

"They said 'Yes, yes'; but it is not in the treaty"
(August 1873)

A government treaty-making council was held on the Crow Agency in Montana Territory from August 11 to August 16, 1873. Blackfoot (c. 1795–1877), though proud of his tribe's battles with their traditional enemies, the Sioux, and of the tribe's allied status with the U.S. Army, objected to the treaty being foisted on the Crows. Blackfoot spoke up on four of the five days of meetings. Three of his speeches follow.

[Second day]
What you have said we have listened to and we think it is true. At Laramie the treaty was made. We did not feel right. We had made a long journey and were tired and sick. They gave us some horses. They thought they were doing a big thing, and making us a big present. But the horses were wild like the antelope. We caught them with the lasso. They jumped and kicked; we held on tight to them, but they got away from us; we were sick hunting them, and when we got home nearly all of them were gone. The commissioners told me that we should have plenty of food given us for forty years. They were big men who talked with us; they were not drunk when they told us. We were men and heard them, and so it ought to be written in the treaty. I told the commissioners at Laramie that I had seen the Sioux commit a great massacre; they killed many white men. But the Sioux are still there and still kill white men. When you whip the Sioux come and tell us of it. You are afraid of the Sioux. Two years ago I went with the soldiers; they were very brave; they were going through the Sioux country to Powder River and Tongue River. We got to Prior Creek, just below here in the Crow country. I wanted to go ahead into the Sioux country, but the soldiers got scared and turned back. I was there and so were others who are here; they know what I say is true. The soldiers said they were going to Tongue River, but they got frightened at the Sioux and turned back. The soldiers were the whirlwind; they went toward the Sioux country, but the whirlwind turned back. Last summer the soldiers went to Prior Creek again; again they said they were going through the Sioux country, but they saw a few Sioux; they were afraid of them; they got scared

SOURCE: 43rd Congress, 1st Session. #1601. Report of the Indian Commission. 501, 504–505, 506–507.

and turned up to the Muscle-Shell, and went back again: again the whirlwind was going through the Sioux country, but again the whirlwind turned back. We are not the whirlwind, but we go to the Sioux; we go into their country; we meet them and fight, but we do not turn back; but we are not the whirlwind. You say the railroad is coming up the Yellowstone; that is like the whirlwind and cannot be turned back. I do not think it will come. The Sioux are on the way and you are afraid of them; they will turn the whirlwind back. If you whip the Sioux, and get them out of its way, the railroad may come, and I will say nothing.

We were born on this side of the Yellowstone and were raised here. It is good land. There is plenty of good land here. Timber and grass and water are plenty, and there is much game in the mountains. You talk about Judith Basin, and say you are going to give us plenty to eat. We do not want to exchange our land. You are my friend. If we were to go to the white man's country and bloody it as they do our country, you would not like it. For many years I have known the whites. You have a big heart, but it is not so with the white men who come into my country. Some of them never sucked their mother's breasts. I think they were raised like the buffalo, and sucked a buffalo cow for their mother. They have no hearts. I was not raised in that way; I am a man. I was raised and sucked milk from my mother's breast. There is no white man's blood on our hands, and I am not ashamed to shake hands with you. What I say is true. I am your friend. The sun sees me and hears what I say. The Great Spirit hears me and knows it is true. Did I ask these white men to come here and crowd me? Buffalo robes are my money; we have some buffalo left yet. If I go to the buffalo country and bring no robes back, the traders will not look at me; they won't be glad to see me and shake hands with me, and say "How," "How," as they would if I had plenty. I think you had better leave Pease with us as he was before. If you put anybody else here, very soon they will kick me in the face with their foot. All the men who have Crow women, we don't want them sent away. They are my friends and I want them to live as I do.

[Third day]

I have said before that we are friends, and that we like each other; yet we have different thoughts in our hearts. The first time I went to Fort Laramie and met the peace commissioners, what each said to the other, we said "Yes, yes." The second time we went, we signed the treaty; but neither of us, my white friends nor the Indian chiefs, said "Yes, yes," to what is in that treaty. What we said to them, and what they said to us, was "Good." We said "Yes, yes," to it; but it is not in the treaty. Shane was there the first time, and what he interpreted to us are not the words that are in the treaty. The first time we went, we did not sign the treaty; we only said "Yes, yes," to each other. The Indian way of making a treaty is to light a pipe, and the Indians and their white friends smoke it.

When we were in council at Laramie, we asked whether we might eat the buffalo for a long time. They said yes. That is not in the treaty. We told them we wanted a big country. They said we should have it; and that is not in the treaty. They promised us plenty of goods, and food for forty years—plenty for all the Crows to eat; but that is not in the treaty. Listen to what I say. We asked, "Shall we and our children get food for forty years?" They said "Yes;" but it is not that way in the treaty. They told us when we got a good man for agent he should stay with us; but it is not so in the treaty. We asked that the white man's road along Powder River be abandoned, and that the grass be permitted to grow in it. They said "Yes, yes;" but it is not in the treaty. The land that we used to own we do not think of taking pay for. We used to own the land in the Mud River Valley. These old Crows you see here were born there. We owned Horse Creek, the Stinking Water, and Heart's Mountains. Many of these Indians were born there. So we owned the country about Powder River and Tongue River, and many of our young men were born there. So we owned the mouth of Muscle-shell, and Crazy Mountain, and Judith Basin; many of our children were born there. So we told the commissioners. They said "Yes, yes;" but there is nothing about it in the treaty. We told them there were many bad Indians, but that we would hold on to the hands of the white man, and would love each other. We told them the Piegans, the Sioux, and other tribes have killed white men. We told them the whites were afraid of them. I asked them to look at us; that we had no arms, and they should not be afraid of the Crows. They said "Yes, yes;" but it is not so written in the treaty.

The treaty, you say, has bought all our land, except on this side of the river. And what do we get for it? I am ashamed about it. We sell our land, and what do we get for it? We get a pair of stockings, and when we put them on they go to pieces. They get some old shirts, and have them washed, and give them to us; we put them on, and our elbows go right through them. They send us tin kettles; we go to get water to carry to our lodges; we dip the water up, but it all runs out again. That is what we get for our land. Why do they not send us annuity goods? We go to the buffalo country and get skins; our wives dress them, and we give them to our friends. We give more presents to our white friends than all the annuity goods we get are worth. And this is what we get for our lands. What goods are given us are no better than we give the whites, and I do not see what we are getting for our lands. We told the commission at Laramie that the Sioux were in our country on Tongue River.

The Sioux and the Crows are at war; yet I went into the Sioux camp alone. They offered to give us two hundred and sixty horses and mules, all taken from white men, if we would join them; but we refused to do so. They took me by the arm, and asked me to stay with them and fight the whites; but I pulled loose from them and would not do so. I told the commission that I was asked to hold the whites with my left hand and the Sioux with my right hand; but now I gave my right hand to the whites, and would hold on to them; they said "Yes, yes." But none of this is in the treaty. We told them we had plenty of fish and game; and when they got scarce we would tell them, and ask help from them.

They said, "Will you sell the Powder River country, Judith Basin, and Wind River country?" I told them no; but that is not in the treaty. When Major Camp came here as agent, we gave him a present of a large number of robes to send to the Great Father. We never heard that the Great Father got those robes; we would like to hear about them. The Crow tribe want Major Pease to remain with us as our agent. Some of the young men want him to take them to see the Great Father at Washington. You ask us to tell you what we want. We want Mexican blankets, elk-teeth, beads, eagle-feathers, and panther and otter skins. We like fine horses and needle-guns; these things are to us what money is to you.

[Fifth day]

On this side of the river and on the other side is our country. If you do not know anything about it, I will tell you about it, for I was raised here. You mark all our country, the streams and mountains, and I would like to tell you about it; and what I say I want you to take to your heart. You make us think a great deal today. I am a man, and am talking to you. All the Indian tribes have not strong arms and brave hearts like we have; they are not so brave. We love you and shake hands with you [taking Mr. Brunot's hand].

We have gone to Judith Basin a great deal, and you wish us to take it for a reservation. All kinds of men go there; trappers and hunters go there poisoning game. The Sioux Indians, Crees, Santees, Mandans, Assineboines, Gros Ventres, Piegans, Pen d'Oreilles, Flatheads, the Mountain Crows, the River Crows, Bannacks, Snakes, and Nez Percé Indians and white people, all go there. You wish us to take the Judith Basin for a reservation. All these Indians will come, and we will likely quarrel; that is what we think about it. Judith Basin is a small basin; a great many people go there; we all go there to eat buffalo. I have told you about the Sioux when they come to fight us. We go a long way from our camp. All Indians are not as strong as we are; they give up and run off. If you have two dogs, if they go to fight, and you catch them and pull apart, when you let them go they fight again. So it is with the Sioux and Crows.

You tell me the railroad is coming up the Yellowstone. If you move this place away from here, the Sioux will be like a whirlwind; they will come and fight the whites; that is true as I tell you. Along Prior Mountain is the Crow trail. We listen to you, and what I tell you is true. The young men do not care what they do. We want some of them to go to Washington with Major Pease, and what they say there will be all right.

I will tell you what we will do; neither of us will live forever; in time both of us will die. We will sell the part of our reservation containing the mountains from Clark's Fork, below the mountains, and the valleys we will not sell. The Crow young men will go to Washington and fix it up, and come back and tell us about it. We will sell the range of mountains to Heart's Mountain and Clark's Fork. The young men will sell it at Washington, and they will say to the Great Father at Washington, that the Crows have a strong heart and are willing to sell their land. When you buy this and give us plenty for it, we will talk about the rest, if you want to buy it. Those mountains are full of mines. The whites think we don't know about the mines, but we do. We will sell you a big country, all the mountains. Now tell us what you are going to give for our mountains. We want plenty for them. Am I talking right? The young men think I am talking right. Everyone here is trying to get plenty. The railroad is coming. It is not here yet. You talk about Judith Basin. I have heard about it. I want to see what you will give for the mountains; then we will talk about the rest of our land.

You think you have peace with the Sioux; I do not think you have. You want to shake hands with them. We want to know whether you are going to fight the Sioux or not; we want to know. We will see what the young men will do at Washington; if they hear what is good, we will do it. The railroad will not be here for some time, and before that we will be part of the time on this side and part of the time on the other side of the river. In the Gallatin Valley, if you sell a house and a little piece of ground, you get paid for it. I know that is the white man's way of doing. The white men are all around us. On the other side of the river all those streams belong to the Crows. When the Sioux come there, we can run them off into the river. We are friends; when our friends get horses stolen, we give them some. Many of our horses are stolen here; four of my horses are gone now; last night some horses were stolen. The Sioux took them along the mountains. On the other side of the gap, there are plenty of houses full of everything. In Gallatin Valley are plenty of cartridges; the Crows have none. If the Sioux come, I do not know what we shall fight them with.

See all these old women! They have no clothing; the young men have no good blankets. We would like the Nez Percés, when they raise camp, to come here; they die with the Crows; they help to fight the Sioux. The last commission told us we could eat buffalo a long time. While we are here, the Flathead Indians take our horses. I would like you to take our part and stop them.

CRAZY HORSE, TASHUNKA WITCO (Oglala Sioux)

"We preferred our own way of living"   (September 5, 1877)

On his deathbed, before his father, mother, and Agent Jesse Lee, Crazy Horse (c. 1842–1877) told his story. Although a man of few words, he was "one of the bravest, gamest, most strategic Indian generals of all frontier history in America, a red man who could not and would not be reconstructed." (Wheeler, 200)

I was not hostile to the white man. Sometimes my young men would attack the Indians who were their enemies and took their ponies. They did it in return. We had buffalo for food, and their hides for clothing and our tepees. We preferred hunting to a life of idleness on the reservations, where we were driven against our will. At times we did not get enough to eat, and we were not allowed to leave the reservation to hunt. We preferred our own way of living. We were no expense to the government then. All we wanted was peace and to be left alone. Soldiers were sent out in the winter, who destroyed our villages. [He referred to the winter before when his village was destroyed by Colonel Reynolds, Third Cavalry.] Then "Long Hair" [Custer] came in the same way. They say we massacred him, but he would have done the same to us had we not defended ourselves and fought to the last. Our first impulse was to escape with our squaws and papooses, but we were so hemmed in that we had to fight. After that I went up on Tongue River with a few of my people and lived in peace. But the government would not let me alone. Finally, I came back to Red Cloud agency. Yet I was not allowed to remain quiet. I was tired of fighting. I went to Spotted Tail agency and asked that chief and his agent to let me live there in peace. I came here with the agent [Lee] to talk with big white chief, but was not given a chance. They tried to confine me, I tried to escape, and a soldier ran his bayonet into me. I have spoken.

SOURCE: Homer W. Wheeler. *Buffalo Days*. Indianapolis: Bobbs-Merrill Co., 1905. 199–200.

YOUNG JOSEPH, "CHIEF JOSEPH" (Nez Percé)

"I will fight no more forever"   (October 5, 1877)

After leading his tribe more than 1,600 miles, and about thirty miles from refuge in Canada, Chief Joseph (1841–1904) surrendered to General Oliver Howard at Eagle Creek, Montana. (See Joseph's detailed account of his tribe and their arduous journey in "An Indian's View of Indian Affairs," the next speech.) His famous words of surrender were recorded on the spot by a U.S. Army interpreter.

Tell General Howard I know his heart. What he told me before I have in my heart. I am tired of fighting. Our chiefs are killed. Looking Glass is dead. Too-hul-hul-sote is dead. The old men are all dead. It is the young men who say yes or no. He who led on the young men is dead. It is cold and we have no blankets. The little children are freezing to death. My people, some of them, have run away to the hills, and have no blankets, no food; no one knows where they are—perhaps freezing to death. I want to have time to look for my children and see how many of them I can find. Maybe I shall find them among the dead. Hear me, my chiefs. I am tired; my heart is sick and sad. From where the sun now stands I will fight no more forever.

SOURCE: 45th Congress, 2nd Session, #1794. Report of the Commissioner of War. 630.

YOUNG JOSEPH, "CHIEF JOSEPH" (Nez Percé)

"An Indian's Views of Indian Affairs" (January 1879)

Joseph (1841–1904) came to Washington, D. C., in January 1879, and described his tribe's history and recent fights with and flight from the U.S. Army.

My friends, I have been asked to show you my heart. I am glad to have a chance to do so. I want the white people to understand my people. Some of you think an Indian is like a wild animal. This is a great mistake. I will tell you all about our people, and then you can judge whether an Indian is a man or not. I believe much trouble and blood would be saved if we opened our hearts more. I will tell you in my way how the Indian sees things. The white man has more words to tell you how they look to him, but it does not require many words to speak the truth. What I have to say will come from my heart, and I will speak with a straight tongue. Ah-cum-kin-i-ma-me-hut (the Great Spirit) is looking at me, and will hear me.

My name is In-mut-too-yah-lat-lat (Thunder Traveling Over the Mountains). I am chief of the Wal-lam-wat-kin band of Chutepa-lu, or Nez Percés (nose-pierced Indians). I was born in eastern Oregon, thirty-eight winters ago. My father was chief before me. When a young man, he was called Joseph by Mr. Spaulding, a missionary. He died a few years ago. There was no stain on his hands of the blood of a white man. He left a good name on the earth. He advised me well for my people.

Our fathers gave us many laws, which they had learned from their fathers. These laws were good. They told us to treat all men as they treated us; that we should never be the first to break a bargain; that it was a disgrace to tell a lie; that we should speak only the truth; that it was a shame for one man to take from another his wife, or his property without paying for it. We were taught to believe that the Great Spirit sees and hears everything, and that he never forgets; that hereafter he will give every man a spirit-home according to his deserts: if he has been a good man, he will have a good home; if he has been a bad man, he will have a bad home. This I believe, and all my people believe the same.

We did not know there were other people besides the Indian until

SOURCE: Young Joseph. "An Indian's Views of Indian Affairs." *North American Review*, April 1879. 415–433.

about one hundred winters ago, when some men with white faces came to our country. They brought many things with them to trade for furs and skins. They brought tobacco, which was new to us. They brought guns with flint stones on them, which frightened our women and children. Our people could not talk with these white-faced men, but they used signs which all people understand. These men were Frenchmen, and they called our people "Nez Percés," because they wore rings in their noses for ornaments. Although very few of our people wear them now, we are still called by the same name. These French trappers said a great many things to our fathers, which have been planted in our hearts. Some were good for us, but some were bad. Our people were divided in opinion about these men. Some thought they taught more bad than good. An Indian respects a brave man, but he despises a coward. He loves a straight tongue, but he hates a forked tongue. The French trappers told us some truths and some lies.

The first white men of your people who came to our country were named Lewis and Clark. They also brought many things that our people had never seen. They talked straight, and our people gave them a great feast, as a proof that their hearts were friendly. These men were very kind. They made presents to our chiefs and our people made presents to them. We had a great many horses, of which we gave them what they needed, and they gave us guns and tobacco in return. All the Nez Percés made friends with Lewis and Clark, and agreed to let them pass through their country, and never to make war on white men. This promise the Nez Percés have never broken. No white man can accuse them of bad faith, and speak with a straight tongue. It has always been the pride of the Nez Percés that they were the friends of the white men. When my father was a young man there came to our country a white man (Rev. Mr. Spaulding) who talked spirit law. He won the affections of our people because he spoke good things to them. At first he did not say anything about white men wanting to settle on our lands. Nothing was said about that until about twenty winters ago, when a number of white people came into our country and built houses and made farms. At first our people made no complaint. They thought there was room enough for all to live in peace, and they were learning many things from the white men that seemed to be good. But we soon found that the white men were growing rich very fast, and were greedy to possess everything the Indian had. My father was the first to see through the schemes of the white men, and he warned his tribe to be careful about trading with them. He had suspicion of men who seemed so anxious to make money. I was a boy then, but I remember well my father's caution. He had sharper eyes than the rest of our people.

Next there came a white officer (Governor Stevens), who invited all the Nez Percés to a treaty council. After the council was opened he made known his heart. He said there were a great many white people in the country, and many more would come; that he wanted the land marked out so that the Indians and white men could be separated. If they were to live in peace it was necessary, he said, that the Indians should have a country set apart for them, and in that country they must stay. My father, who represented his band, refused to have anything to do with the council, because he wished to be a free man. He claimed that no man owned any part of the earth, and a man could not sell what he did not own.

Mr. Spaulding took hold of my father's arm and said, "Come and sign the treaty." My father pushed him away, and said: "Why do you ask me to sign away my country? It is your business to talk to us about spirit matters, and not to talk to us about parting with our land." Governor Stevens urged my father to sign his treaty, but he refused. "I will not sign your paper," he said; "you go where you please, so do I; you are not a child, I am no child; I can think for myself. No man can think for me. I have no other home than this. I will not give it up to any man. My people would have no home. Take away your paper. I will not touch it with my hand."

My father left the council. Some of the chiefs of the other bands of the Nez Percés signed the treaty, and then Governor Stevens gave them presents of blankets. My father cautioned his people to take no presents, for "after a while," he said, "they will claim that you have accepted pay for your country." Since that time four bands of the Nez Percés have received annuities from the United States. My father was invited to many councils, and they tried hard to make him sign the treaty, but he was firm as the rock, and would not sign away his home. His refusal caused a difference among the Nez Percés.

Eight years later (1863) was the next treaty council. A chief called Lawyer, because he was a great talker, took the lead in this council, and sold nearly all the Nez Percés country. My father was not there. He said to me: "When you go into council with the white man, always remember your country. Do not give it away. The white man will cheat you out of your home. I have taken no pay from the United States. I have never sold our land." In this treaty Lawyer acted without authority from our band. He had no right to sell the Wallowa (winding water) country. That had always belonged to my father's own people, and the other bands had never disputed our right to it. No other Indians ever claimed Wallowa.

In order to have all people understand how much land we owned, my father planted poles around it and said:

"Inside is the home of my people—the white man may take the land outside. Inside this boundary all our people were born. It circles around the graves of our fathers, and we will never give up these graves to any man."

The United States claimed they had bought all the Nez Percés country outside of Lapwai Reservation, from Lawyer and other chiefs, but we continued to live on this land in peace until eight years ago, when white men began to come inside the bounds my father had set. We warned them against this great wrong, but they would not leave our land, and some bad blood was raised. The white men represented that we were going upon the war-path. They reported many things that were false.

The United States Government again asked for a treaty council. My father had become blind and feeble. He could no longer speak for his people. It was then that I took my father's place as chief. In this council I made my first speech to white men. I said to the agent who held the council:

"I did not want to come to this council, but I came hoping that we could save blood. The white man has no right to come here and take our country. We have never accepted any presents from the Government. Neither Lawyer nor any other chief had authority to sell this land. It has always belonged to my people. It came unclouded to them from our fathers, and we will defend this land as long as a drop of Indian blood warms the hearts of our men."

The agent said he had orders, from the Great White Chief at Washington, for us to go upon the Lapwai Reservation, and that if we obeyed he would help us in many ways. "You *must* move to the agency," he said. I answered him: "I will not. I do not need your help; we have plenty, and we are contented and happy if the white man will let us alone. The reservation is too small for so many people with all their stock. You can keep your presents; we can go to your towns and pay for all we need; we have plenty of horses and cattle to sell, and we won't have any help from you; we are free now; we can go where we please. Our fathers were born here. Here they lived, here they died, here are their graves. We will never leave them." The agent went away, and we had peace for a little while.

Soon after this my father sent for me. I saw he was dying. I took his hand in mine. He said: "My son, my body is returning to my mother earth, and my spirit is going very soon to see the Great Spirit Chief. When I am gone, think of your country. You are the chief of these people. They look to you to guide them. Always remember that your father never sold his country. You must stop your ears whenever you are asked to sign a treaty selling your home. A few years more, and white men will be all around you. They have their eyes on this land. My son, never forget my dying words. This country holds your father's body. Never sell the bones of your father and your mother." I pressed my father's hand and told him I would protect his grave with my life. My father smiled and passed away to the spirit-land.

I buried him in that beautiful valley of winding waters. I love that land more than all the rest of the world. A man who would not love his father's grave is worse than a wild animal.

For a short time we lived quietly. But this could not last. White men had found gold in the mountains around the land of winding water. They stole a great many horses from us and we could not get them back because we were Indians. The white men told lies for each other. They drove off a great many of our cattle. Some white men branded our young cattle so they could claim them. We had no friend who would plead our cause before the law councils. It seemed to me that some of the white men in Wallowa were doing these things on purpose to get up a war. They knew that we were not strong enough to fight them. I labored hard to avoid trouble and bloodshed. We gave up some of our country to the white men, thinking that then we could have peace. We were mistaken. The white man would not let us alone. We could have avenged our wrongs many times, but we did not. Whenever the Government has asked us to help them against other Indians, we have never refused. When the white men were few and we were strong we could have killed them all off, but the Nez Percés wished to live at peace.

If we have not done so, we have not been to blame. I believe that the old treaty has never been correctly reported. If we ever owned the land we own it still, for we never sold it. In the treaty councils the commissioners have claimed that our country had been sold to the Government. Suppose a white man should come to me and say, "Joseph, I like your horses, and I want to buy them." I say to him, "No, my horses suit me, I will not sell them." Then he goes to my neighbor, and says to him: "Joseph has some good horses. I want to buy them, but he refuses to sell." My neighbor answers, "Pay me the money, and I will sell you Joseph's horses." The white man returns to me, and says, "Joseph, I have bought your horses, and you must let me have them." If we sold our lands to the Government, this is the way they were bought.

On account of the treaty made by the other bands of the Nez Percés, the white men claimed my lands. We were troubled greatly by white men crowding over the line. Some of these were good men, and we lived on peaceful terms with them, but they were not all good.

Nearly every year the agent came over from Lapwai and ordered us on to the reservation. We always replied that we were satisfied to live in

Wallowa. We were careful to refuse the presents or annuities which he offered.

Through all the years since the white men came to Wallowa we have been threatened and taunted by them and the treaty Nez Percés. They have given us no rest. We have had a few good friends among white men, and they have always advised my people to bear these taunts without fighting. Our young men were quick-tempered, and I have had great trouble in keeping them from doing rash things. I have carried a heavy load on my back ever since I was a boy. I learned then that we were but few, while the white men were many, and that we could not hold our own with them. We were like deer. They were like grizzly bears. We had a small country. Their country was large. We were contented to let things remain as the Great Spirit Chief made them. They were not; and would change the rivers and mountains if they did not suit them.

Year after year we have been threatened, but no war was made upon my people until General Howard came to our country two years ago and told us that he was the white war-chief of all that country. He said: "I have a great many soldiers at my back. I am going to bring them up here, and then I will talk to you again. I will not let white men laugh at me the next time I come. The country belongs to the Government, and I intend to make you go upon the reservation."

I remonstrated with him against bringing more soldiers to the Nez Percés country. He had one house full of troops all the time at Fort Lapwai.

The next spring the agent at Umatilla agency sent an Indian runner to tell me to meet General Howard at Walla Walla. I could not go myself, but I sent my brother and five other head men to meet him, and they had a long talk.

General Howard said: "You have talked straight, and it is all right. You can stay in Wallowa." He insisted that my brother and his company should go with him to Fort Lapwai. When the party arrived there General Howard sent out runners and called all the Indians in to a grand council. I was in that council. I said to General Howard, "We are ready to listen." He answered that he would not talk then, but would hold a council next day, when he would talk plainly. I said to General Howard: "I am ready to talk today. I have been in a great many councils, but I am no wiser. We are all sprung from a woman, although we are unlike in many things. We can not be made over again. You are as you were made, and as you were made you can remain. We are just as we were made by the Great Spirit, and you can not change us; then why should children of one mother and one father quarrel—why should one try to cheat the other? I do not believe that the Great Spirit

Chief gave one kind of men the right to tell another kind of men what they must do."

General Howard replied: "You deny my authority, do you? You want to dictate to me, do you?"

Then one of my chiefs—Too-hool-hool-suit—rose in the council and said to General Howard: "The Great Spirit Chief made the world as it is, and as he wanted it, and he made a part of it for us to live upon. I do not see where you get authority to say that we shall not live where he placed us."

General Howard lost his temper and said: "Shut up! I don't want to hear any more of such talk. The law says you shall go upon the reservation to live, and I want you to do so, but you persist in disobeying the law" (meaning the treaty). "If you do not move, I will take the matter into my own hand, and make you suffer for your disobedience."

Too-hool-hool-suit answered: "Who are you, that you ask us to talk, and then tell me I shan't talk? Are you the Great Spirit? Did you make the world? Did you make the sun? Did you make the rivers to run for us to drink? Did you make the grass to grow? Did you make all these things, that you talk to us as though we were boys? If you did, then you have the right to talk as you do."

General Howard replied, "You are an impudent fellow, and I will put you in the guard-house," and then ordered a soldier to arrest him.

Too-hool-hool-suit made no resistance. He asked General Howard: "Is that your order? I don't care. I have expressed my heart to you. I have nothing to take back. I have spoken for my country. You can arrest me, but you can not change me or make me take back what I have said."

The soldiers came forward and seized my friend and took him to the guard-house. My men whispered among themselves whether they should let this thing be done. I counseled them to submit. I knew if we resisted that all the white men present, including General Howard, would be killed in a moment, and we would be blamed. If I had said nothing, General Howard would never have given another unjust order against my men. I saw the danger, and, while they dragged Too-hool-hool-suit to prison, I arose and said: "*I am going to talk now*. I don't care whether you arrest me or not." I turned to my people and said: "The arrest of Too-hool-hool-suit was wrong, but we will not resent the insult. We were invited to this council to express our hearts, and we have done so." Too-hool-hool-suit was prisoner for five days before he was released.

The council broke up for that day. On the next morning General Howard came to my lodge and invited me to go with him and White-Bird and Looking-Glass to look for land for my people. As we rode along we came to some good land that was already occupied by Indians and white people. General Howard, pointing to this land, said: "If you will come on to the reservation, I will give you these lands and move these people off."

I replied: "No. It would be wrong to disturb these people. I have no right to take their homes. I have never taken what did not belong to me. I will not now."

We rode all day upon the reservation, and found no good land unoccupied. I have been informed by men who do not lie that General Howard sent a letter that night, telling the soldiers at Walla Walla to go to Wallowa Valley, and drive us out upon our return home.

In the council, next day, General Howard informed me, in a haughty spirit, that he would give my people *thirty days* to go back home, collect all their stock, and move on to the reservation, saying, "If you are not here in that time, I shall consider that you want to fight, and will send my soldiers to drive you on."

I said: "War can be avoided, and it ought to be avoided. I want no war. My people have already been the friends of the white man. Why are you in such a hurry? I can not get ready to move in thirty days. Our stock is scattered, and Snake River is very high. Let us wait until fall, then the river will be low. We want time to hunt up our stock and gather supplies for winter."

General Howard replied, "If you let the time run over one day, the soldiers will be there to drive you on to the reservation, and all your cattle and horses outside of the reservation at that time will fall into the hands of the white men."

I knew I had never sold my country, and that I had no land in Lapwai; but I did not want bloodshed. I did not want my people killed. I did not want anybody killed. Some of my people had been murdered by white men, and the white murderers were never punished for it. I told General Howard about this, and again said I wanted no war. I wanted the people who lived upon the lands I was to occupy at Lapwai to have time to gather their harvest.

I said in my heart that, rather than have war, I would give up my country. I would give up my father's grave. I would give up everything rather than have the blood of white men upon the hands of my people.

General Howard refused to allow me more than thirty days to move my people and their stock. I am sure that he began to prepare for war at once.

When I returned to Wallowa I found my people very much excited upon discovering that the soldiers were already in the Wallowa Valley. We held a council, and decided to move immediately, to avoid bloodshed.

Too-hool-hool-suit, who felt outraged by his imprisonment, talked for war, and made many of my young men willing to fight rather than be driven like dogs from the land where they were born. He declared that blood alone would wash out the disgrace General Howard had put upon him. It required a strong heart to stand up against such talk, but I urged my people to be quiet, and not to begin a war.

We gathered all the stock we could find, and made an attempt to move. We left many of our horses and cattle in Wallowa, and we lost several hundred in crossing the river. All of my people succeeded in getting across in safety. Many of the Nez Percés came together in Rocky Cañon to hold a grand council. I went with all my people. This council lasted ten days. There was a great deal of war-talk, and a great deal of excitement. There was one young brave present whose father had been killed by a white man five years before. This man's blood was bad against white men, and he left the council calling for revenge.

Again I counseled peace, and I thought the danger was past. We had not complied with General Howard's order because we could not, but we intended to do so as soon as possible. I was leaving the council to kill beef for my family, when news came that the young man whose father had been killed had gone out with several other hot-blooded young braves and killed four white men. He rode up to the council and shouted: "Why do you sit here like women? The war has begun already." I was deeply grieved. All the lodges were moved except my brother's and my own. I saw clearly that the war was upon us when I learned that my young men had been secretly buying ammunition. I heard then that Too-hool-hool-suit, who had been imprisoned by General Howard, had succeeded in organizing a war-party. I knew that their acts would involve all my people. I saw that the war could not then be prevented. The time had passed. I counseled peace from the beginning. I knew that we were too weak to fight the United States. We had many grievances, but I knew that war would bring more. We had good white friends, who advised us against taking the war-path. My friend and brother, Mr. Chapman, who has been with us since the surrender, told us just how the war would end. Mr. Chapman took sides against us, and helped General Howard. I do not blame him for doing so. He tried hard to prevent bloodshed. We hoped the white settlers would not join the soldiers. Before the war commenced we had discussed this matter all over, and many of my people were in favor of warning them that if they took no part against us they should not be molested in the event of war being begun by General Howard. This plan was voted down in the war-council.

There were bad men among my people who had quarreled with white men, and they talked of their wrongs until they roused all the bad hearts in the council. Still I could not believe that they would begin the war. I know that my young men did a great wrong, but I ask, Who was first to blame? They had been insulted a thousand times; their fathers and brothers had been killed; their mothers and wives had been disgraced; they had been driven to madness by whisky sold to them by white men; they had been told by General Howard that all their horses and cattle which they had been unable to drive out of Wallowa were to fall into the hands of white men; and, added to all this, they were homeless and desperate.

I would have given my own life if I could have undone the killing of white men by my people. I blame my young men and I blame the white men. I blame General Howard for not giving my people time to get their stock away from Wallowa. I do not acknowledge that he had the right to order me to leave Wallowa at any time. I deny that either my father or myself ever sold that land. It is still our land. It may never again be our home, but my father sleeps there, and I love it as I love my mother. I left there, hoping to avoid bloodshed.

If General Howard had given me plenty of time to gather up my stock, and treated Too-hool-hool-suit as a man should be treated, there *would have been no war.*

My friends among white men have blamed me for the war. I am not to blame. When my young men began the killing, my heart was hurt. Although I did not justify them, I remembered all the insults I had endured, and my blood was on fire. Still I would have taken my people to the buffalo country without fighting, if possible.

I could see no other way to avoid a war. We moved over to White Bird Creek, sixteen miles away, and there encamped, intending to collect our stock before leaving; but the soldiers attacked us, and the first battle was fought. We numbered in that battle sixty men, and the soldiers a hundred. The fight lasted but a few minutes, when the soldiers retreated before us for twelve miles. They lost thirty-three killed, and had seven wounded. When an Indian fights, he only shoots to kill, but soldiers shoot at random. None of the soldiers were scalped. We do not believe in scalping, nor in killing wounded men. Soldiers do not kill many Indians unless they are wounded and left upon the battle-field. Then they kill Indians.

Seven days after the first battle, General Howard arrived in the Nez Percés country, bringing seven hundred more soldiers. It was now war in earnest. We crossed over Salmon River, hoping General Howard would follow. We were not disappointed. He did follow us, and we got back between him and his supplies, and cut him off for three days. He sent out two companies to open the way. We attacked them, killing one officer, two guides, and ten men.

We withdrew, hoping the soldiers would follow, but they had got fighting enough for that day. They intrenched themselves, and next day we attacked them again. The battle lasted all day, and was renewed next morning. We killed four and wounded seven or eight.

About this time General Howard found out that we were in his rear. Five days later he attacked us with three hundred and fifty soldiers and settlers. We had two hundred and fifty warriors. The fight lasted twenty-seven hours. We lost four killed and several wounded. General Howard's loss was twenty-nine men killed and sixty wounded.

The following day the soldiers charged upon us, and we retreated with our families and stock a few miles, leaving eighty lodges to fall into General Howard's hands.

Finding that we were outnumbered, we retreated to Bitter Root Valley. Here another body of soldiers came upon us and demanded our surrender. We refused. They said, "You can not get by us." We answered, "We are going by you without fighting if you will let us, but we are going by you anyhow." We then made a treaty with these soldiers. We agreed not to molest any one, and they agreed that we might pass through the Bitter Root country in peace. We bought provisions and traded stock with white men there.

We understood that there was to be no more war. We intended to go peaceably to the buffalo country, and leave the question of returning to our country to be settled afterward.

With this understanding we traveled on for four days, and, thinking that the trouble was all over, we stopped and prepared tent-poles to take with us. We started again, and at the end of two days we saw three white men passing our camp. Thinking that peace had been made, we did not molest them. We could have killed or taken them prisoners, but we did not suspect them of being spies, which they were.

That night the soldiers surrounded our camp. About daybreak one of my men went out to look after his horses. The soldiers saw him and shot him down like a coyote. I have since learned that these soldiers were not those we had left behind. They had come upon us from another direction. The new white war-chief's name was Gibbon. He charged upon us while some of my people were still asleep. We had a hard fight. Some of my men crept around and attacked the soldiers from the rear. In this battle we lost nearly all our lodges, but we finally drove General Gibbon back.

Finding that he was not able to capture us, he sent to his camp a few miles away for his big guns (cannons), but my men had captured them and all the ammunition. We damaged the big guns all we could, and carried away the powder and lead. In the fight with General Gibbon we lost fifty women and children and thirty fighting men. We remained long enough to bury our dead. The Nez Percés never make war on women and children; we could have killed a great many women and children while the war lasted, but we would feel ashamed to do so cowardly an act.

We never scalp our enemies, but when General Howard came up and joined General Gibbon, their Indian scouts dug up our dead and scalped them. I have been told that General Howard did not order this great shame to be done.

We retreated as rapidly as we could toward the buffalo country. After six days General Howard came close to us, and we went out and attacked him, and captured nearly all his horses and mules (about two hundred and fifty head). We then marched on to the Yellowstone Basin.

On the way we captured one white man and two white women. We released them at the end of three days. They were treated kindly. The women were not insulted. Can the white soldiers tell me of one time when Indian women were taken prisoners, and held three days and then released without being insulted? Were the Nez Percés women who fell into the hands of General Howard's soldiers treated with as much respect? I deny that a Nez Percé was ever guilty of such a crime.

A few days later we captured two more white men. One of them stole a horse and escaped. We gave the other a poor horse and told him he was free.

Nine days' march brought us to the mouth of Clarke's Fork of the Yellowstone. We did not know what had become of General Howard, but we supposed that he had sent for more horses and mules. He did not come up, but another new war-chief (General Sturgis) attacked us. We held him in check while we moved all our women and children and stock out of danger, leaving a few men to cover our retreat.

Several days passed, and we heard nothing of General Howard, or Gibbon, or Sturgis. We had repulsed each in turn, and began to feel secure, when another army, under General Miles, struck us. This was the fourth army, each of which outnumbered our fighting force, that we had encountered within sixty days.

We had no knowledge of General Miles's army until a short time before he made a charge upon us, cutting our camp in two, and capturing nearly all of our horses. About seventy men, myself among them, were cut off. My little daughter, twelve years of age, was with me. I gave her a rope, and told her to catch a horse and join the others who were cut off from the camp. I have not seen her since, but I have learned that she is alive and well.

I thought of my wife and children, who were now surrounded by soldiers, and I resolved to go to them or die. With a prayer in my mouth to the Great Spirit Chief who rules above, I dashed unarmed through the line of soldiers. It seemed to me that there were guns on every side, before and behind me. My clothes were cut to pieces and my horse was wounded, but I was not hurt. As I reached the door of my lodge, my wife handed me my rifle, saying: "Here's your gun. Fight!"

The soldiers kept up a continuous fire. Six of my men were killed in one spot near me. Ten or twelve soldiers charged into our camp and got possession of two lodges, killing three Nez Percés and losing three of their men, who fell inside our lines. I called my men to drive them back. We fought at close range, not more than twenty steps apart, and drove the soldiers back upon their main line, leaving their dead in our hands. We secured their arms and ammunition. We lost, the first day and night, eighteen men and three women. General Miles lost twenty-six killed and forty wounded. The following day General Miles sent a messenger into my camp under protection of a white flag. I sent my friend Yellow Bull to meet him.

Yellow Bull understood the messenger to say that General Miles wished me to consider the situation; that he did not want to kill my people unnecessarily. Yellow Bull understood this to be a demand for me to surrender and save blood. Upon reporting this message to me, Yellow Bull said he wondered whether General Miles was in earnest. I sent him back with my answer, that I had not made up my mind, but would think about it and send word soon. A little later he sent some Cheyenne scouts with another message. I went out to meet them. They said they believed that General Miles was sincere and really wanted peace. I walked on to General Miles's tent. He met me and we shook hands. He said, "Come, let us sit down by the fire and talk this matter over." I remained with him all night; next morning Yellow Bull came over to see if I was alive, and why I did not return.

General Miles would not let me leave the tent to see my friend alone.

Yellow Bull said to me: "They have got you in their power, and I am afraid they will never let you go again. I have an officer in our camp, and I will hold him until they let you go free."

I said: "I do not know what they mean to do with me, but if they kill me you must not kill the officer. It will do no good to avenge my death by killing him."

Yellow Bull returned to my camp. I did not make any agreement that day with General Miles. The battle was renewed while I was with him. I was very anxious about my people. I knew that we were near Sitting Bull's camp in King George's land, and I thought maybe the Nez Percés who had escaped would return with assistance. No great damage was done to either party during the night.

On the following morning I returned to my camp by agreement, meeting the officer who had been held a prisoner in my camp at the flag of truce. My people were divided about surrendering. We could have escaped from Bear Paw Mountain if we had left our wounded, old women, and children behind. We were unwilling to do this. We had never heard of a wounded Indian recovering while in the hands of white men.

On the evening of the fourth day General Howard came in with a small escort, together with my friend Chapman. We could now talk understandingly. General Miles said to me in plain words, "If you will come out and give up your arms, I will spare your lives and send you to your reservation." I do not know what passed between General Miles and General Howard.

I could not bear to see my wounded men and women suffer any longer; we had lost enough already. General Miles had promised that we might return to our own country with what stock we had left. I thought we could start again. I believed General Miles, or *I never would have surrendered.* I have heard that he has been censured for making the promise to return us to Lapwai. He could not have made any other terms with me at that time. I would have held him in check until my friends came to my assistance, and then neither of the generals nor their soldiers would have ever left Bear Paw Mountain alive.

On the fifth day I went to General Miles and gave up my gun, and said, "From where the sun now stands I will fight no more." My people needed rest—we wanted peace.

I was told we could go with General Miles to Tongue River and stay there until spring, when we would be sent back to our country. Finally it was decided that we were to be taken to Tongue River. We had nothing to say about it. After our arrival at Tongue River, General Miles received orders to take us to Bismarck. The reason given was, that subsistence would be cheaper there.

General Miles was opposed to this order. He said: "You must not blame me. I have endeavored to keep my word, but the chief who is over me has given the order, and I must obey it or resign. That would do you no good. Some other officer would carry out the order."

I believe General Miles would have kept his word if he could have done so. I do not blame him for what we have suffered since the surrender. I do not know who is to blame. We gave up all our horses—over eleven hundred—and all our saddles—over one hundred—and we have not heard from them since. Somebody has got our horses.

General Miles turned my people over to another soldier, and we were taken to Bismarck. Captain Johnson, who now had charge of us, received an order to take us to Fort Leavenworth. At Leavenworth we were placed on a low river bottom, with no water except river-water to drink and cook with. We had always lived in a healthy country, where the mountains were high and the water was cold and clear. Many of my people sickened and died, and we buried them in this strange land. I can not tell how much my heart suffered for my people while at Leavenworth. The Great Spirit Chief who rules above seemed to be looking some other way, and did not see what was being done to my people.

During the hot days (July, 1878) we received notice that we were to be moved farther away from our own country. We were not asked if we were willing to go. We were ordered to get into the railroad-cars. Three of my people died on the way to Baxter Springs. It was worse to die there than to die fighting in the mountains.

We were moved from Baxter Springs (Kansas) to the Indian Territory, and set down without our lodges. We had but little medicine, and we were nearly all sick. Seventy of my people have died since we moved there.

We have had a great many visitors who have talked many ways. Some of the chiefs (General Fish and Colonel Stickney) from Washington came to see us, and selected land for us to live upon. We have not moved to that land, for it is not a good place to live.

The Commissioner Chief (E. A. Hayt) came to see us. I told him, as I told every one, that I expected General Miles's word would be carried out. He said it "could not be done; that white men now lived in my country and all the land was taken up; that, if I returned to Wallowa, I could not live in peace; that law-papers were out against my young men who began the war, and that the Government could not protect my people." This talk fell like a heavy stone upon my heart. I saw that I could not gain anything by talking to him. Other law chiefs (Congressional Committee) came to see me and said they would help me to get a healthy country. I did not know who to believe. The white people have too many chiefs. They do not understand each other. They do not all talk alike.

The Commissioner Chief (Mr. Hayt) invited me to go with him and hunt for a better home than we have now. I like the land we found (west of the Osage reservation) better than any place I have seen in that country; but it is not a healthy land. There are no mountains and rivers. The water is warm. It is not a good country for stock. I do not believe my people can live there. I am afraid they will all die. The Indians who occupy that country are dying off. I promised Chief Hayt to go there, and do the best I could until the Government got ready to make good General Miles's word. I was not satisfied, but I could not help myself.

Then the Inspector Chief (General McNiel) came to my camp and we had a long talk. He said I ought to have a home in the mountain country north, and that he would write a letter to the Great Chief at Washington. Again the hope of seeing the mountains of Idaho and Oregon grew up in my heart.

At last I was granted permission to come to Washington and bring my friend Yellow Bull and our interpreter with me. I am glad we came. I have shaken hands with a great many friends, but there are some things I want to know which no one seems able to explain. I can not understand how the Government sends a man out to fight us, as it did General Miles, and then breaks his word. Such a Government has something wrong about it. I can not understand why so many chiefs are allowed to talk so many different ways, and promise so many different things. I have seen the Great Father Chief (the President), the next Great Chief (Secretary of the Interior), the Commissioner Chief (Hayt), the Law Chief (General Butler), and many other law chiefs (Congressmen), and they all say they are my friends, and that I shall have justice, but while their mouths all talk right I do not understand why nothing is done for my people. I have heard talk and talk, but nothing is done. Good words do not last long unless they amount to something. Words do not pay for my dead people. They do not pay for my country, now overrun by white men. They do not protect my father's grave. They do not pay for all my horses and cattle. Good words will not give me back my children. Good words will not make good the promise of your War Chief General Miles. Good words will not give my people good health and stop them from dying. Good words will not get my people a home where they can live in peace and take care of themselves. I am tired of talk that comes to nothing. It makes my heart sick when I remember all the good words and all the broken promises. There has been too much talking by men who had no right to talk. Too many misrepresentations have been made, too many misunderstandings have come up between the white men about the Indians. If the white man wants to live in peace with the Indian he can live in peace. There need be no trouble. Treat all men alike. Give them all the same law. Give them all an even chance to live and grow. All men were made by the same Great Spirit Chief. They are all brothers. The earth is the mother of all people, and all people should have equal rights upon it. You might as well expect the rivers to run backward as that any man who was born a free man should be contented when penned up and denied liberty to go where he pleases. If you tie a horse to a stake, do you expect he will grow fat? If you pen an Indian up on a small spot of earth, and compel him to stay there, he will not be contented, nor will he grow and prosper. I have asked some of the great white chiefs where they get their authority to say to the Indian that he shall stay in one place, while he sees white men going where they please. They can not tell me.

I only ask of the Government to be treated as all other men are treated. If I can not go to my own home, let me have a home in some country where my people will not die so fast. I would like to go to Bitter Root Valley. There my people would be healthy; where they are now they are dying. Three have died since I left my camp to come to Washington.

When I think of our condition my heart is heavy. I see men of my race treated as outlaws and driven from country to country, or shot down like animals.

I know that my race must change. We can not hold our own with the white men as we are. We only ask an even chance to live as other men live. We ask to be recognized as men. We ask that the same law shall work alike on all men. If the Indian breaks the law, punish him by the law. If the white man breaks the law, punish him also.

Let me be a free man—free to travel, free to stop, free to work, free to trade where I choose, free to choose my own teachers, free to follow the religion of my fathers, free to think and talk and act for myself—and I will obey every law, or submit to the penalty.

Whenever the white man treats the Indian as they treat each other, then we will have no more wars. We shall all be alike—brothers of one father and one mother, with one sky above us and one country around us, and one government for all. Then the Great Spirit Chief who rules above will smile upon this land, and send rain to wash out the bloody spots made by brothers' hands from the face of the earth. For this time the Indian race are waiting and praying. I hope that no more groans of wounded men and women will ever go to the ear of the Great Spirit Chief above, and that all people may be one people.

In-mut-too-yah-lat-lat has spoken for his people.

SITTING BULL, TATANKA YOTANKA (Hunkpapa Sioux)

"Behold, my friends, the spring is come" (1875)

The chief and wise-man of the Sioux, Sitting Bull (c. 1830–1890) was their greatest leader and a sharp-witted and poetic speaker. At an Indian council at the Powder River, Sitting Bull described his mistrust of the American people.

Behold, my friends, the spring is come; the earth has gladly received the embraces of the sun, and we shall soon see the results of their love! Every seed is awakened, and all animal life. It is through this mysterious power that we too have our being, and we therefore yield to our neighbors, even to our animal neighbors, the same right as ourselves to inhabit this vast land.

Yet hear me, friends! we have now to deal with another people, small and feeble when our forefathers first met with them, but now great and overbearing. Strangely enough, they have a mind to till the soil, and the love of possessions is a disease in them. These people have made many rules that the rich may break, but the poor may not! They have a religion in which the poor worship, but the rich will not! They even take tithes of the poor and weak to support the rich and those who rule. They claim this mother of ours, the Earth, for their own use, and fence their neighbors away from her, and deface her with their buildings and their refuse. They compel her to produce out of season, and when sterile she is made to take medicine in order to produce again. All this is sacrilege.

This nation is like a spring freshet; it overruns its banks and destroys all who are in its path. We cannot dwell side by side. Only seven years ago we made a treaty by which we were assured that the buffalo country should be left to us forever. Now they threaten to take that from us also. My brothers, shall we submit? or shall we say to them: "First kill me, before you can take possession of my fatherland!"

SOURCE: Charles A. Eastman (Ohiyesa). *Indian Heroes and Great Chieftains.* Boston: Little, Brown, 1918. 119–121. [Reprint edition. Mineola, New York: Dover Publications, 1997. 53.]

SITTING BULL, TATANKA YOTANKA (Hunkpapa Sioux)

"You come here to tell us lies, but we don't want to hear them" (October 17, 1878)

After the Battle of the Little Big Horn on June 25, 1876, at which he, Crazy Horse and 1,800 other Sioux and Cheyenne warriors wiped out an army led by General George Custer, Sitting Bull (c. 1830–1890), facing the repercussions of the U.S. Army, decided to escape to Canada. In 1878, the U.S. Government sent representatives to Canada to try to convince him and his band to return to a reservation. But they warned him: "Should you attempt to return with arms in your hands, you must be treated as enemies of the United States."

For sixty-four years you have kept me and my people and treated us bad. What have we done that you should want us to stop? We have done nothing. It is all the people on your side that have started us to do all these depredations. We could not go anywhere else, and so we took refuge in this country. It was on this side of the country we learned to shoot, and that is the reason why I came back to it again. I would like to know why you came here. In the first place, I did not give you the country, but you followed me from one place to another, so I had to leave and come over to this country. I was born and raised in this country with the Red River Half-Breeds, and I intend to stop with them. I was raised hand in hand with the Red River Half-Breeds, and we are going over to that part of the country, and that is the reason why I have come over here. [Shaking hands with the British officers.] That is the way I was raised, in the hands of these people here, and that is the way I intend to be with them. You have got ears, and you have got eyes to see with them, and you see how I live with these people. You see me? Here I am! If you think I am a fool you are a bigger fool than I am. This house is a medicine-house. You come here to tell us lies, but we don't want to hear them. I don't wish any such language used to me; that is, to tell me such lies in my Great Mother's house. Don't you say two more words. Go back home where you came from. This country is mine, and I intend to stay here, and to raise this country full of grown people. See these people here. We were raised with them. [Again

SOURCE: 45th Congress, 2nd Session, House Executive Document 1. #1800. "Sitting Bull Commission." 724.

shaking hands with the British officers.] That is enough; so no more. You see me shaking hands with these people.

The part of the country you gave me you ran me out of. I have now come here to stay with these people, and I intend to stay here. I wish you to go back, and to "take it easy" going back. [As Sitting Bull got up to leave this meeting, a U.S. government representative asked, "Shall I say to the President that you refuse the offers that he has made to you? Are we to understand from what you have said that you refuse those offers?" Sitting Bull answered: "I could tell you more, but that is all I have to tell you. If we told you more—why, you would not pay any attention to it. That is all I have to say. This part of the country does not belong to your people. You belong on the other side; this side belongs to us." Nevertheless, in July 1881, Sitting Bull—with his people hungry and ill, and Canada regarding them as unwanted refugees—surrendered at Fort Buford, Montana.]

SITTING BULL, TATANKA YOTANKA (Hunkpapa Sioux)

"The life my people want is a life of freedom"   (c. 1882)

A journalist visited Sitting Bull (c. 1830–1890), among his braves, two wives and several children, in his tepee while the chief, after his surrender, was a prisoner of war at Fort Randall in 1881-1883. These are the remarks that Sitting Bull made to him.

I have lived a long time, and I have seen a great deal, and I have always had a reason for everything I have done. Every act of my life has had an object in view, and no man can say that I have neglected facts or failed to think.

I am one of the last chiefs of the independent Sioux nation, and the place I hold among my people was held by my ancestors before me. If I had no place in the world, I would not be here, and the fact of my existence entitles me to exercise any influence I possess. I am satisfied that I was brought into this life for a purpose; otherwise, why am I here?

This land belongs to us, for the Great Spirit gave it to us when he put us here. We were free to come and go, and to live in our own way. But white men, who belong to another land, have come upon us, and are forcing us to live according to their ideas. That is an injustice; we have never dreamed of making white men live as we live.

White men like to dig in the ground for their food. My people prefer to hunt the buffalo as their fathers did. White men like to stay in one place. My people want to move their tepees here and there to the different hunting grounds. The life of white men is slavery. They are prisoners in towns or farms. The life my people want is a life of freedom. I have seen nothing that a white man has, houses or railways or clothing or food, that is as good as the right to move in the open country, and live in our own fashion. Why has our blood been shed by your soldiers?

[Sitting Bull drew a square on the ground with his thumb nail. The Indians craned their necks to see what he was doing.]

There! Your soldiers made a mark like that in our country, and said that we must live there. They fed us well, and sent their doctors to heal our sick. They said that we should live without having to work. But they told us that we must go only so far in this direction, and only so far in that direction. They gave us meat, but they took away our liberty. The

---

SOURCE: James Creelman. *On the Great Highway: The Wanderings and Adventures of a Special Correspondent.* Boston: Lothrop Publishing Co., 1901. 299–302.

white men had many things that we wanted, but we could see that they did not have the one thing we liked best,—freedom. I would rather live in a tepee and go without meat when game is scarce than give up my privileges as a free Indian, even though I could have all that white men have. We marched across the lines of our reservation, and the soldiers followed us. They attacked our village, and we killed them all. What would you do if your home was attacked? You would stand up like a brave man and defend it. That is our story. I have spoken.

SITTING BULL, TATANKA YOTANKA (Hunkpapa Sioux)

"All of this land belongs to me" (August 21, 1883)

At the Standing Rock Agency in Dakota Territory, Sitting Bull (c. 1830–1890) bristled at the disrespectful manner of the U.S. Senators' select committee chairman: "You say you know I am Sitting Bull, but do you know what position I hold?" "I do not know any difference between you and the other Indians at this agency," replied the chairman. Sitting Bull answered: "I am here by the will of the Great Spirit, and by his will I am a chief. My heart is red and sweet, and I know it is sweet, because whatever passes near me puts out its tongue to me; and yet you men have come here to talk with us, and you say you do not know who I am. I want to tell you that if the Great Spirit has chosen any one to be the chief of this country it is myself." Finally, Sitting Bull told the senators, "You have conducted yourselves like men who have been drinking whiskey, and I came here to give you advice." And with that, Sitting Bull waved his hand, and he and the other Indians left the room. He later returned to apologize and make the following speech.

I came in with a glad heart to shake hands with you, my friends, for I feel that I have displeased you; and I am here to apologize to you for my bad conduct and to take back what I said. I will take it back because I consider I have made your hearts bad. I heard that you were coming here from the Great Father's house some time before you came, and I have been sitting here like a prisoner waiting for someone to release me. I was looking for you everywhere, and I considered that when we talked with you it was the same as if we were talking with the Great Father; and I believe that what I pour out from my heart the Great Father will hear. What I take back is what I said to cause the people to leave the council, and want to apologize for leaving myself. The people acted like children, and I am sorry for it. I was very sorry when I found out that your intentions were good and entirely different from what I supposed they were. Now I will tell you my mind and I will tell everything straight. I know the Great Spirit is looking down upon me from above and will hear what I say, therefore I will do my best to talk straight; and I am in hopes that someone will listen to my wishes and help me to carry them out.

I have always been a chief, and have been made chief of all the land.

SOURCE: 48th Congress, Official Document 283. #2174. "Condition of the Tribes in Montana and Dakota." 78–81.

Thirty-two years ago I was present at councils with the white man, and at the time of the Fort Rice council I was on the prairie listening to it, and since then a great many questions have been asked me about it, and I always said wait; and when the Black Hills council was held, and they asked me to give up that land, I said they must wait. I remember well all the promises that were made about that land because I have thought a great deal about them since that time. Of course I know that the Great Spirit provided me with animals for my food, but I did not stay out on the prairie because I did not wish to accept the offers of the Great Father, for I sent in a great many of my people and I told them that the Great Father was providing for them and keeping his agreements with them, and I was sending the Indians word all the time I was out that they must remember their agreements and fulfill them, and carry them out straight. When the English authorities were looking for me I heard that the Great Father's people were looking for me too. I was not lost. I knew where I was going all the time.

Previous to that time, when a Catholic priest called "White Hair" [meaning Bishop Marty] came to see me, I told him all these things plainly. He told me the wishes of the Great Father, and I made promises which I meant to fulfill, and did fulfill; and when I went over into the British possessions he followed me, and I told him everything that was in my heart, and sent him back to tell the Great Father what I told him; and General Terry sent me word afterwards to come in, because he had big promises to make me, and I sent him word that I would not throw my country away; that I considered it all mine still, and I wanted him to wait just four years for me; that I had gone over there to attend to some business of my own, and my people were doing just as any other people would do. If a man loses anything and goes back and looks carefully for it he will find it, and that is what the Indians are doing now when they ask you to give them the things that were promised them in the past; and I do not consider that they should be treated like beasts, and that is the reason I have grown up with the feelings I have. Whatever you wanted of me I have obeyed, and I have come when you called me. The Great Father sent me word that whatever he had against me in the past had been forgiven and thrown aside, and he would have nothing against me in the future, and I accepted his promises and came in; and he told me not to step aside from the white man's path, and I told him I would not, and I am doing my best to travel in that path.

I feel that my country has gotten a bad name, and I want it to have a good name; it used to have a good name; and I sit sometimes and wonder who it is that has given it a bad name. You are the only people now who can give it a good name, and I want you to take good care of my country and respect it. When we sold the Black Hills we got a very small price for it, and not what we ought to have received. I used to think that the size of the payments would remain the same all the time, but they are growing smaller all the time. I want you to tell the Great Father everything I have said, and that we want some benefit from the promises he has made to us; and I don't think I should be tormented with anything about giving up any part of my land until those promises are fulfilled—I would rather wait until that time, when I will be ready to transact any business he may desire.

I consider that my country takes in the Black Hills, and runs from the Powder River to the Missouri; and that all of this land belongs to me. Our reservation is not as large as we want it to be, and I suppose the Great Father owes us money now for land he has taken from us in the past. You white men advise us to follow your ways, and therefore I talk as I do. When you have a piece of land, and anything trespasses on it, you catch it and keep it until you get damages, and I am doing the same thing now; and I want you to tell all this to the Great Father for me. I am looking into the future for the benefit of my children, and that is what I mean, when I say I want my country taken care of for me. My children will grow up here, and I am looking ahead for their benefit, and for the benefit of my children's children, too; and even beyond that again.

I sit here and look around me now, and I see my people starving, and I want the Great Father to make an increase in the amount of food that is allowed us now, so that they may be able to live. We want cattle to butcher—I want to kill three hundred head of cattle at a time. That is the way you live, and we want to live the same way. This is what I want you to tell the Great Father when you go back home. If we get the things we want our children will be raised like the white children. When the Great Father told me to live like his people I told him to send me six teams of mules, because that is the way white people make a living, and I wanted my children to have these things to help them to make a living. I also told him to send me two spans of horses with wagons, and everything else my children would need. I also asked for a horse and buggy for my children; I was advised to follow the ways of the white man, and that is why I asked for those things. I never ask for anything that is not needed. I also asked for a cow and a bull for each family, so that they can raise cattle of their own. I asked for four yokes of oxen and wagons with them. Also a yoke of oxen and a wagon for each of my children to haul wood with. It is your own doing that I am here; you sent me here, and advised me to live as you do, and it is not right for me to live in poverty. I asked the Great Father for hogs, male and female, and for male and female sheep for my children to raise from. I did not leave out anything in the way of animals that the white men have; I asked for every one of them. I want you to tell the Great Father to send me some agricultural implements, so that I will not be obliged to work bare-handed. Whatever he sends to this agency our agent will take care of for us, and we will be satisfied because we know he will keep everything right. Whatever is sent here for us he will be pleased to take care of for us. I want to tell you that our rations have been reduced to almost nothing, and many of the people have starved to death.

Now I beg of you to have the amount of rations increased so that our children will not starve, but will live better than they do now. I want clothing too, and I will ask for that too. We want all kinds of clothing for our people. Look at the men around here and see how poorly dressed they are. We want some clothing this month, and when it gets cold we want more of it to protect us from the weather. That is all I have to say.

SITTING BULL, TATANKA YOTANKA (Hunkpapa Sioux)

"What treaty that the whites have kept has the red man broken?" (n.d.)

In 1889, the Ghost Dance religion (see Short Bull and Kicking Bear, pages 185 and 188) swept through reservations across the West. Sitting Bull (c. 1830–1890), though not a participant, defended those who wished to practice it. On December 15, 1890, at the instigation of the agent of the local reservation, who resented Sitting Bull's influence, Indian police officers attempted to arrest him but wound up shooting and killing him. In the following speech, which is undated, he expresses his discouragement with American treaties and with the whites' perceptions of him.

What treaty that the whites have kept has the red man broken? Not one. What treaty that the whites ever made with us red men have they kept? Not one. When I was a boy the Sioux owned the world. The sun rose and set in their lands. They sent ten thousand horsemen to battle. Where are the warriors today? Who slew them? Where are our lands? Who owns them? What white man can say I ever stole his lands or a penny of his money? Yet they say I am a thief. What white woman, however lonely, was ever when a captive insulted by me? Yet they say I am a bad Indian. What white man has ever seen me drunk? Who has ever come to me hungry and gone unfed? Who has ever seen me beat my wives or abuse my children? What law have I broken? Is it wrong for me to love my own? Is it wicked in me because my skin is red; because I am a Sioux; because I was born where my fathers lived; because I would die for my people and my country?

SOURCE: W[illis]. Fletcher Johnson. *Life of Sitting Bull and History of the Indian War of 1890–'91.* Philadelphia: Edgewood Publishing Co., 1891. 201.

STANDING BEAR (Ponca)

"We lived on our land as long as we can remember"
(c. 1880)

In a case of careless treaty-making, the U.S. Government granted the Sioux, traditional enemies of the Poncas, the Poncas' tribal lands. To "correct" the error, the government decided to remove the Poncas to Oklahoma, with the Poncas allowed their pick of the available lands in Indian Territory. Standing Bear's odyssey of 1876, which he narrates in the testimony below, came about when a government agent showed him, White Eagle, and other Ponca representatives unsatisfactory locations for their resettlement. When the Poncas rejected the proffered lands, the agent refused to bring them back to Nebraska. They returned on their own, walking five hundred miles in forty-two days, and discovering, on their arrival, that some of the Poncas had been threatened into removal. The rest of the tribe was forced to follow them soon after. In the spring of 1879, after a brutal winter in Oklahoma, Standing Bear and thirty members of his band trekked back to Nebraska to bury Standing Bear's son, whose last request was to be buried on their traditional lands. The Poncas took refuge with the Omahas, before Standing Bear (c. 1830–1908) was jailed for defying the removal. His testimony about the underhanded tactics of the government agent helped regain tribal lands for the Poncas in Nebraska, which the Sioux graciously gave back. Those Poncas who returned to Nebraska became known as the Northern Poncas.

We lived on our land as long as we can remember. No one knows how long ago we came there. The land was owned by our tribe as far back as memory of men goes.

We were living quietly on our farms. All of a sudden one white man came. We had no idea what for. This was the inspector. He came to our tribe with Rev. Mr. Hinman. These two, with the agent, James Lawrence, they made our trouble.

They said the President told us to pack up—that we must move to the Indian Territory.

The inspector said to us: "The President says you must sell this land. He will buy it and pay you the money, and give you new land in the Indian Territory."

SOURCE: Helen Hunt Jackson. *A Century of Dishonor: A Sketch of the United States Government's Dealings with Some of the Indian Tribes.* New York, Harper and Brothers, 1881. 199–204.

We said to him: "We do not know your authority. You have no right to move us till we have had council with the President."

We said to him: "When two persons wish to make a bargain, they can talk together and find out what each wants, and then make their agreement."

We said to him: "We do not wish to go. When a man owns anything, he does not let it go till he has received payment for it."

We said to him: "We will see the President first."

He said to us: "I will take you to see the new land. If you like it, then you can see the President, and tell him so. If not, then you can see him and tell him so." And he took all ten of our chiefs down. I went, and Bright Eyes' uncle went. He took us to look at three different pieces of land. He said we must take one of the three pieces, so the President said. After he took us down there he said: "No pay for the land you left."

We said to him: "You have forgotten what you said before we started. You said we should have pay for our land. Now you say not. You told us then you were speaking truth." All these three men took us down there. The man got very angry. He tried to compel us to take one of the three pieces of land. He told us to be brave. He said to us: "If you do not accept these, I will leave you here alone. You are one thousand miles from home. You have no money. You have no interpreter, and you cannot speak the language." And he went out and slammed the door. The man talked to us from long before sundown till it was nine o'clock at night.

We said to him: "We do not like this land. We could not support ourselves. The water is bad. Now send us to Washington, to tell the President, as you promised."

He said to us: "The President did not tell me to take you to Washington; neither did he tell me to take you home."

We said to him: "You have the Indian money you took to bring us down here. That money belongs to us. We would like to have some of it. People do not give away food for nothing. We must have money to buy food on the road."

He said to us: "I will not give you a cent."

We said to him: "We are in a strange country. We cannot find our way home. Give us a pass, that people may show us our way."

He said: "I will not give you any."

We said to him: "This interpreter is ours. We pay him. Let him go with us."

He said: "You shall not have the interpreter. He is mine, and not yours."

We said to him: "Take us at least to the railroad; show us the way to that."

And he would not. He left us right there. It was winter. We started for home on foot. At night we slept in hay-stacks. We barely lived till morning, it was so cold. We had nothing but our blankets. We took the ears of corn that had dried in the fields; we ate it raw. The soles of our moccasins wore out. We were barefoot in the snow. We were nearly dead when we reached the Otoe Reserve. It had been fifty days. We stayed there ten days to strengthen up, and the Otoes gave each of us a pony. The agent of the Otoes told us he had received a telegram from the inspector, saying that the Indian chiefs had run away; not to give us food or shelter, or help in any way. The agent said: "I would like to understand. Tell me all that has happened. Tell me the truth."

Then we told our story to the agent and to the Otoe chiefs—how we had been left down there to find our way.

The agent said: "I can hardly believe it possible that any one could have treated you so. That inspector was a poor man to have done this. If I had taken chiefs in this way, I would have brought them home; I could not have left them there."

In seven days we reached the Omaha Reservation. Then we sent a telegram to the President: asked him if he had authorized this thing. We waited three days for the answer. No answer came.

In four days we reached our own home. We found the inspector there. While we were gone, he had come to our people and told them to move.

Our people said: "Where are our chiefs? What have you done with them? Why have you not brought them back? We will not move till our chiefs come back."

Then the inspector told them: "Tomorrow you must be ready to move. If you are not ready you will be shot." Then the soldiers came to the doors with their bayonets, and ten families were frightened. The soldiers brought wagons; they put their things in and were carried away. The rest of the tribe would not move.

When we got there, we asked the inspector why he had done this thing, and he got very angry.

Then we said to him: "We did not think we would see your face again, after what has passed. We thought never to see your face any more. But here you are."

We said to him: "This land is ours. It belongs to us. You have no right to take it from us. The land is crowded with people, and only this is left to us."

We said to him: "Let us alone. Go away from us. If you want money, take all the money which the President is to pay us for twelve years to come. You may have it all, if you will go and leave us our lands."

Then, when he found that we would not go, he wrote for more soldiers to come.

Then the soldiers came, and we locked our doors, and the women and children hid in the woods. Then the soldiers drove all the people [to] the other side of the river, all but my brother Big Snake and I. We did not go; and the soldiers took us and carried us away to a fort and put us in jail. There were eight officers who held council with us after we got there. The commanding officer said: "I have received four messages telling me to send my soldiers after you. Now, what have you done?"

Then we told him the whole story. Then the officer said: "You have done no wrong. The land is yours; they had no right to take it from you. Your title is good. I am here to protect the weak, and I have no right to take you; but I am a soldier, and I have to obey orders."

He said: "I will telegraph to the President, and ask him what I shall do. We do not think these three men had any authority to treat you as they have done. When we own a piece of land, it belongs to us till we sell it and pocket the money."

Then he brought a telegram, and said he had received answer from the President. The President said he knew nothing about it.

They kept us in jail ten days. Then they carried us back to our home. The soldiers collected all the women and children together; then they called all the chiefs together in council; and then they took wagons and went round and broke open the houses. When we came back from the council we found the women and children surrounded by a guard of soldiers.

They took our reapers, mowers, hay-rakes, spades, ploughs, bedsteads, stoves, cupboards, everything we had on our farms, and put them in one large building. Then they put into the wagons such things as they could carry. We told them that we would rather die than leave our lands; but we could not help ourselves. They took us down. Many died on the road. Two of my children died. After we reached the new land, all my horses died. The water was very bad. All our cattle died; not one was left. I stayed till one hundred and fifty-eight of my people had died. Then I ran away with thirty of my people, men and women and children. Some of the children were orphans. We were three months on the road. We were weak and sick and starved. When we reached the Omaha Reserve the Omahas gave us a piece of land, and we were in a hurry to plough it and put in wheat. While we were working the soldiers came and arrested us. Half of us were sick. We would rather have died than have been carried back; but we could not help ourselves.

WHITE EAGLE (Ponca)

"We were as grass that is trodden down"   (January 1881)

In January 1881, a Presidential commission, including generals George Crook and Nelson A. Miles, investigated the Poncas' forced removal to Indian Territory from northern Nebraska. White Eagle (1841–1914), who had become chief of the Southern Poncas, described further details of the 1876 odyssey he undertook with Standing Bear (see page 176).

WHITE EAGLE: My friend, as you have asked the question, I will tell you. It is as I told the Great Father. When I lived up there the Dakotas made attacks upon me, killed some of my people, and stole some of my ponies, and I was thinking that I could get pay for that. A white man came there suddenly after Christmas to see us. We didn't get any news he was coming; he came suddenly. They called us all to the church and there they told us the purpose of his coming. This is the fifth winter since that time. "The Great Father at Washington says you are to move, and for that reason I've come," said he. "These Dakotas are causing you a great deal of trouble, and they'll put you out of patience very soon." "My friends, you have caused us to hear these things very suddenly," I said. "When the Great Father has any business to transact with us he generally sends for us to come to Washington and there we transact it. When the Great Father has any plans on foot he generally sends word to all the people, but you have come very suddenly." "No; the Great Father says you have to go," said he. "My friend, I want you to send a letter to the Great Father, and if he really says this I desire him to send for us," I said. "If it be so, and I hear of it the right way, I'll say his words are straight. The Great Father can't be surpassed." "I'll send a letter to him," said he. He struck the wire. He sent the message by telegraph and it reached the Great Father very soon. "Your Great Father says you are to come with ten of your chiefs," said he. "You are to go and see the land, and after passing through a part you are to come to Washington." We consented to that proposition and went. "You are to look at the Warm Land (Indian Territory) and if you see any land that is good there you are to tell him about it," said he, "and also about any bad land there; tell him about both."

And so we went there to the Warm Land. We went to the terminus

SOURCE: 46th Congress, 3rd Session, Senate Executive Document 30. #1941. "Message from the President of the United States." 14–16.

of the railroad and passed through the land of the Osages and on to the
land full of rocks, and next morning we came to the land of the Kaws;
and leaving the Kansas reservation we came to Arkansas City, and so,
having visited the lands of two of these Indian tribes and seen this land
full of rocks and how low the trees were, I came to this town of the
whites. We were sick twice and we saw how the people of that land
were, and we saw those stones and rocks, and we thought those two
tribes were not able to do much for themselves. And he said to us the
next morning, "We'll go to the Shicaska River and see that;" and I said,
"My friend, I've seen these lands and I've been sick on the journey.
From this on I'll stop on this journey, seeing these lands, and will go
and see the Great Father. Run to the Great Father. Take me with you
to see the Great Father. These two tribes are poor and sick, and these
lands are poor; therefore, I've seen enough of them." "No," said he,
"come and see these other lands in the Indian Territory." "My friend,"
said I, "take me, I beg, to see the Great Father. You said formerly we
could tell him whatever we saw, good or bad, and I wish to tell him."
"No," said he, "I don't wish to take you to see him. If you take part of
this land I'll take you to see him; if not, not." "If you will not take me
to see the Great Father," said I, "take me home to my own country."
"No," said he, "notwithstanding what you say, I'll not take you to see
the Great Father. He did not say I should take you back to your own
country." "How in the world shall I act," said I. "You are unwilling to
take me to the Great Father, and you don't want to take me back to my
own country. You said formerly that the Great Father had called me,
but now it is not so; you have not spoken the truth; you have not spoken the straight word." "No," said he, "I'll not take you to your homes;
walk there if you want to."

"It makes my heart feel said," said I, "as I do not know this land." We
thought we should die, and felt that I should cry, but I remembered
that I was a man.

After saying this, the white man, being in a bad humor, went up
stairs. After he had gone up stairs, we chiefs sat considering what to do.
We said, "He does not speak of taking us to see the Great Father or of
taking us to our own country. We don't think the Great Father has
caused this." We had one interpreter there with us, and we said, "As he
will not take us back, we want him to give us a piece of paper to show
the whites, as we don't know the land." The interpreter went up stairs
to see the man and came back and said, "He will not give you the
paper. He does not wish to make it for you." We sent the interpreter
back again and said: "We want some money from that due us from the
Great Father, so we can make our way home." When he came back
he said, "He does not wish to give you the money." He said, "The

interpreter and three others, half-breeds, must stay. The rest of you can go on foot." We sat talking with each other and said, "Although the Great Father has not caused this, yet if we stay here what man will give us food? Let us go towards our own home." He said to those who were part white and who could act as interpreters, "You must not go to your homes." Two of these half-breeds, Michel and the Lone Chief, remained. Another, Big Elk, said to the full-bloods, "Wherever you go I'll go and die." We said, "He has behaved shamefully towards us, and now, at night, let us go," and so we went towards our home. This man, Standing Bear, said, "Beware, lest they say of us these men have stolen off."

We did not know the land; we were without food; we were without moccasins, and we said, "Why should we die? What have we done?" I thought we should die. Passing on, I was sick on the way—very sick. At last we came to the land of the Otoes, and on the way we lived on corn. For ten days we stayed with the Otoes and they gave us food. Passing on our homeward way, we reached the Omahas, and from that place we soon reached our home.

When we got home we found that he had anticipated us and was there in advance of us. When we reached home we found that he had ordered the Poncas who were there to get ready to move. Having called us, we went there to him. "Move ye," said he; "prepare to remove." We were unwilling. Said I, "I've come back weary; every one of us is unwilling to move; this removal is difficult. Much money will be lost, fall to the ground. Stop your speaking; that is enough," said I. "No," said he, "the Great Father wishes you to remove at once, and you must move to the Indian Territory." "If you wish to speak saucy to us and scold us, scold us," said I. Some soldiers came there. "Only this day will I speak about it," said he. "I will leave this matter in the hands of the leader of the soldiers," said he, "surrender my charge to him." I said, "There are white people traveling around and some of them may come here and look at my body and say, 'Why did they kill him?' and they will say 'Because he did not go.' And I wish the Great Father to know it. I want no trouble with the white soldiers. If the soldiers should shoot at me, I'd not take revenge; I'll not shoot back." "My friend, stop saying that; I do not want it that way," said he.

They separated the half-breeds from the pure bloods, and talked separately to them, and suddenly they were carried away. The white man came with the rations intended for us, but we did not take and eat of them. They had taken away some of our people in advance and we sat without eating. We commenced plowing our land, thinking the affair was ended, so we commenced to dig up our land. I wanted to see some of the leading men of the whites, but I could not see any of them. On the other side of the Niobrara River, at the town of Niobrara, was a white man, one who was a lawyer. I went to see him. "Alas, my friend, I want to find out—I want you to send a message to the Great Father, but I haven't any money. If you will send to him quickly, I'll give you this horse." He sent the message, but none ever came back, although I'd given him the pony. Then I said to this lawyer, "My friend, I want you to go to the Great Father." "I have no money," said he. "My friend, I have thirty-two horses, I'll give them to you." "Well, bring them to me," said the white man. Driving the horses before me, I took them to the white man and gave them to him. He sold the ponies and went to the Great Father and returned. This white man sent a letter to me. In it he said, "I've been to see the Great Father." He sent the first letter before he returned and he was on his way home when he sent a second letter, saying, "My friend, I am sick and on my way home."

It came to pass a person came there. A white man came with a half-breed interpreter back from the party of Poncas first removed; not the first white man, but another. He called us to come across the Niobrara River. It was a place not quite at the town of Niobrara, but a little north-west of it, between the bank of river and town. He spoke gently and softly to us. "My friend, I've come back to you that we may go; that we may remove." At that time we were very tired. Before we returned home a young Ponca, a young man, came to us and said, "The soldiers have come to the lodges." We had not yet seen them. Buffalo and myself said to the young men, "Come to decision; if you say we are to remove we are to remove." The Ponca women were afraid of the soldiers. The soldiers came to the borders of the village and forced us across the Niobrara to the other side, just as one would drive a herd of ponies; and the soldiers pushed us on until we came to the Platte River. They drove us on in advance just as if we were a herd of ponies, and I said, "If I have to go, I'll go to that land. Let the soldiers go away, our women are afraid of them." And so I reached the Warm Land, and so I've been there up to this time. And this is the end.

[GENERAL CROOK: Ask him if he was satisfied after he got down there.]

WHITE EAGLE: We found the land there was bad and we were dying one after another, and we said, "What man will take pity on us?" And our animals died. O, it was very hot. "This land is truly sickly, and we'll be apt to die here, and we hope the Great Father will take us back again." That is what we said. There were one hundred of us died there, and then we who are here came to Washington to see the Great Father. In the winter we came here—in September, 1877. "My friend," we said to the Great Father, "you have brought us up very well, but you have treated us very meanly, and we wish you to send us back to our own land." The three Great Fathers sat listening to this; one of them is not here now. "No, that is very difficult; you have come from a great distance." "Not so, Great Father; it is very difficult for us. I did not cause this myself, to dwell at so great a distance. Some of us have died already. We are walking Indians, I said, and walk to our homes. The land being very small where we are, when we put out our horses someone comes and steals them away from us. I am speaking of troubles, but down here where I am living, it seems as if I had leaped into difficulties." He said, "Search around for other lands. Those all belong to the Indians; those in Indian Territory." He gave me a paper authorizing me to search for other lands. There were three lands mentioned in the paper. I did not go. These men went. They came back, saying, "These lands are very good." They all came back, saying, "We have found good land and will move there." But the Great Father didn't send us there and so we sat waiting. There was an agent with us and he didn't want us to go. He wished to keep us in the land of the Quapaws. "This land is very bad," we said. "The Great Father has told us to hunt for land and we'll go and not listen to anything the agent may say." About ten lodges remained, waiting for instructions to move; the rest moved off, and those who went to the new lands, being without provisions, nearly starved to death. The agent had the provisions with him, but gave them to those who remained with him. And we said, "We'll send a message by telegraph to the Great Father. We'll abandon this old agent and get a new one." I arrived there. The land was good, but in the summer we were sick again.

After the 4th of July we were as grass that is trodden down; we and our stock. Then came the cold weather, and how many died we did not know. Next year there was not quite so much sickness, but from last spring up to this time we have not had sickness. We had made a turn in our course; turned over a new leaf, and we think now that God has pity on us and that we'll have better times. A bad agent and sickness and the wind blowing all these bad things upon us were very hard to bear, but we have now a good agent and are doing better. The agent having spoken gently to me, and having spoken to me about working, I wished to remain where we are, and so he wrote the letter. For five winters I've been looking for someone to help me, and now the sickness is going away and now we think we will dwell in the land where we are. I said to my agent, "Write this business for me; the land we had I'll sell, and I will dwell in this land. We wish you to write and say we desire a firm paper for our lands."

SHORT BULL, TATANKAPTECELAN (Brulé Sioux)

"We prefer to stay here and die, if necessary, to loss of liberty" (Fall 1890)

The Ghost Dance was a religion founded on the vision of a Nevada Paiute named Wovoka: he believed that if the participants danced hard enough and long enough, all the buffalo would come back, all the Indians' ancestors would come to life, and all the white people would be buried. With every tribe in America devastated by war, disease, or removal, the Ghost Dance was an immediately popular activity. In the following speech, Short Bull (c. 1846–1915) resisted the entreaties of the Indians No Neck and Louis Shangraux to return to his agency on the condition of giving up the Ghost Dance.

I have risen today to tell you something of importance. You have heard the words of the brothers from the agency camps, and if you have done as myself you have weighed them carefully. If the Great Father would permit us to continue the dance, would give more rations, and quit taking away portions of the reservation, I would be in favor of returning. But even if you [turning to Shangraux] say that he will, how can we discern whether you are telling the truth? We have been lied to so many times that we will not believe any words that your agent sends to us. If we return he will take away our guns and ponies, put some of us in jail for stealing cattle and plundering houses. We prefer to stay here and die, if necessary, to loss of liberty. We are free now and have plenty of beef, can dance all the time in obedience to the command of Great Wakantanka. We tell you to return to your agent and say to him that the Dakotas in the Bad Lands are not going to come in.

SOURCE: James P. Boyd. *Recent Indian Wars under the Lead of Sitting Bull and Other Chiefs; with a Full Account of the Messiah Craze and Ghost Dances.* Philadelphia: Publishers Union, 1892. 207–208.

SHORT BULL, TATANKAPTECELAN (Brulé Sioux)

"We must continue the dance"   (November 1890)

Short Bull (c. 1846–1915), in describing his Ghost-Dance vision, encouraged the Sioux near the Rosebud Agency to continue on their new religious path.

My friends and relatives: I will soon start the thing in running order. I have told you that this would come to pass in two seasons, but since the whites are interfering so much I will advance the time from what my Father above told me. The time will be shorter, therefore you must not be afraid of anything. Some of my relatives have no ears so I will have them blown away. Now there will be a true tree sprout up, and then all the members of your religion and the tribe must gather together. That will be the place where we will see our relatives. But before this time we will have the balance of the moon, at the end of which time the earth will shiver very hard. Whenever this thing occurs I will start the wind to blow. We are the ones who will then see our fathers, mothers and everybody. We are the tribe of Indians and the ones who are living the sacred life. God, our Father, Himself has told and commanded and shown me to do these things. Our Father in heaven has placed a mark at each point of the four winds. First, a clay pipe, which lies at the setting of the sun and represents the Sioux tribe; second, there is a holy arrow lying at the north, which represents the Cheyenne tribe; third, at the rising of the sun there lies hail, representing the Arrapaho tribe; and fourth, there lies a pipe and nice feather at the south, which represents the Crow tribe. My Father has shown me these things, therefore we must continue the dance. There may be soldiers to surround you, but pay no attention to them. Continue the dance. If the soldiers surround you four deep, those upon whom I put holy spirits will sing a song which I have taught you, and some of them will drop dead. Then the rest will start to run, but their horses will sink into the earth. The riders will jump from their horses, but they will sink into the earth and you can do what you desire for them.

Now, you must know this—that all the soldiers and the race will be dead. There will be only five hundred of them left living on the earth. My friends and relatives, this is straight and true. Now, we must gather

SOURCE: James P. Boyd. *Recent Indian Wars under the Lead of Sitting Bull and Other Chiefs; with a Full Account of the Messiah Craze and Ghost Dances.* Philadelphia: Publishers Union, 1892. 222–224.

at Pass Creek when the tree is sprouting. Then we will go among our dead relatives. You must not take any earthly things with you. Their women and men must disrobe themselves.

My Father above has told us to do this and we must do as he says. You must not be afraid of anything. The guns are the only things that we are afraid of, but they belong to our Father in Heaven. He will see that they do not harm. Whatever white men may tell you do not listen to them; my relations, this is all. I will now raise my hand up to my Father and close what He has said to you through me.

KICKING BEAR (Oglala Sioux)

"I bring you word from your fathers, the ghosts, that they are now marching to join you" (1890)

Kicking Bear (1853–1904) and ten other Sioux went to meet Wovoka, the Nevada Paiute and major prophet of the Ghost Dance, in the spring of 1890. The U.S. Government found the Native/Christian religion so alarming that it outlawed it and took reprisals against the Indians practicing it. Kicking Bear was one of the Sioux evangelists of the Ghost Dance, and the Indian agent James McLaughlin exiled him from the reservation. Thousands of U.S. Army troops, anticipating uprisings, converged on Pine Ridge Reservation. At Wounded Knee Creek, on December 29, 1890, two weeks after the killing of Sitting Bull, the U.S. Army massacred a band of Sioux led by Big Foot, who had already announced they were giving up the Ghost Dance so they could return to the reservation. The massacre was devastating but not forgotten; eighty-three years later members of the American Indian Movement made a stand at Wounded Knee. (See Russell Means, page 213.) In the following speech, Kicking Bear described his vision of the Messiah.

My brothers, I bring to you the promise of a day in which there will be no white man to lay his hand on the bridle of the Indian's horse; when the red men of the prairie will rule the world and not be turned from the hunting-grounds by any man. I bring you word from your fathers, the ghosts, that they are now marching to join you, led by the Messiah who came once to live on earth with the white men, but was cast out and killed by them. I have seen the wonders of the spirit-land, and have talked with the ghosts. I traveled far and am sent back with a message to tell you to make ready for the coming of the Messiah and return of the ghosts in the spring.

In my tepee on the Cheyenne reservation I arose after the corn-planting, sixteen moons ago, and prepared for my journey. I had seen many things and had been told by a voice to go forth and meet the ghosts, for they were to return and inhabit the earth. I traveled far on the cars of the white men, until I came to the place where the railroad stopped. There I met two men, Indians, whom I had never seen before, but who greeted me as a brother and gave me meat and bread. They had three horses, and we rode without talking for four days, for I knew

SOURCE: James McLaughlin. *My Friend the Indian*. Boston: Houghton Mifflin, 1910. 185–189.

they were to be witnesses to what I should see. Two suns had we traveled, and had passed the last signs of the white man—for no white man had ever had the courage to travel so far—when we saw a strange and fierce-looking black man, dressed in skins. He was living alone, and had medicine with which he could do what he wished. He would wave his hands and make great heaps of money; another motion, and we saw many spring wagons, already painted and ready to hitch horses to; yet another motion of the hands, and there sprung up before us great herds of buffalo. The black man spoke and told us that he was the friend of the Indian; that we should remain with him and go no farther, and we might take what we wanted of the money, and spring wagons, and the buffalo. But our hearts were turned away from the black man, my brothers, and we left him and traveled for two days more.

On the evening of the fourth day, when we were weak and faint from our journey, we looked for a camping-place, and were met by a man dressed like an Indian, but whose hair was long and glistening like the yellow money of the white man. His face was very beautiful to see, and when he spoke my heart was glad and I forgot my hunger and the toil I had gone through. And he said, "How, my children. You have done well to make this long journey to come to me. Leave your horses and follow me." And our hearts sang in our breasts and we were glad. He led the way up a great ladder of small clouds, and we followed him up through an opening in the sky. My brothers, the tongue of Kicking Bear is straight and he cannot tell all that he saw, for he is not an orator, but the forerunner and herald of the ghosts. He whom we followed took us to the Great Spirit and his wife, and we lay prostrate on the ground, but I saw that they were dressed as Indians. Then from an opening in the sky we were shown all the countries of the earth and the camping-grounds of our fathers since the beginning; all were there, the tepees, and the ghosts of our fathers, and great herds of buffalo, and a country that smiled because it was rich and the white man was not there. Then he whom we had followed showed us his hands and feet, and there were wounds in them which had been made by the whites when he went to them and they crucified him. And he told us that he was going to come again on earth, and this time he would remain and live with the Indians, who were his chosen people.

Then we were seated on rich skins, of animals unknown to me, before the open door of the tepee of the Great Spirit, and told how to say the prayers and perform the dances I am now come to show my brothers. And the Great Spirit spoke to us saying:

"Take this message to my red children and tell it to them as I say it. I have neglected the Indians for many moons, but I will make them my people now if they obey me in this message. The earth is getting old, and I will make it new for my chosen people, the Indians, who are to inhabit it, and among them will be all those of their ancestors who have died, their fathers, mothers, brothers, cousins and wives—all those who hear my voice and my words through the tongues of my children. I will cover the earth with new soil to a depth of five times the height of a man, and under this new soil will be buried the whites, and all the holes and the rotten places will be filled up. The new lands will be covered with sweet-grass and running water and trees, and herds of buffalo and ponies will stray over it, that my red children may eat and drink, hunt and rejoice. And the sea to the west I will fill up so that no ships may pass over it, and the other seas will I make impassable. And while I am making the new earth the Indians who have heard this message and who dance and pray and believe will be taken up in the air and suspended there, while the wave of new earth is passing; then set down among the ghosts of their ancestors, relatives, and friends. Those of my children who doubt will be left in undesirable places, where they will be lost and wander around until they believe and learn the songs and the dance of the ghosts. And while my children are dancing and making ready to join the ghosts, they shall have no fear of the white man, for I will take from the whites the secret of making gunpowder, and the powder they now have on hand will not burn when it is directed against the red people, my children, who know the songs and the dances of the ghosts; but that powder which my children, the red men, have, will burn and kill when it is directed against the whites and used by those who believe. And if a red man die at the hands of the whites while he is dancing, his spirit will only go to the end of the earth and there join the ghosts of his fathers and return to his friends next spring. Go then, my children, and tell these things to all the people and make all ready for the coming of the ghosts."

We were given food that was rich and sweet to taste, and as we sat there eating, there came up through the clouds a man, tall as a tree and thin like a snake, with great teeth sticking out of his mouth, his body covered with short hair, and we knew at once it was the Evil Spirit. And he said to the Great Spirit, "I want half the people of the earth." And the Great Spirit answered and said, "No, I cannot give you any; I love them all too much." The Evil Spirit asked again and was again refused, and asked the third time, and the Great Spirit then told him that he could have the whites to do what he liked with, but that he would not let him have any Indians, as they were his chosen people for all future time. Then we were shown the dances and taught the songs that I am bringing to you, my brothers, and were led down the ladder of clouds by him who had taken us up. We found our horses and rode back to the railroad, the Messiah flying along in the air with us and teaching us the songs for the new dances. At the railroad he left us and told us to return to our people, and tell them, and all the people of the red nations, what we had seen; and he promised us that he would return to the clouds no more, but would remain at the end of the earth and lead the ghosts of our fathers to meet us when the next winter is passed.

Part III.

TWENTIETH CENTURY

CELSA APAPAS (Cupa)

"If you give us the best place in the world, it is not so good for us as this" (1901)

Celsa Apapas attended a meeting of the Sequoya League, a group of Southern Californians who bought traditional lands for the local Indians but who were, in this case, unable to afford the exorbitant price the heirs of the white "owner" were asking for the Cupeños' former land, Warner's Ranch (Agua Caliente). Apapas spoke for her chief, Cecilio Blacktooth, in the words that follow. In 1903, the Cupeños were forced to move to the Pala reservation, near San Bernardino.

We thank you for coming here to talk to us in a way we can understand. It is the first time anyone has done so. You ask us to think what place we like best next to this place, where we always lived. You see that graveyard out there? There are our fathers and our grandfathers. You see that Eagle-nest mountain and that Rabbit-hole mountain? When God made them, He gave us this place. We have always been here. We do not care for any other place. It may be good, but it's not ours. We have always lived here. We would rather die here. Our fathers did. We cannot leave them. Our children were born here—how can we go away? If you give us the best place in the world, it is not so good for us as this. The captain [Cecilio Blacktooth, a Cupa elder] he say his people cannot go anywhere else; they cannot live anywhere else. Here they always lived; their people always lived here. There is no other place. This is our home. We ask you to get it for us. If Harvey Downey say he own the place, that is wrong. The Indians always here. Everybody knows this Indian land. These Hot Springs always Indian. We cannot live anywhere else. We were born here and our fathers are buried here. We do not think of any place after this. We want this and not any other place.

[*A representative of the Sequoya League asked: "But if the Government cannot buy this place for you, then what would you like next best?"*]

There is no other place for us. We do not want you to buy any other place. If you will not buy this place, we will go into the mountains like quail, and die there, the old people and the women and children. Let the Government be glad and proud. It can kill us. We do not fight. We do what it says. If we cannot live here, we want to go into the mountains and die. We do not want any other home.

SOURCE: Zepherin Englehardt. *San Luis Rey Mission*. San Francisco: James Barry, 1921. 191–192.

CARLOS MONTEZUMA, WASSAJA (Apache)

"Light on the Indian Situation" (October 5, 1912)

At Ohio State University, Montezuma (c. 1867–1923) narrated the story of his amazing life for the Society of American Indians (an organization of, for the most part, college-educated professional Native Americans). He was a doctor and long-time advocate for Native American rights and independence.

Senator Smith of Arizona, when a member of the House of Representatives, said, "There is more hope of educating the rattlesnake, than of educating the Apaches." I am an Apache.

When I was ushered into civilization the warning among the palefaces was: "Look out! an Indian is an Indian. If you do not get the first drop on him, he will drop you."

Rounding up the Apaches by the soldiers and Indian scouts was worse than catching bears and rattlesnakes. The Apaches were destroyed in bunches while caged in caves and gulches. If they stampeded they were shot down like dogs. They were deceived into surrender and then killed. Indian scouts were paid for making midnight massacre raids on Apache camps and taking [as] prisoners their children who were sold into captivity.

In one of these midnight raids made by the Pimas in 1871 many Apaches were slaughtered, and I was captured. That dark memorable night with all its awful horrors of massacre is indelibly impressed upon my mind.

The next morning, as from a supernatural stupor I awoke in another world. Childlike, I cried as if my heart would break. I wanted to go to my mother and my father. Not so. Life had another mission for me.

Two days on horseback under the broiling sun brought us to the Pimas' homes, where I was kept for several days.

To celebrate their victory, about four hundred Pimas danced around me and then helped me onto a horse and carried me off to be sold.

I was purchased for the sum of $30 by Mr. Carlos Gentile, who was on his way east, at Adamsville, Arizona. He legally adopted me and cared for me as his own. In the east we traveled from place to place and within one year landed in Chicago.

Here I entered the public school before I could speak with much

SOURCE: *The Quarterly Journal of the Society of American Indians.* January-April, 1913. 50–55.

intelligence in English. I made rapid progress, because I was a lone Apache in school with English-speaking children. Very soon, unconsciously, I took on their ways. I could do nothing else. In school, in the streets and in whatever way I turned I was led to become like my schoolmates. I was carried by the current of my environment. I was lost in it and had to stick to it. In my earlier days I had become Apache in speech and habit because I had associated with those who spoke only the Apache Indian language.

My public school education was not only in Chicago but also in a little red country schoolhouse near Galesburg, Illinois, where I grasped the rudiments of farm life during a two years' stay.

I was taken to Brooklyn, New York. There I studied with the children of other races learning to become American citizens; and then came west to Urbana, Illinois, where I was tutored and prepared for the state university.

While a student at the university without money, to pay part of my expenses I helped around the house—gardened, took care of a horse, and worked at whatever I could find to do outside of my study hours. During vacations I worked on a farm. Graduating in the spring of 1884, I came back to Chicago.

Here, like all new comers, I experienced that even with a university degree it was not an easy task to convince the people that you can do anything. After many days of fruitless search I found a "job," not a "position," where I worked only for my meals and a place in the store to sleep.

Through kind friends my tuition was remitted to me at the Chicago Medical College. For five years alternately behind the counter and attending lectures I finally graduated in medicine and obtained my coveted license to practice medicine and surgery. After several months of private practice I entered the Indian service as physician and clerk at the Fort Stevenson Indian School in North Dakota. Here I saw an Indian school for the first time. One year later I was transferred to Western Shoshone Agency in Nevada as agency physician. There I saw in full what deterioration a reservation is for the Indians. I watched these Indians, cut off from civilized life, trying to become like Yankees with the aid of a few government employees. Because of my own experience I was now able to fully realize how their situation held them to their old Indian life, and often wondered why the government held them so arbitrarily to their tribal life, when better things were all around them.

After three years and a half of hard service in Nevada I was sent to the Colville Agency in Washington, where I had the honor of being physician to the Chief Moses band of Columbia River Indians and

Chief Joseph's band of Nez Percés, these two chiefs being among the greatest in our history.

Though I longed to help these Indians, yet my heart yearned for civilization, and, as God would have it, I received without solicitation a call from the east—a call to become resident physician at the renowned Carlisle Indian School in Pennsylvania. Here I had the blessed privilege of working with those who had at heart the real uplift of my people.

Two and one-half years at this institution under that famous God-fearing man, General Pratt, was an inspiration. At that time this school was a lighthouse for all the Indians. It was a stepping stone to all its students helping them to go out into every avenue of civilized American life.

That I might better acquaint myself with all human kind by coming in contact with all races of all climes; that I might see with my own eyes the world's progress; and that I might exert the energies with which God had blessed me and developed in me to the best interest of my fellow men, I resigned my position at Carlisle. Again coming back to Chicago I started at the bottom of my profession, equipped with a firm determination to learn and struggle on. After sixteen years of the steady and persistent practice of medicine, I believe that I am justified in feeling a merited pride in that I can refer with confidence of support to hundreds of the best physicians and surgeons in Chicago and elsewhere, who are my friends and know me, my work and my observance of its professional ethics.

To draw the *lesson* from this recital of my life, I wish you to note that I am not a Reservation Indian. I never was a Reservation Indian. The world was my sphere of action and not the limitations, nearly as binding as a prison, of a strictly Bureau-ruled reservation. It may have been cruel to have been forced away from paternal love, care and protection, but after all these years, to me it has proven the greatest blessing. I studied in public schools and not in Indian schools. I did not spend a few hours in a Reservation schoolroom and the rest of the time in Indian camps. At an early age I was compelled to earn my own way in life. The government never paid one cent for my education. I have no trouble with the Indian Bureau about my money, my property or my rights as a citizen. Indian Bureau care and restrictions are unknown to me. I obey the laws of the State and Nation under whose protection I live, and so have widest freedom.

Rather than go back to my people I stayed in the east. I had to make my civilized life good within one generation and not in thousands and thousands of years.

Such is the embodiment of my life and that is why I ask the same liberty for my noble race—the American Indians. In these forty years' absence from my people I have not forgotten them. They have been in my heart day and night. For them my pen and tongue have not been idle.

You cannot treat on Temperance without thinking of Frances Willard; on the Salvation Army without keeping in mind General Booth; nor can you grasp the Indian situation without bringing in Gen. R. H. Pratt. The ex-president "who can do no wrong" relieved the general from the Indian service; from the institution he founded, loved and to which he gave twenty-five years of the best of his life. The bard that had kept the best interests of the Indians intact, went down. At that moment the steering of the Indian ship was given into hands opposed to General Pratt's ideals and it has been heading wrong ever since. It is drifting and we only can help it to sail in the right direction and for the right port by dropping out these past eight years and beginning again where we then left off.

Colonization, segregation and reservation are the most damnable creations of men. They are the home, the very hothouse of personal slavery—and are no place for the free and the "home of the brave."

I do not desire to criticize the individuals composing the guiding power of the Indian Bureau of our government, but I am unalterably opposed to the system itself.

I firmly believe that the only true solution of the so-called "Indian problem" is the entire wiping out of the reservation system; of the absolute free association of the Indian race with the paleface. Let us have an opportunity of joining with them on the basis on which all other races have been placed. No race on earth has contended so long, so diligently, so persistently for "equal rights" as has ours. No race on earth has ever survived such handicaps, oppression and the denial of any basis of freedom as has ours. Look back in history and find if you can, any race that ever inhabited this earth, who have contended against a greater force than ours for a period of four hundred years; and we are still struggling and fighting for liberty and equal privilege. God only knows the trials, tribulations, slavery and oppressions to which the Indian race has been obliged to submit and yet is valiantly fighting to overcome. If it were not for the sturdiness, the physical and moral strength of our ancestors,—would it be possible for us here today—descendants of the greatest aboriginal race in the world—still to contend for liberty and freedom?

Years and years ago the Indian only knew that truth and righteousness governed all things. But a century and more of deceit and hypocrisy has naturally taught him to distrust the paleface, through their unfulfilled promises and double dealing.

Only as an exception has a paleface appeared who in truth and in fact was a friend. Yet with all our oppression, with all the deceit that has been practiced upon us, I challenge any paleface who can meet the fidelity "even unto death" that is today and has always existed in the heart of every Indian in this country.

All who understand the Indian as a man know that his possibilities, given half a chance, are limitless. They know that there is nothing in the world we can not master. For four hundred years we have pleaded, begged—yes, sacrificed our lives—to receive fair treatment. We knew little of murder, rape, assassination and other crimes until the paleface taught us these things in their most exquisite form. History records where we, time after time, have sought peaceful solution of our rights and interests and as many times and more have we been deceived, cheated and defrauded. Is it surprising that we fought? Will a rat forced into a corner die without a fight?

The Indian Bureau system is wrong. It must by virtue of its powers be oppressive. It is not human and therefore can not be just. If the good government as our guardian has failed to place us where we rightfully belong in this world, remember that the fault lies there and not with the Indian. Therefore, it behooves every member of this Society and all Indians throughout the country to compel the government to realize its injustice. We educated Indians must awaken and express ourselves.

How often have I looked unto Heaven and said: "Oh, Lord, how long, how long!" when it seemed as though there was no shadow of hope for my people and that even God had forsaken us. But not so, my brothers and sisters, God is near and will help us. The light that comes from an Indian's heart is not yet dead. We still have among us men and women with the spirit of Red Jacket, Logan and Pocahontas, and the dawn of a better day is here.

Cease not to pray that He will yet give us an administration that will legislate and administer the end of reservation prison life for our people and open as wide opportunities for them into American civilization as it gives to all other races, and then will we be free to work out our own salvation.

CHAUNCEY YELLOW ROBE (Sioux)

"The Indian and the Wild West Show"   (October 1913)

At the Third Annual Conference of the Society of American Indians in Denver, Yellow Robe spoke on the issue of cultural degradation.

I am glad that the circumstances enabled me to be present upon this convention; and as I look about this gathering, of the leaders of my own race, it is a great inspiration to me to think that we are assembled here in the interest of our common cause.

I have come to this convention with a question that is familiar to you all—The Wild West Indian Show.

Before I go any further to speak upon this subject I wish to ask one question: Is there anyone here that will tell me that the Wild West Show is a good thing for the Indian? If this Society is in favorable accord with such a practice, I am willing to form a new Wild West Show right here among the members of this Society to take the place of the celebrated Buffalo Bill, whose last camping ground was Denver.

The Indian is not to be censured for the Wild West Indian Show, for his condition and the present life which the Indian is forced to lead has drawn him into such shows. What benefit has the Indian derived from these Wild West Shows? None, but what are degrading, demoralizing and degenerating, and all their influences fall far short of accomplishing the ideals of citizenship and civilized state of affairs which we most need to know. Tribal habits and customs are apt to be degraded for show purposes, because the Indian Bureau under our government is constantly encouraging the Indian to degenerate by permitting hundreds of them to leave their homes for fraudulent savage demonstrations before the world. All these Wild West Shows are exhibiting the Indian worse than he ever was, and deprive him of his high manhood and individuality.

We see the Indian. He is pictured in the lowest degree of humanity. He is exhibited as a savage in every motion picture theatre in the country. We see the Indian, in his full native costume, stamped on the five-dollars bills as a reminder of his savagery. We see a monument of the Indian in New York harbor as a memorial of his vanishing race. The Indian wants no such memorial monument, for he is not yet dead.

SOURCE: *The Quarterly Journal of the Society of American Indians.* January–March, 1914. 39–40.

The name of the North American Indian will not be forgotten as long as the rivers flow and the hills and the mountains shall stand, and though we have progressed, we have not vanished.

At every celebration upon the reservation borders the Indian is in demand for show exhibitions. I have had the privilege of witnessing some of these occasions where the Indian is induced by pay to perform the naked war dance before the intelligent people who call themselves Christians. Under these circumstances is it any wonder that sometimes it is considered that the Indian does not possess the adaptability for Anglo-Saxon civilization?

The fact is here demonstrated that the Indian is truly a man, and that he can become adapted to the highest state of development and achievement. Every effort should be made to lead him through the paths of education and Christianity to self-supporting and independent American citizenship. It is for us who feel more deeply and trust in our God to consider our own difficult questions, to hope that the day is not far distant when the reservation system and all these hindrances that concern us will be removed, and that all of our people will enjoy the same privilege of citizenship that you and I do.

DELOS LONEWOLF (Kiowa)

"How to Solve the Problem" (1915)

At a conference of the Society of American Indians, Lonewolf spoke out in favor of the controversial use of peyote and of giving his people more autonomy in a number of ways.

I have been listening here to these speeches. I have been thinking of the Indians that are talking. From their talk I can make out they were raised among the white people; that is, the principal speakers; and then I heard a white man (R. D. Hall) talk about these Indians and he was raised among the Indians! The man said something about the students. Of course these other speakers were raised among the white people and some of them live there yet. I am one of the returned students; a graduate of the Carlisle Indian school. I have been among the Indians, among my people, ever since I graduated at Carlisle in 1896. What I want to say is not what Indians tell me or what I learned from the Quakers. I am going to tell what I know from personal experience. I listened to the speeches about peyote yesterday. I had a word to say about it, but I thought it was not best at the time. Now you Christian people who are trying to civilize the Indians, why don't you take your civilization and your Christianity to the lost Indians who are using peyote. Right there is where the fault comes in. This thing of talking about peyote killing the Indians, there is no such thing. I used peyote for fifteen years. I have been right in with these "lost Indians" as a Christian Indian. There is a certain time when the Indians reach out, a certain time about three o'clock when the influence comes on them, they naturally reach out to get hold of something, their worship, right then I have been brave enough to go there, not what the Christian people or missionary or anybody else say, but I talk Jesus Christ to them and through my influence and through the instrument of peyote some of the hardest cases that the missionary or anybody else could not reach they have been converted and introduced into Christian churches.

Now as to abolishing Indian Bureau and things like that; the position I have taken is on record. The Secretary of the Interior wrote several personal letters to me. One asked me several questions and one of them was, "Do you think that Government ought to turn Indians loose, and state in full why you think so?" He said in the beginning he wanted this information because he wanted to help the Indians in the best way and

SOURCE: *The American Indian Magazine.* July–September, 1916. 257–259.

the best way possible, and here is the answer I wrote him. I feel just like [Carlos] Montezuma about freedom but because *of the conditions I could not recommend turning the Indians loose today,* but here is the recommendation I wrote to him. I said, "If you want to help us, leave our land and our restrictions just like they are until the trust period runs out, which is about nine or ten years from now, but give us more liberal use of our funds." I was talking about the younger people, say people about fifty years and down. But over that, of course, the government will have to take care of them. I was speaking for the young people, I said, "Give us our money, and if we are good enough to work, and let us have the privilege to handle our own money. Give us our money and if we use it all and blow it just like you been saying we would do, then we got no place to look to for any more. Then we will have to go to work, and that is our only salvation." *Work is the only salvation for Indians.* I spoke about handling our own allotments. If you will let us lease them, practical experience will teach us better and quicker than any of the best teachers and instructors you can send out among us. I said if Indian makes a bad deal in leasing his land, next time he will see and he will make a better trade and at the end of his trust period he will know just how to handle his allotment and he will get on well just like anybody else. Here is another statement I made; *as long as we have undivided money in the United States Treasury we will not do much work.* That is the trouble with everybody, I don't care who it is. You white people if you have got your living coming from somebody somewhere you will not exert yourself at all. Let us have what is ours and give us a chance to work.

JIM BECENTI (Navajo)

"We are starving for education"   (January 30, 1947)

Jim Becenti spoke at an Office of Indian Affairs meeting in Phoenix about employment problems.

It is hard for us to go outside the reservation where we meet strangers. I have been off the reservation ever since I was sixteen. Today I am sorry I quit the Santa Fe R.R. I worked for them in 1912–13. You are enjoying life, liberty, and happiness on the soil the American Indian had, so it is your responsibility to give us a hand, brother. Take us out of distress. I have never been to vocational school. I have very little education. I look at the white man who is a skilled laborer. When I was a young man I worked for a man in Gallup as a carpenter's helper. He treated me as his own brother. I used his tools. Then he took his tools and gave me a list of tools I should buy and I started carpentering just from what I had seen.

We have no alphabetical language. We see things with our eyes and can always remember it. I urge that we help my people to progress in skilled labor as well as common labor. The hope of my people is to change our ways and means in certain directions, so they can help you someday as taxpayers. If not, as you are going now, you will be burdened the rest of your life. The hope of my people is that you will continue to help so that we will be all over the United States and have a hand with you, and give us a brotherly hand so we will be happy as you are. Our reservation is awful small. We did not know the capacity of the range until the white man come and say "you raise too much sheep, got to go somewhere else," resulting in reduction to a skeleton where the Indians can't make a living on it. For eighty years we have been confused by the general public, and what is the condition of the Navajo today? Starvation! We are starving for education. Education is the main thing and the only thing that is going to make us able to compete with you great men here talking to us.

SOURCE: *The American Indian.* Volume IV, Number 8 (1948). 42.

CLYDE WARRIOR (Ponca)

"We are poor in spirit because we are not free"
(February 3, 1967)

President Lyndon B. Johnson's National Advisory Commission on Rural Poverty conducted three public hearings. Clyde Warrior, a founding member of the National Indian Youth Council, came from the nonreservation Native American community in Ponca City, Oklahoma, to speak about the drawbacks of government assistance and to suggest changes for existing programs.

Most members of the National Indian Youth Council can remember when we were children and spent many hours at the feet of our grandfathers listening to stories of the time when the Indians were a great people, when we were free, when we were rich, when we lived the good life. At the same time we hear stories of droughts, famines, and pestilence among Indian people. But it is only recently that we realized that there was surely great material deprivation in those days, and that our old people felt rich because they were free. They were rich in the things of spirit. But if there is one thing that characterizes Indian life today it is poverty of the spirit. We still have human passion and depth of feeling, which is something rare today, but we are poor in spirit because we are not free, free in the most basic sense of the word. We as American Indians are not allowed to make those basic human choices and decisions about our personal life and about the best need of our communities, which is the mark of free, mature people.

We sit on our front porches or in our yards, and the world and our lives in it pass us by without our desires or aspirations having any effect. We are not free. We do not make choices. Our choices are made for us; we are the poor. For those of us who live on reservations these choices and decisions are made by Federal administrators, bureaucrats, and their yes men, euphemistically called tribal governments. Those of us who live in nonreservation areas have our lives controlled by local white power elites. We have many rulers. They are called social workers, cops, school teachers, churches, et cetera, and recently OEO employees, because in the meeting they tell us what is good for us and how they programmed us, for they come into our homes and instruct

SOURCE: *Rural Poverty: Hearings Before the National Advisory Committee on Rural Poverty, Memphis, Tennessee.* Washington, D. C., September 1967. 144–147.

us, and their manners are not what one would always call polite by Indian standards, or perhaps by any standards. We are rarely accorded respect as fellow human beings. Our children come home from school to us with shame in their hearts and a sneer on their lips for their home and parents. We are the "poverty problem," and that is true; and perhaps it is also true that our lack of reasonable choices, our lack of freedom, our poverty of spirit is not unconnected with our material poverty.

The National Indian Youth Council realizes there is a great struggle going on in America now between those who want more "local" control of programs and those who would keep the power and the purse strings in the hands of the Federal Government. We are unconcerned with that struggle because we know that no one is arguing that the dispossessed, the poor, be given any control over their own destiny. The local white power elites who protest the loudest against Federal control are the very ones who would keep us poor in spirit and worldly goods in order to enhance their own personal and economic station in the world. Nor have those of us on reservations fared any better under the paternalistic control of Federal administrators. In fact, we shudder at the specter of what seems to be the forming alliances in Indian areas between Federal administrators and local elites.

Some of us fear that this is the shape of things to come in the War on Poverty effort. Certainly it is in those areas where such an alliance is taking place, that the poverty program seems to be "working well." That is to say, it is in those areas of the country where the Federal Government is getting the least "static," and where Federal money is being used to bolster the local power structure and local institutions. By "everybody being satisfied," I mean the people who count, and the Indian or poor does not count.

Let us take the Headstart program as an instance. We are told in the not-so-subtle racist vocabulary of the modern middle class that our children are "deprived." Exactly what they are deprived of seems to be unstated. We give our children love, warmth, and respect in our homes and the qualities necessary to be a warm human being. Perhaps many of them get into trouble in their teens because we have given them too much warmth, love, passion, and respect. Perhaps they have a hard time reconciling themselves to being a number on an IBM card. Nevertheless, many educators and politicians seem to assume that we, the poor, the Indians, are not capable of handling our own affairs and even raising our own children and that State institutions must do that job for us and take them away from us as soon as they can. My grandmother said last week, "Train your child well now for soon she will belong to her teacher and the schools."

Many of our fears about the Headstart program which we had from listening to the vocabulary of educators and their intentions were not justified, however. In our rural areas the program seems to have turned out to be just a federally subsidized kindergarten which no one takes too seriously. It has not turned out to be, as we feared, an attempt to rethread the twisted head of the child from a poor home. Headstart, as a program, may not have fulfilled the expectations of elitist educators in our educational colleges, and the poor may not be ecstatic over the results, but local powers are overjoyed. This is the one program which has not upset anyone's applecart and which has strengthened local institutions in an acceptable manner, acceptable at least to our local "patrons."

Fifty years ago the Federal Government came into our communities and by force carried most of our children away to distant boarding schools for ten or twelve years. My father and many of my generation lived their childhoods in an almost prisonlike atmosphere. Many returned unable even to speak their own language. Some returned to become drunks. Most of them had become white haters or that most pathetic of all modern Indians, Indian haters. Very few ever became more than very confused, ambivalent, and immobilized individuals, never able to reconcile the tensions and contradictions built inside themselves by outside institutions. As you can imagine, we have little faith in such kinds of Federal programs devised for our betterment, nor do we see education as a panacea for all ills.

In recent days, however, some of us have been thinking that perhaps the damage done to our community by forced assimilation and directed acculturative programs was minor compared to the situation in which our children find themselves. There is a whole generation of Indian children who are growing up in the American school system. They still look to their relatives, my generation and my father's, to see if they are worthy people. Their judgment and definition of what is worthy is now the judgment which most Americans make. They judge worthiness as competence and competence as worthiness. And I am afraid my fathers and I do not fare well in the light of this situation and judgment. Our children are learning that their people are not worthy and thus that they individually are not worthy. But even if by some stroke of good fortune prosperity was handed to us on a platter, that still would not soften the negative judgment our youngsters have of their people and themselves. As you know, people who feel themselves to be unworthy and feel they cannot escape this unworthiness turn to drink and crime and self-destructive acts. Unless there is some way that we as Indian individuals and communities can prove ourselves competent and worthy in the eyes of our youngsters there will be a generation of Indians grow[ing] to adulthood whose reactions to their situation will make previous social ills seem like a Sunday school picnic.

For the sake of our children, for the sake of the spiritual and material well-being of our total community, we must be able to demonstrate competence to ourselves. For the sake of our psychic stability as well as our physical well-being, we must be free men and exercise free choices. We must make decisions about our own destinies. We must be able to learn and profit by our own mistakes. Only then can we become competent and prosperous communities. We must be free in the most literal sense of the word, not sold or coerced into accepting programs for our own good, not of our own making or choice. Too much of what passes for grassroots democracy on the American scene is really a slick job of salesmanship. It is not hard for sophisticated administrators to sell tinsel and glitter programs to simple people, programs which are not theirs, which they do not understand, and which cannot but ultimately fail to contribute to already strong feelings of inadequacy.

Community development must be just what the word implies, community development. It cannot be packaged programs wheeled into Indian communities by outsiders which Indians can "buy" or once again brand themselves as unprogressive if they do not "cooperate." Even the best of outside programs suffer from one very large defect: If the program falters, helpful outsiders too often step in to smooth over the rough spots. At that point any program ceases to belong to the people involved and ceases to be a learning experience for them. Programs must be Indian creations, Indian choices, Indian experiences. Even the failures must be Indian experiences because only then will Indians understand why a program failed and not blame themselves for some personal inadequacy. A better program built upon the failure of an old program is the path of progress. But to achieve this experience, competence, worthiness, sense of achievement, and the resultant material prosperity, Indians must have the responsibility in the ultimate sense of the word. Indians must be free in the sense that other, more prosperous Americans are free. Freedom and prosperity are different sides of the same coin and there can be no freedom without complete responsibility. And I do not mean the fictional responsibility and democracy of passive consumers of programs—programs which emanate from and whose responsibility for success rests in the hands of outsiders, be they Federal administrators or local white elitist groups.

Many of our young people are captivated by the lure of the American city with its excitement and promise of unlimited opportunity. But even if educated they come from powerless and inexperienced communities and many times carry with them a strong sense of unworthiness. For many of them the promise of opportunity ends in the gutter on the skid rows of Los Angeles and Chicago. They should and must be given a better chance to take advantage of the opportunities they have. They must grow up in a decent community with a strong sense of personal adequacy and competence.

America cannot afford to have whole areas and communities of people in such dire social and economic circumstances. Not only for her economic well-being, but for her moral well-being as well. America has given a great social and moral message to the world and demonstrated, perhaps not forcefully enough, that freedom and responsibility as an ethic is inseparable from and, in fact, the cause of the fabulous American standard of living. America has not, however, been diligent enough in promulgating this philosophy within her own borders. American Indians need to be given this freedom and responsibility which most Americans assume as their birthright. Only then will poverty and powerlessness cease to hang like the sword of Damocles over our heads, stifling us. Only then can we enjoy the fruits of the American system and become participating citizens—Indian Americans rather than American Indians.

We hope this commission pays close attention to the three supplementary sections of this testimony and pays heed to the recommendations therein.

Perhaps the National Indian Youth Council's real criticism is against a structure created by bureaucratic administrators who are caught in this American myth that all people assimilate into American society, that economics dictates assimilation and integration. When from the experience of the National Indian Youth Council, and in reality—which we cannot emphasize and recommend strongly enough—the fact is that no one integrates and disappears into American society. What ethnic groups do is not integrate into American society and economy individually, but enter into the mainstream of American society as a people, and in particular as communities of people. The solution to Indian poverty is not government programs, but in the competence of the person and his people. The real solution to poverty is encouraging the competence of the community as a whole.

The National Indian Youth Council recommends for openers that to really give these people—"the poor, the dispossessed, the Indians"—complete freedom and responsibility, is to let it become a reality, not a much-heard-about dream, and let the poor decide for once what is best for themselves.

We recommend that funds or subsidy or whatever it's called be provided for indigent tribes and communities so that they themselves decide what they would like to do and what they deem best for their community. Of course, we realize within the present structure this is not possible. So we further recommend that another avenue of thought be tried, such as junking the present structure and creating another, since it is typical of bureaucratic societies that when one takes upon himself to improve a situation, one immediately, unknowingly, falls into a structure of thinking that in order to improve any situation you take the existing avenues of so-called improvement and reinforce the existing condition, thereby reinforcing and strengthening the ills that are implicit in the very structure of that society.

DAVID COURCHENE, LEADING THUNDERBIRD
(Manitoba Indian Brotherhood)

"We know we can't turn back the clock" (1969)

The President of the Manitoba Indian Brotherhood spoke about the causes of some of the present-day dilemmas facing Native Americans.

A hundred years of submission and servitude, of protectionism and paternalism have created psychological barriers for Indian people that are far more difficult to break down and conquer than are the problems of economic and social poverty. Paternalistic programs of the past, based largely on the idea that we must shelter and protect the ignorant savage, have created complex problems to those who want to shelter and protect themselves. . . . Where once the Indian roamed, the factories, farms, and dwellings of a European horde block passage. We are dispossessed of our ancient ways and faced with life in a city. . . .

We know that we can't turn back the clock. We know that we can't live for long in a wilderness that is fast being ransacked of fish and fur to feed and clothe the luxury-minded dwellers of the city. So, we too must enter the confines of the city and try as best we might to make our way.

But, understand, oh white man; understand, lovely lady dressed in fur! It is hard, very hard, to know that the land that once was ours will never ever again be our hunting grounds. It is hard to bear the crime-filled streets and the liquor-selling bars where once was only peaceful grass and sobriety. We understand that we must change—and we are changing—but remember: it once was our land, our life, and it is hard.

SOURCE: Annette Rosenstiel. *Red & White: Indian Views of the White Man, 1492–1982.* New York: Universe Books, 1983. 173.

RUSSELL MEANS (Oglala Sioux)

"The spirits of Big Foot and his people are all around us"
(1973)

Means (b. 1939) was a founder of the American Indian Movement (AIM), which, in 1973, in their seventy-one day occupation of Wounded Knee, galvanized support from many tribes but at the same time encountered armed assault from a tribal government and the U.S. Government. During that occupation, Means spoke about the revival of the Ghost Dance.

The white man says that the 1890 massacre was the end of the wars with the Indian, that it was the end of the Indian, the end of the Ghost Dance. Yet here we are at war, we're still Indians, and we're Ghost Dancing again. And the spirits of Big Foot and his people are all around us. They suffered through here once before, in the snow and the cold, and they were hungry, they were surrounded at that time with the finest weapons the United States had available to them, brand new machine guns and cannons.

What came to me was that Big Foot and his band were like a grandfather. It was time for them to go to sleep, but they had a child that was just born. And this child had to grow and learn all kinds of new things before it once again could return here to Wounded Knee. World War I came along, and the United States asked the American Indian if they would fight their war for them. So we went out and saw around the world what was happening, and we came back. Then another war happened. This time they not only took Indians into the army, but into the defense plants all across America, and into the big cities. And we learned the ways of the white man, right here in this country, found out about the white man to bring that knowledge back for the use of our people. But we still had patience, and all this time we had been watching the white men.

When armed white men were fighting in the labor movement, riots and armed clashes with the pigs, we watched that. And in the '50s when the Communist scare was going throughout the country. And white man was fighting white man, arresting him and putting him in jail. And in the '60s, we watched the black man, that black cloud that Black Elk prophesied would cover this country. Then the 1970s came. And as a people we are beginning to see . . .

SOURCE: *Voices from Wounded Knee: In the Words of the Participants.* Mohawk Nation, via Rooseveltown, New York: Akwesasne Notes, 1974. 89–90.

213

RUSSELL MEANS (Oglala Sioux)

"We are people who live in the belly of the monster"
(September 20, 1977)

Means (b. 1939), who has become famous as a defender of the rights of native peoples worldwide as well as an actor and author, addressed United Nations affiliates and members of the Human Rights Commission in Geneva, Switzerland.

We are people who live in the belly of the monster. The monster being the U.S.A. Every country in the Western Hemisphere follows the lead of the monster. I come not to turn the other cheek. We have turned it now for almost five hundred years, and we realize that here in Geneva, this is our first small step into the international community. . . . The President of the U.S.—to show you what a racist he is—[talks] about human rights while my people are suffering genocide. Not only in the U.S. but in the entire Hemisphere—planned genocide by governments. We have brought documents to Geneva that support this charge.

We are approaching the international community this first time for support and assistance to stop not only this rape of our sacred mother earth, but also to stop the genocide of a whole people. A people with international rights backed up especially in North America by treaties between the U.S. and Indian Nations. The U.S., the monster, and its multinational corporations have dictated foreign policy in this world. They no longer care about the future as witnessed by the Dene [Navajo], by my people, by Central and South America. . . .

You see, there is only one color of mankind that is not allowed to participate in the international community, and that color is red. The black, the white, the brown, the yellow—all participate in one form or another. We no longer, until this day, have had a voice within the international community.

Someone once said you can tell the power of a country by the oppression its people will tolerate. No longer are we going to tolerate the monster.

SOURCE: Annette Rosenstiel. *Red & White: Indian Views of the White Man, 1492–1982.* New York: Universe Books, 1983. 181–182.

OREN LYONS (Onondaga)

"Sovereignty and the Natural World Economy"   (1991)

At the 1991 conference of the Aboriginal Law Association of McGill University in Montreal, Canada, Oren Lyons (b. 1930), a Six Nations Iroquois spokesperson, discussed America's five-hundred-year history of land ownership.

Sovereignty is a term that we hear being used all the time and particularly in relation to Indians. It is a term that should be applied to Indians. However, I have noticed in the past ten years or so a certain change in terminology. Nationally and internationally, the term "sovereignty" is often being replaced by the term "autonomy." I have noticed this in relation to the Nicaraguan conflict and the Mesquitoe Indians.

What is the difference between the two terms? What is sovereignty? We have always taken a rather simplistic view. We said that sovereignty is the act thereof. You are as sovereign as you are able to be. Generally, sovereignty is applied to nations and today, to nation-states. Indians have always perceived themselves to be nations, sovereign and independent. Further, we apply sovereignty even further than nations. We apply it to individuals in the form of respect. Indian People, of all people, understand the concept of freedom and being born free with rights.

Columbus landed here five hundred years ago. Across America and the world there was a tremendous preparation for 1992. I know that the President of the United States set aside some eighty-two million dollars for this "celebration" as they call it, and Spain has spent even more than that. All of the world has become involved: the Catholic Church, for obvious reasons, Italy, the United States, as well as Latin America. Everybody is pointing to the year 1992.

Why? Since 1992 is a year of assessment, where we stand back and look at five hundred years of activity in the western hemisphere and assess what condition we are in. It can be a year of atonement for what happened to the Indigenous Peoples who caught the brunt of this invasion, or it can be a year of commitment to see that the next five hundred years are going to be better than the last five hundred.

This process of reflection will have to involve Indian nations. We

SOURCE: Oren Lyons. *Justice for Natives: Searching for Common Ground.* Edited by Andrea P. Morrison with Irwin Cotler. Montreal: McGill-Queen's University Press, 1997. 157–161.

have to make our own assessment of our condition. We have to present a position to challenge this idea of a celebration, to challenge this idea of a discovery. Discovery is a very arrogant perception; we were "discovered," sort of like the flora and fauna of North America. In truth, there were free nations here with a real understanding of government and community, of the process and great principles of life. In fact, on the landfall of Christopher Columbus, freedom was rampant in North, Central and South America. Everybody was free and living in a natural world economy where they had economic security in perpetuity. They had adjusted themselves to working with the land, and understood that every year that the land renewed itself.

Now, coming across the water were people with a different perception about economy. As a matter of fact, up to the present day, the Governments of Canada and the United States have spent their time trying to get our people involved in this economy. They have spent a lot of time trying to tell us about the importance of private property as opposed to community property. We hear terms like development, progressive development, sustainable development, but our perception is that if you do not operate around the real laws of the universe, you are challenging fundamental cycles that you depend on for life.

So, there was obviously a conflict between Christopher Columbus' perception, and the people that he met. All of the writing says the First Peoples were healthy, happy and well-fed, and not overly inclined to warfare. Yet, the process of domination began immediately. He said: these would make good slaves. That was his first message back to the Queen: we can make slaves of these people since they are easily subjugated, and they do not know much about warfare. Any ten of my men can take over this island with the technology and weapons we have brought over.

The basic conflict relates to economy because Indian Nations operated on the basis of a natural world economy. They had Thanksgiving ceremonies that went around the clock and around the calendar year. Something was always coming up so there was always Thanksgiving in a land-based economy. It was part of the structure of a community. It was an instruction to respect what was growing. This was true across the Americas. Yet, our white brother kept telling us there was a better way: get rich. Our people had a hard time with that. They said, "No, our land is held in common, everyone owns the land. Water is free, air is free, everything you need for life sustenance is free." And he said, "I would like to buy your land." They said, "What do you mean by buying?" Now we have people "buying" his argument. We have people, our own people, who are now willing to "sell" long-term sovereignty for short-term personal gain.

As we sit back and assess these last five hundred years, let us look at what has happened to our people. How have the Indian Nations fared? How have our children? How are our institutions? Are they holding up? How are our principles? Are they holding up? We have to look at ourselves because as tough as these last five hundred years have been, the next five hundred or even fifty years are going to be tougher.

There is a fundamental issue here that we have to look at because human beings are displacing life around the world. Huge populations are displacing life whether it is trees, the elephants in Africa, the tigers in India or the buffalo in this country. They are not here anymore. Yet, there are more and more people. There is a displacement going on here of things a fundamental economy needs. The Indians understood one thing: they understood that the law of flesh, blood and bones is common to all living beings. We are under one common law here. We are animals, but we are animals with intellect. Intellect is what makes us dangerous because we have the foreknowledge of death. Animals know when death is coming, and they prepare for it. Yet, we know from a very young age that we are going to die. This is a tremendous knowledge, but how do you use that knowledge? How do you work with it?

When one speaks of generations the way the Indians speak of them, we must see that the next generations, those faces coming from the earth, have the same good that we have and can enjoy the same law that we do. Well, in assessing five hundred years in this country, we see that the next seven generations are not going to enjoy that. Every day, at least six species of life become extinct. So, when you talk about the philosophy of sovereignty, you must talk of longevity and the future. This is the common sense that comes from the long experience of Indian Nations being in one place: if you do not work with the laws that surround you, you will not survive. It is quite simple. We know that there is no mercy in the natural law whatsoever. It will exact retribution in direct ratio to violation. You cannot discuss this—there are no lawyers, only the retribution. The problem here is that we visit this retribution on our children and on our grandchildren. We leave them the problem of our excesses. What do we say to greedy individuals that say sovereignty is money?

I never believed the white man when he said his way was better. I never believed it. I always believed that our way was better, maybe just because I knew more about it. The truth is, if we sit back and really look at it, there is some hard news here for all of us no matter who we are.

When we speak of sovereignty, we have to have a large conceptualization of what it is we are talking about. With Indian Nations, it is not just a political term, it is also a spiritual term. It may be even be more spiritual than political. One of our people once said that spirituality is the highest form of politics. So, let us keep the parameters of what we are talking about clear.

The parameters are beyond the oceans that surround us, and they are beyond our time here on earth. The parameters we are discussing reverberate into the future. If your economy does not function within those parameters then you are shortchanging those future generations we talked about. Maybe it is only the Indians that talk about the seventh generation. I do not know. Since we have talked about it a lot, I have heard it again and again. I hear it from strangers, I hear it from strange places. Why not? It seems to us common law and common sense. So, let us say that sovereign is common sense in its most basic fundamental form: common sense and respect for all life.

Land is the issue, land has always been the issue. We cannot trade our jurisdiction over lands and territories for money. Our lands and our right to govern ourselves are all we have. If we gamble our lands for money, jurisdiction and taxation, we will lose because that is the white man's game.

FICTION

THE QUEEN OF SPADES AND OTHER STORIES, Alexander Pushkin. 128pp. 0-486-28054-3

THE STORY OF AN AFRICAN FARM, Olive Schreiner. 256pp. 0-486-40165-0

FRANKENSTEIN, Mary Shelley. 176pp. 0-486-28211-2

THE JUNGLE, Upton Sinclair. 320pp. (Available in U.S. only.) 0-486-41923-1

THREE LIVES, Gertrude Stein. 176pp. (Available in U.S. only.) 0-486-28059-4

THE BODY SNATCHER AND OTHER TALES, Robert Louis Stevenson. 80pp. 0-486-41924-X

THE STRANGE CASE OF DR. JEKYLL AND MR. HYDE, Robert Louis Stevenson. 64pp. 0-486-26688-5

TREASURE ISLAND, Robert Louis Stevenson. 160pp. 0-486-27559-0

GULLIVER'S TRAVELS, Jonathan Swift. 240pp. 0-486-29273-8

THE KREUTZER SONATA AND OTHER SHORT STORIES, Leo Tolstoy. 144pp. 0-486-27805-0

THE WARDEN, Anthony Trollope. 176pp. 0-486-40076-X

FATHERS AND SONS, Ivan Turgenev. 176pp. 0-486-0073-5

ADVENTURES OF HUCKLEBERRY FINN, Mark Twain. 224pp. 0-486-28061-6

THE ADVENTURES OF TOM SAWYER, Mark Twain. 192pp. 0-486-40077-8

THE MYSTERIOUS STRANGER AND OTHER STORIES, Mark Twain. 128pp. 0-486-27069-6

HUMOROUS STORIES AND SKETCHES, Mark Twain. 80pp. 0-486-29279-7

AROUND THE WORLD IN EIGHTY DAYS, Jules Verne. 160pp. 0-486-41111-7

CANDIDE, Voltaire (François-Marie Arouet). 112pp. 0-486-26689-3

GREAT SHORT STORIES BY AMERICAN WOMEN, Candace Ward (ed.). 192pp. 0-486-28776-9

"THE COUNTRY OF THE BLIND" AND OTHER SCIENCE-FICTION STORIES, H. G. Wells. 160pp. (Not available in Europe or United Kingdom.) 0-486-29569-9

THE ISLAND OF DR. MOREAU, H. G. Wells. 112pp. (Not available in Europe or United Kingdom.) 0-486-29027-1

THE INVISIBLE MAN, H. G. Wells. 112pp. (Not available in Europe or United Kingdom.) 0-486-27071-8

THE TIME MACHINE, H. G. Wells. 80pp. (Not available in Europe or United Kingdom.) 0-486-28472-7

THE WAR OF THE WORLDS, H. G. Wells. 160pp. (Not available in Europe or United Kingdom.) 0-486-29506-0

ETHAN FROME, Edith Wharton. 96pp. 0-486-26690-7

SHORT STORIES, Edith Wharton. 128pp. 0-486-28235-X

THE AGE OF INNOCENCE, Edith Wharton. 288pp. 0-486-29803-5

THE PICTURE OF DORIAN GRAY, Oscar Wilde. 192pp. 0-486-27807-7

JACOB'S ROOM, Virginia Woolf. 144pp. (Not available in Europe or United Kingdom.) 0-486-40109-X

MONDAY OR TUESDAY: Eight Stories, Virginia Woolf. 64pp. (Not available in Europe or United Kingdom.) 0-486-29453-6

NONFICTION

POETICS, Aristotle. 64pp. 0-486-29577-X

POLITICS, Aristotle. 368pp. 0-486-41424-8

NICOMACHEAN ETHICS, Aristotle. 256pp. 0-486-40096-4

MEDITATIONS, Marcus Aurelius. 128pp. 0-486-29823-X

THE LAND OF LITTLE RAIN, Mary Austin. 96pp. 0-486-29037-9

THE DEVIL'S DICTIONARY, Ambrose Bierce. 144pp. 0-486-27542-6

THE ANALECTS, Confucius. 128pp. 0-486-28484-0

CONFESSIONS OF AN ENGLISH OPIUM EATER, Thomas De Quincey. 80pp. 0-486-28742-4

THE SOULS OF BLACK FOLK, W. E. B. Du Bois. 176pp. 0-486-28041-1

DOVER·THRIFT·EDITIONS

NONFICTION

ᴀʀʀᴀᴛɪᴠᴇ ᴏꜰ ᴛʜᴇ Lɪꜰᴇ ᴏꜰ Fʀᴇᴅᴇʀɪᴄᴋ Dᴏᴜɢʟᴀss, Frederick Douglass. 96pp. 0-486-28499-9

ꜱᴇʟꜰ-Rᴇʟɪᴀɴᴄᴇ ᴀɴᴅ Oᴛʜᴇʀ Essᴀʏs, Ralph Waldo Emerson. 128pp. 0-486-27790-9

ᴛʜᴇ Lɪꜰᴇ ᴏꜰ Oʟᴀᴜᴅᴀʜ Eǫᴜɪᴀɴᴏ, ᴏʀ Gᴜsᴛᴀᴠᴜs Vᴀssᴀ, ᴛʜᴇ Aꜰʀɪᴄᴀɴ, Olaudah Equiano. 192pp. 0-486-40661-X

ᴛʜᴇ Aᴜᴛᴏʙɪᴏɢʀᴀᴘʜʏ ᴏꜰ Bᴇɴᴊᴀᴍɪɴ Fʀᴀɴᴋʟɪɴ, Benjamin Franklin. 144pp. 0-486-29073-5

ᴛᴏᴛᴇᴍ ᴀɴᴅ Tᴀʙᴏᴏ, Sigmund Freud. 176pp. (Not available in Europe or United Kingdom.) 0-486-40434-X

Lᴏᴠᴇ: A Book of Quotations, Herb Galewitz (ed.). 64pp. 0-486-40004-2

Pʀᴀɢᴍᴀᴛɪsᴍ, William James. 128pp. 0-486-28270-8

ᴛʜᴇ Sᴛᴏʀʏ ᴏꜰ Mʏ Lɪꜰᴇ, Helen Keller. 80pp. 0-486-29249-5

Tᴀᴏ Tᴇ Cʜɪɴɢ, Lao Tze. 112pp. 0-486-29792-6

Gʀᴇᴀᴛ Sᴘᴇᴇᴄʜᴇs, Abraham Lincoln. 112pp. 0-486-26872-1

ᴛʜᴇ Pʀɪɴᴄᴇ, Niccolò Machiavelli. 80pp. 0-486-27274-5

ᴛʜᴇ Sᴜʙᴊᴇᴄᴛɪᴏɴ ᴏꜰ Wᴏᴍᴇɴ, John Stuart Mill. 112pp. 0-486-29601-6

Sᴇʟᴇᴄᴛᴇᴅ Essᴀʏs, Michel de Montaigne. 96pp. 0-486-29109-X

ᴜᴛᴏᴘɪᴀ, Sir Thomas More. 96pp. 0-486-29583-4

ʙᴇʏᴏɴᴅ Gᴏᴏᴅ ᴀɴᴅ Eᴠɪʟ: Prelude to a Philosophy of the Future, Friedrich Nietzsche. 176pp. 0-486-29868-X

ᴛʜᴇ Bɪʀᴛʜ ᴏꜰ Tʀᴀɢᴇᴅʏ, Friedrich Nietzsche. 96pp. 0-486-28515-4

ᴄᴏᴍᴍᴏɴ Sᴇɴsᴇ, Thomas Paine. 64pp. 0-486-29602-4

ꜱʏᴍᴘᴏsɪᴜᴍ ᴀɴᴅ Pʜᴀᴇᴅʀᴜs, Plato. 96pp. 0-486-27798-4

ᴛʜᴇ Tʀɪᴀʟ ᴀɴᴅ Dᴇᴀᴛʜ ᴏꜰ Sᴏᴄʀᴀᴛᴇs: Four Dialogues, Plato. 128pp. 0-486-27066-1

A Mᴏᴅᴇsᴛ Pʀᴏᴘᴏsᴀʟ ᴀɴᴅ Oᴛʜᴇʀ Sᴀᴛɪʀɪᴄᴀʟ Wᴏʀᴋs, Jonathan Swift. 64pp. 0-486-28759-9

Cɪᴠɪʟ Dɪsᴏʙᴇᴅɪᴇɴᴄᴇ ᴀɴᴅ Oᴛʜᴇʀ Essᴀʏs, Henry David Thoreau. 96pp. 0-486-27563-9

Wᴀʟᴅᴇɴ; ᴏʀ, Lɪꜰᴇ ɪɴ ᴛʜᴇ Wᴏᴏᴅs, Henry David Thoreau. 224pp. 0-486-28495-6

Nᴀʀʀᴀᴛɪᴠᴇ ᴏꜰ Sᴏᴊᴏᴜʀɴᴇʀ Tʀᴜᴛʜ, Sojourner Truth. 80pp. 0-486-29899-X

ᴛʜᴇ Tʜᴇᴏʀʏ ᴏꜰ ᴛʜᴇ Lᴇɪsᴜʀᴇ Cʟᴀss, Thorstein Veblen. 256pp. 0-486-28062-4

Dᴇ Pʀᴏꜰᴜɴᴅɪs, Oscar Wilde. 64pp. 0-486-29308-4

Oꜱᴄᴀʀ Wɪʟᴅᴇ's Wɪᴛ ᴀɴᴅ Wɪsᴅᴏᴍ: A Book of Quotations, Oscar Wilde. 64pp. 0-486-40146-4

Uᴘ ꜰʀᴏᴍ Sʟᴀᴠᴇʀʏ, Booker T. Washington. 160pp. 0-486-28738-6

A Vɪɴᴅɪᴄᴀᴛɪᴏɴ ᴏꜰ ᴛʜᴇ Rɪɢʜᴛs ᴏꜰ Wᴏᴍᴀɴ, Mary Wollstonecraft. 224pp. 0-486-29036-0

PLAYS

Pʀᴏᴍᴇᴛʜᴇᴜs Bᴏᴜɴᴅ, Aeschylus. 64pp. 0-486-28762-9

ᴛʜᴇ Oʀᴇsᴛᴇɪᴀ Tʀɪʟᴏɢʏ: Agamemnon, The Libation-Bearers and The Furies, Aeschylus. 160pp. 0-486-29242-8

Lʏsɪsᴛʀᴀᴛᴀ, Aristophanes. 64pp. 0-486-28225-2

Wʜᴀᴛ Eᴠᴇʀʏ Wᴏᴍᴀɴ Kɴᴏᴡs, James Barrie. 80pp. (Not available in Europe or United Kingdom.) 0-486-29578-8

ᴛʜᴇ Cʜᴇʀʀʏ Oʀᴄʜᴀʀᴅ, Anton Chekhov. 64pp. 0-486-26682-6

ᴛʜᴇ Sᴇᴀ Gᴜʟʟ, Anton Chekhov. 64pp. 0-486-40656-3

ᴛʜᴇ Tʜʀᴇᴇ Sɪsᴛᴇʀs, Anton Chekhov. 64pp. 0-486-27544-2

ᴜɴᴄʟᴇ Vᴀɴʏᴀ, Anton Chekhov. 64pp. 0-486-40159-6

ᴛʜᴇ Wᴀʏ ᴏꜰ ᴛʜᴇ Wᴏʀʟᴅ, William Congreve. 80pp. 0-486-27787-9

ʙᴀᴄᴄʜᴀᴇ, Euripides. 64pp. 0-486-29580-X

Mᴇᴅᴇᴀ, Euripides. 64pp. 0-486-27548-5

DOVER · THRIFT · EDITIONS

PLAYS

ELECTRA, Sophocles. 64pp. 0-486-28482-4

MISS JULIE, August Strindberg. 64pp. 0-486-27281-8

THE PLAYBOY OF THE WESTERN WORLD AND RIDERS TO THE SEA, J. M. Synge. 80pp. 0-486-27562-0

THE DUCHESS OF MALFI, John Webster. 96pp. 0-486-40660-1

THE IMPORTANCE OF BEING EARNEST, Oscar Wilde. 64pp. 0-486-26478-5

LADY WINDERMERE'S FAN, Oscar Wilde. 64pp. 0-486-40078-6

BOXED SETS

FAVORITE JANE AUSTEN NOVELS: *Pride and Prejudice, Sense and Sensibility* and *Persuasion* (Complete and Unabridged), Jane Austen. 800pp. 0-486-29748-9

BEST WORKS OF MARK TWAIN: Four Books, Dover. 624pp. 0-486-40226-6

EIGHT GREAT GREEK TRAGEDIES: Six Books, Dover. 480pp. 0-486-40203-7

FIVE GREAT ENGLISH ROMANTIC POETS, Dover. 496pp. 0-486-27893-X

GREAT AFRICAN-AMERICAN WRITERS: Seven Books, Dover. 704pp. 0-486-29995-3

GREAT WOMEN POETS: 4 Complete Books, Dover. 256pp. (Available in U.S. only. 0-486-28388-7

MASTERPIECES OF RUSSIAN LITERATURE: Seven Books, Dover. 880pp. 0-486-40665-2

SIX GREAT AMERICAN POETS: Poems by Poe, Dickinson, Whitman, Longfellow, Frost, and Millay, Dover. 512pp. (Available in U.S. only.) 0-486-27425-X

FAVORITE NOVELS AND STORIES: Four Complete Books, Jack London. 568pp. 0-486-42216-X

FIVE GREAT SCIENCE FICTION NOVELS, H. G. Wells. 640pp. 0-486-43978-X

FIVE GREAT PLAYS OF SHAKESPEARE, Dover. 496pp. 0-486-27892-1

TWELVE PLAYS BY SHAKESPEARE, William Shakespeare. 1,173pp. 0-486-44336-1